Praise for the first edition:

"This is an excellent resource for those teaching courses in human development, specifically courses needed by individuals seeking licensing and accreditation (e.g., social work, psychology) from licensing boards with defined cognitive objectives in the area of human growth and development (e.g., CACREP). In addition, the book is valuable for those wishing to get up to speed on the topic of moral development and those struggling with individuals with moral issues. Summing Up: Highly recommended. Upper-division undergraduates, graduate students, professionals, general readers."

R.E. Osborne, *Texas State University,*
in CHOICE, September 2014

"*Moral Development* is a unique book in that it so effectively provides extensive coverage of the theoretical side of moral development but also serves as a very useable guide for those who are interested in moral development from an educational or therapeutic standpoint."

Michelle Stroffolino Schmidt, *PsycCRITIQUES*

"Vozzola masterfully delves into controversial areas with finesse, examines unresolved disputes without hesitation and throughout it all maintains a friendly writing style. The book will engage students, broaden their imaginations, and guide them in practical application. I plan to use it in my courses and strongly endorse it for every undergraduate course addressing moral development!"

Darcia Narvaez, *University of Notre Dame, USA*

"Elly Vozzola leads aspiring professionals through the hills and valleys of moral psychology. Hers is a thoughtful survey of the evolution of moral development accompanied by useful triggers for reflection and discussion. As a textbook it is invitingly written and I would warmly commend it to teachers wishing to introduce their students to a sensitive account of moral development."

James Cor

"*Moral Development* is just the sort of l for. Clear, accessible, and comprehensi into the current debates in the fiel evolutionary theory in a clear and live.

Sharon Lamb, *University of Massachusetts-Boston, USA*

Dear Rosemary and Don,
Thanks for all your support and encouragement over the years (as well as listening to all my stories). I hope you enjoy this book.
Annie Benland

"Many students struggle with combining theory and practice and this book serves as a nice model of this important connection.... [It] provides the reader with concrete examples of how moral development is carried out in therapy....This book adds a great deal to the existing literature in the field in an accessible and useful manner."

Stefanie Sinno, *Muhlenberg College, USA*

"Vozzola has a lively writing style, which students will appreciate... By using very practical examples and memorable interview quotations, Vozzola provides a very interesting survey of the variety of perspectives and a compelling case for their usefulness.... I would use and recommend it. I believe it would be very useful to students and teachers."

John R. Snarey, *Emory University, USA*

"The writing style... is personal and "down to earth"... like reading a good novel.... Most texts review Piaget, Kohlberg and Gilligan.... This text goes beyond that in terms of both theory and application.... It is appropriate for graduate and upper division undergraduate courses.... I would consider adopting this book.... After providing a theoretical foundation... the author then looks at the current research from a cultural perspective and... helps the student apply both theory and research in order to utilize the knowledge learned."

Rebecca J. Glover, *University of North Texas, USA*

"In this work, Elizabeth Vozzola tackles an important challenge: to provide a balanced, comprehensive review of moral development theory and applications for a broad audience. She is up to the task, building on her decades of experience in the field to offer, in under 200 pages, an integrated and thoughtful outline that will be especially relevant for advanced undergraduate and graduate students preparing for work in education and the helping professions... The book incorporates various integrative and pedagogical features, including interviews with prominent theorists in the field, and well-presented tables that compare and contrast salient features of relevant theories and programmes. This text will also prove useful for those in cognate fields who want a current overview of moral development and education. Vozzola's writing style is informal and she shares many incidents from her own journey as a teacher in the field... Vozzola's goal is to prime moral interest and provide tools for the journey. To this end she succeeds admirably, providing a historical sweep of the field of moral development and a sense of its complexity and potential. I suspect the book will prompt many new to the field to rethink their moral assumptions as well as consider further study."

Jay W. Brandenberger, *University of Notre Dame,*
Journal of Moral Education

Moral Development

Moral Development offers a comprehensive overview of classic and current theories of moral development and applications of these theories in various counseling and educational settings. It examines changes across time and experience in how people understand right and wrong, and individual differences in moral judgements, emotions, and actions.

Elizabeth C. Vozzola and Amie K. Senland review the latest research in the field and integrate classic work with contemporary perspectives on assessment and treatment. Part 1 provides an understanding of a range of theories, explaining their strengths and challenges, and offering examples of how these theories apply to helping professionals. It covers Freud, Piaget, Kohlberg, Rest, Gilligan, Nodding, Bandura, Turiel, Nucci, Narvaez, Haidt, and Shweder. Part 2 highlights promising applications of moral development theory in education and counseling. Fully updated with new chapters on faith development and moral and prosocial development in infancy and early childhood, the text explores specific approaches to helping clients with a variety of clinical or developmental challenges and provides an excellent resource for courses addressing the CACREP program objectives for Human Growth and Development. It also integrates issues of gender, ethnicity, and culture throughout to prepare readers for practicing in a global culture and presents a new perspective: the cultural developmental approach. Illustrated throughout with examples that highlight applications of moral development concepts in today's media, it also includes interviews from some of today's leading theorists and practitioners.

Ideal as a text for advanced courses on moral development and moral psychology, as well as courses on human, child, social and personality development taught in psychology, counseling, education, human development, family studies, social work, and religion. Its applied approach also appeals to mental health and school counselors.

Elizabeth C. Vozzola is a Professor Emerita of Psychology and former Director of the Honors Program at the University of Saint Joseph in West Hartford, CT, USA.

Amie K. Senland is a Lecturer and Laboratory Coordinator of Psychology at Trinity College in Hartford, CT, USA.

Moral Development
Theory and Applications

Second Edition

**Elizabeth C. Vozzola and
Amie K. Senland**

NEW YORK AND LONDON

Second edition published 2022
by Routledge
605 Third Avenue, New York, NY 10158

and by Routledge
4 Park Square, Milton Park, Abingdon, Oxon, OX14 4RN

Routledge is an imprint of the Taylor & Francis Group, an informa business

First edition published by Routledge 2014

Library of Congress Cataloging-in-Publication Data
A catalog record has been requested for this book

ISBN: 978-0-367-27196-1 (hbk)
ISBN: 978-0-367-27197-8 (pbk)
ISBN: 978-0-429-29546-1 (ebk)

DOI: 10.4324/9780429295461

Typeset in Bembo
by MPS Limited, Dehradun

Elly Vozzola: This book is dedicated to my late parents, Elly van den Berge Vozzola and Peter John Vozzola, who gave me such important lessons in "how to live and what to do;" to my life partner, Paul Cimbala, for all the years of love, support, and encouragement; and to my two sons, Vincenzo and Peter, for growing into fine young men whose many talents are filtered through loving hearts.

Amie Senland: This book is dedicated to my parents, Karin and Aage, who have taught me many life lessons and provided me with much support and encouragement through the years.

Contents

Figures and Tables

Figure

Tables

About the Authors

 **Elizabeth (Elly) C. Vozzola, Ph.D.**, is a Professor of Psychology Emerita and former Director of the Honors Program at the University of Saint Joseph in West Hartford, Connecticut, USA. She earned a master's degree in community counseling at Winona State University, where Tim Hatfield introduced her to Lawrence Kohlberg's stage theory and Norm Sprinthall's conception of deliberate psychological education (DPE)—concepts that sparked her lifelong interest in moral development theory and applications. She earned a second master's and doctorate in Applied Developmental Psychology at Fordham University, where she had the privilege of working with Ann Higgins-D'Alessandro and completing a doctoral internship in one of Kohlberg's just community schools. Her scholarly projects have included studies of college faculty's moral reasoning about affirmative action, children's moral understanding of the Harry Potter series, emerging adults' moral perceptions of the Twilight Saga, student and faculty perceptions of the long-term influence of the Scarsdale Alternative School's just community, and explorations of moral exemplars such as Atticus Fitch and Abraham Lincoln. She lives in West Hartford, CT, with her husband, Civil War historian Paul Cimbala, and two political cats, Franklin and Eleanor.

 **Amie K. Senland, Ph.D.**, is a Lecturer and Laboratory Coordinator in Psychology at Trinity College in Hartford, Connecticut, USA. She earned her master's and doctorate in Applied Developmental Psychology at Fordham University, where she also had the honor of working with Ann Higgins-D'Alessandro, who nurtured and guided her interest in moral development. Amie's scholarly projects have included studies of children's understanding of the

Harry Potter series, the moral reasoning and empathy of adolescents and young adults with autism spectrum disorder, and college students' faith development. She lives in CT, where she enjoys hiking, raising Monarch butterflies, and spending time with her cat, Olaf, who was rescued as a 6-week-old kitten during a snowstorm.

Preface

Overview

This book is written to provide an overview of moral development theories and applications for upper-level undergraduate and master's level students, especially those in applied fields such as psychology, counseling, social work, nursing/allied health, and education. The book can be used as the main text for courses on moral development or as a supplementary text for any developmental, theory, or practice course where there is an emphasis on moral development. Because of its practical nature, the book may also appeal to professionals in related fields.

This book looks at the field of **moral development,** in two ways: (1) **changes across time and experience in how people understand right and wrong;** as well as (2) **individual differences in moral judgments, emotions, and actions**. Some perspectives stress that principles of moral conduct are set by society, others that they are actively constructed by the developing child, and still others that there is a significant biological underpinning to our moral judgments, emotions, and behavior.

In the years since the first edition was published, the rise of neurological/ biological, evolutionary developmental, cultural developmental, and emotion-based/implicit explanations of morality; as well as new challenges to classic universalist theories necessitate revisiting and updating the text. Co-author Amie Senland has selected some of the most important examples of research and theory in these areas as well as writing two entirely new chapters on (a) prosocial and moral development in early childhood, and (b) faith development.

For a comparatively small speciality area, moral development can boast of an extensive, often complex theoretical and research base. As such, it was necessary to limit the considerations to a manageable domain of information. The book focuses primarily on approaches with particularly well-researched and direct links to applications. We hope that the brief discussions of relevant theories and research whet your appetite to pursue further readings on your own. The current book makes no claim to providing an in-depth review of theory and research but rather is offered as a synthesis of a rich, wide set of moral development resources that focuses on examples and perspectives with particular relevance to helping professionals.

After decades of researching and teaching about moral development, we continue to be impressed with people's hunger for and appreciation of moral development and moral education. Elly has presented similar versions of the material in some of these chapters to groups ranging from parent groups in urban schools to undergraduates, graduate students, and veteran teachers and counselors. The backgrounds could not be more different or the engagement and insights more similar. The intense motivation to learn about moral development arises, we believe, because all see immediate applications of the knowledge to their lives and their professions.

We have attempted always to ask the question: What information would be useful to someone who wanted to take his or her knowledge of moral development out into the world? The second edition's continued stress on application reflects our sincere hope that whether you are a professional reading the book to enhance your practice or a student reading it in a course, you make the connections between theory and the pressing moral issues of our time. You will notice that discussion questions throughout the text challenge you to make those connections. We also share our own ideas on "what to do and how to live" in the concluding chapter.

One unique feature of the book is to acknowledge that although most texts address issues of gender and ethnicity, students will be practicing in settings (and a world) in which understanding issues of **global culture** will be the new necessity. The chapter on global perspectives on morality (Chapter 7) not only frames the ideas of some of the major theorists writing on cultural developmental aspects of morality (e.g., Jensen, 2015a, 2020a), but also includes examples of novel perspectives from China, Latin America, and Africa, as well as the Islamic world. Thus, while issues related to gender and ethnicity are integrated throughout the text, the global perspective has been given a special focus.

Special Features

Each chapter ends with several discussion questions. These questions are intended to help you make personal connections to the ideas and concepts in the chapters. Chapters also end with a brief list of additional resources. Exploration of the resources can be used for class-enrichment activities, extra credit, or sources for papers on course topics. Many chapters feature "Interviews with Discipline Leaders" boxes in which leading developmental theorists, practitioners, and researchers discuss their work. We hope that learning more about the work that has been particularly meaningful to the field's leaders helps to bring their research and theories alive for you.

Once we have covered the theoretical material, you will begin to see "Dilemma of the Day" boxes that are designed to help you apply theory to real-world situations. The dilemma exercises are designed to help you begin to think about your own moral principles and can be used for class discussions or short writing assignments.

The applications chapters include "Morality in the Media" boxes with recommendations for films or books that exemplify concepts from the chapter. One course assignment that many students find particularly meaningful is to write a brief analysis paper in which they examine the characters and themes of films or novels through the lens of moral development theories.

You will find summary tables of theory strengths and weaknesses within Chapters 2, 3, and 12, tables of key concepts in Chapters 4 and 5, and brief tables connecting applications to their theoretical roots within Chapters 9 and 10. These tables are intended to provide you with brief overviews of the chapter's ideas that should be helpful aids to better understanding of the theories as well as providing a resource to refer back to as you read the later application chapters. To help you understand the studies that gave rise to or support these theories, the text reviews the latest research methods techniques used in the field.

Other highlights are numerous demonstrations of how theory is used by today's helping professionals that will help readers make connections between theory and moral issues of our time. The strong emphasis on application in Part II integrates the classic theories covered in Part I with contemporary research on assessment and treatment. The application chapters also highlight cutting-edge research on the moral and empathic development of antisocial youth, psychopaths, and individuals diagnosed on the autism spectrum and a new chapter on faith development.

Finally, for graduate counseling classes, this text can provide an excellent resource for courses addressing the Council for Accreditation of Counseling and Related Educational Programs (CACREP) objectives related to the common core area of Human Growth and Development. Many chapters directly address the objective that skilled counselors should be able to demonstrate knowledge of cognitive structural theories of moral, intellectual, and ethical development.

Contents

Part I of this book explores not only the classic theories upon which the modern field of moral development rests, but also newer theories and directions that are rarely covered in traditional developmental textbooks. Every major developmental textbook covers Freud, Piaget, Kohlberg, Haidt and Gilligan, but here you will see important but lesser known theories, such as Nodding's care ethic, Bandura's theory of moral disengagement, and Turiel's domain theory. As teachers, we always try to end a class by pulling out the key "big ideas" we have been discussing. Thus, the concluding chapter of Part I summarizes key points and evaluates the strengths and weaknesses of various theoretical approaches.

In **Part II**, we highlight promising applications of moral development theory in the fields of education, counseling and faith development. For example, character education programs that are based on sound developmental theory hold promise for meeting the challenges facing public education today. If you are planning on a career in teaching, you'll find some of the suggested additional resources especially useful. With tight licensing requirements dictating curricular offerings in the professional programs, few counselors, psychologists, or social workers today get the deep grounding in moral development theory and practice that could help them better evaluate their clients' cognitive, emotional, and behavioral challenges. Chapters 10 and 11 present specific approaches to helping clients with diverse problems, ranging from dysfunctional or developmentally inappropriate schemas to serious behavior problems such as conduct disorder and psychopathy.

Acknowledgments

Elizabeth (Elly) Vozzola: Although the final interpretations (and any misinterpretations) are wholly our own, we owe a debt of gratitude to the scholars who were so generous in talking with us about their work: Lene Arnett-Jensen, Marv Berkowitz, John Gibbs, Rick Halstead, Hyemin Han, Tim Hatfield, Ann Higgins D'Alessandro, Dan Lapsley, Darcia Narvaez, Don Reed, Bob Selman, Norm Sprinthall, and Steve Thoma. I would also like to thank the reviewers of the first edition: Sam A. Hardy, Brigham Young University: Stefanie Sinno, Muhlenberg College; John R. Snarey, Emory University; and two anonymous reviewers.

Through the many years I worked on the two editions of this book, my family, friends, and colleagues have been uniformly supportive (and patient). The long but non-exhaustive list of beloved cheerleaders includes Vincenzo & Anahid, Peter, Casey, Anne & Alan, Mark & Tema, Tim, Norm & Lois, Becky, Lance, Mary, Tonya, Lisa, MJ, Wayne, Ann, Mark, Rick, Kevin, Joan, Karen, Agnes, and Ken. Special thanks are due to my eagle-eyed former proofreader, now co-author, Gen Next moral scholar Amie Senland, for her insightful updating of all references and brilliant writing and editing skills, and to our supportive, patient and generous editors: Debra Riegert (first edition) and Helen Pritt (second edition) for helping us to hone the material into a polished final product. We especially appreciated the skillful organizational skills of editorial assistant Shreya Bajpai who brought us through the home stretch of this project. Most of all, I thank my best friend and life partner, the lead guitarist of many a past rock and blues band (and, oh yes, respected Civil War historian), Paul Cimbala.

Amie Senland: I also wish to thank Helen Pritt (second edition) and her assistant, Shreya Bajpai, for their assistance throughout this project, as well as their patience and support as we revised the second edition during a pandemic. I would especially like to thank Hyemin Han, who I had the privilege of interviewing for the second edition. Special thanks to my mentors over the years who have helped me to hone my understanding of the field of moral development, including Elly Vozzola and Ann Higgins-D'Alessandro; as well as Dina Anselmi and David Reuman, who have fostered my growth in teaching practice. Finally, I thank my family, as well as my friends, for their patience and support as I have worked on this second edition.

Part I

Moral Development in the 21st Century: Theoretical Roots and New Directions

1 Introduction

Humans have been pondering questions of morality for as long as we have records of their queries. Meno asks Socrates, "Can you tell me, Socrates, whether virtue is acquired by teaching or by practice;... [or] whether it comes to man by nature, or in what other way?" (Plato, 380 BCE). In the relatively recent field of psychology, cognitive developmentalists have developed one set of answers, and thinkers from behavioral, psychoanalytic, social learning, and evolutionary perspectives yet others.

A second edition of this text was important because of the current paradigm shift of theory and research within the field. The earlier dominant constructionist paradigm has been challenged, and some believe, replaced, by theories from evolutionary, biological, personality, and cultural psychology. Many researchers no longer hold to classic universal theories and stress the need to look at morality through specific cultural lenses.

For the purposes of this book, we use the term **morality** in the general language usage of **principles of right and wrong actions and judgments.** This book looks at a special area of morality, the field of **moral development,** in two ways: (1) **changes across time and experience in how people understand right and wrong;** as well as (2) **individual differences in moral judgments, emotions, and actions.** Some perspectives stress that principles of moral conduct are set by society, others that they are actively constructed by the developing child, and still others that there is a significant biological underpinning to our moral judgments, emotions, and behavior.

Part I of this book explores not only the classic theories upon which the modern field of moral development rests, but also newer theories and directions that are rarely covered in traditional developmental textbooks. In Chapter 2, we attempt to give you a deep and broad understanding of the work of two seminal thinkers: Freud and Piaget. The cliché that "We stand on the shoulders of giants" is particularly apt when we consider that any contemporary theory must grapple with describing the emotional and cultural components of morality described by Freud, as well as the cognitive and structural components described by Piaget.

In Chapter 3, we present the theories from two of the field's most

DOI: 10.4324/9780429295461-2

influential thinkers, Lawrence Kohlberg and James Rest, who, like Piaget, focused specifically on the rational side of morality. Although Kohlberg's theory is better known to the general public, it has been the broader conception of morality, eventually developed by Rest and his colleagues at the University of Minnesota, that has better stood the test of time and future research.

Chapters 4 and 5 fill in a major gap in the treatment of moral development found in most textbooks. Textbooks tend to present Freud, Piaget, Kohlberg, and Gilligan but neglect to cover the dynamic current state of theory and research. It's as if your knowledge of a living family came only from hearing the stories about their most famous ancestors. In Chapter 4, we look at how classic cognitive-developmental theories have faced substantive challenges not only from care theorists such as Carol Gilligan and Nel Noddings, but also from a perspective called domain theory as well as from the emerging area of moral self/moral personality. In Chapter 5, we turn to the rise of important new theories from neuroscience and evolutionary perspectives. In the second edition, we made substantive additions to these sections to introduce you to cutting-edge research in the areas of emotion-based/implicit moral reasoning and Evolutionary Development ("Evo-Devo").

The second edition also features a wholly new chapter (i.e., 6) that explores the vibrant field of research into the origins of pro-social behavior and morality in infancy and early childhood. This work extends and complements theories discussed in the previous chapter.

A unique feature of the book is to acknowledge that, although issues of gender and ethnicity now tend to be integrated into textbooks and training across the professions (diversity classes are ubiquitous in professional programs), students will be practicing in settings (and a world) in which understanding issues of global culture will be the new necessity. For example, students in the public schools in Elly's suburban American hometown of West Hartford come from homes in which 80 different languages are spoken. No professional can hope to come to a deep understanding of dozens of cultures, but Chapter 7 frames specific examples of moral development theory, research, and issues within an overarching frame of core moral values that can help the practitioner make sense of the multitude of cultural variations that she or he will face in practice. This chapter has been substantially revised to incorporate contemporary research and theory from cultural-development psychology.

The concluding chapter of Part I summarizes key points and evaluates the strengths and weaknesses of various theoretical approaches. We cover a lot of theoretical and research ground in this section, and it is important to pull back from all that exposition and ask, "So what does all this mean?" How can we make sense of all these seemingly contradictory ideas? Chapter 8 attempts to answer those questions while acknowledging the reality of ongoing controversies and gaps in our knowledge base.

In **Part II**, we highlight promising applications of moral development theory in the fields of education and counseling. We added a new chapter on faith development that has applications not only for religious education but also for college and university curricula and programming.

We need to acknowledge from the very beginning that we cannot conceivably present you with a comprehensive picture of the enormous field of moral education research and practice. But in Chapter 9, we do attempt to give you a Cook's Tour of past accomplishments and future directions in moral and character education that should give interested students a framework from which to pursue additional resources in more depth.

Schools, however, are not the only, or even the most powerful, source of moral messages. Certainly, families and peers play a large role but, increasingly, young people are immersed in a world of media. Thus, in Chapter 9 we also share some recent research on how media's moral messages are perceived across development. Research from a major Common Sense Census Media survey in 2015 found that 8- to 18-year-old young people are spending, on average, between 42 and 63 hours per week on various media sources from Facebook to reality TV (Rideout, 2016).

In Chapter 10, we move to a consideration of how counselors and therapists have integrated moral development theories into their practice. We briefly summarize the perspectives of practitioners who focused on "giving psychology away" through school-based interventions aimed at promoting moral development for all students and then turn to more specific individual and group counseling techniques. The chapter ends by offering Halstead's conceptual model for assessing client core issues as well as current research on promoting well-being and treating Post Traumatic Stress Disorder (PTSD).

Many moral development theories (e.g., Hoffman, 2000; Selman, 1976, 2003) posit the importance of perspective-taking and/or empathy for healthy moral development. Thus, we thought it would be useful to follow the overview of developmental counseling with a chapter (Chapter 11) that shows you in some detail what can happen when moral or empathic development goes seriously awry. After presenting Martin Hoffman's theory of empathic development and Albert Bandura's theory of moral disengagement, we give you some examples of how developmental deficits play out in individuals diagnosed with conduct disorder, autism spectrum disorders, and psychopathy.

Another chapter new to this second edition brings you classic theories and contemporary research in the field of faith development. Major surveys of religious participation in the United States have shown a stark decline in religious attendance and a rise in those who identify as religiously unaffiliated, yet faith and religious participation vary widely across cultures and sub-cultures (Pew Research Center [PEW], 2015a, 2019). Faith remains an integral component of life and meaning for many people, and Chapter 12 explores its manifestations across development as well as its relationship to moral development.

The book concludes with a reflection on Tolstoy's perennial questions: How to live and what to do? Just as Chapter 8 attempted to make sense of the diverse theoretical perspectives in Part I, Chapter 13 attempts to pull out some general themes from Part II about how theory can best inform practice, not only in the areas of education and practice examined in the text, but also across the wide range of settings in which a background in moral development might help you better understand yourself and others.

William Perry (1970) proposed that college students move through a series of epistemological positions—a fancy term for the process of changes in the way they think about what knowledge is and how it is gained. In brief, many students come to college as dualistic thinkers looking for black/white right/wrong answers to questions. They believe that experts and textbooks have the answers and that their job as students is to memorize the information and give it back. We call this "learning as regurgitation." The multiple perspectives students encounter in college, both from professors and fellow students, shake their certainty in "right" answers and move most of them into a stage of relativism in which they understand that different people may hold different perspectives. Students at this epistemological stage often drive their professors slightly crazy with their characteristic comment, "That's just your opinion." Eventually, most students, especially in work in their major field, come to realize that all opinions are *not* equal and that there are guidelines for determining the strengths and weaknesses of evidence and arguments. This moves students into a stage of commitment in relativism in which they are willing to say, "Here I stand—these perspectives and interpretations make the most sense to me given the evidence we now have. I realize I need to remain open to possible future evidence, but, for now, here I stand."

This book reflects our own "Here we stand" position on the topics presented. A central goal has been to introduce you to the foundations of the knowledge base in moral development. Roger Straughan (1985, reprinted in Puka, 1994) once wrote a critique of Kohlberg's theory, cleverly entitled "How to Reach Stage 6 and Remain a Bastard." This text's stress on application reflects our own sincere hope that whether you are a professional reading the book to enhance your practice or a student reading it in a course, you make the connections between theory and the pressing moral issues of our time. Our goal has been to spark your interest to such an extent that you feel motivated to implement some of the field's ideas in your own professional life. In a world fraught with challenges at every level—from the struggles of stressed families to the international scourges of terrorism, genocide, bigotry, ignorance, pandemics, and war—we need a committed core of helping professionals dedicated to promoting both justice and care.

2 Classic Theories of Morality: Freud and Piaget

When Elly's son Peter was 7, he accidentally hit his cousin Jason in the head with a baseball bat while swinging at a pitch. The boys' parents heard a set of yells outside the window and saw Jason, bat in hand, in hot pursuit of Peter. The grownups separated the warring parties, heard out the victim's claims, and were about to demand that Peter offer the obligatory apology when he turned to Jason and burst out: "OK, OK, just hit me back!" Someone grabbed the bat from Jason just in time, but clearly both boys would have been quite satisfied with their brand of Old Testament justice.

Through the lens of cognitive-developmental theory, this story provides a nearly perfect illustration of the type of "eye for an eye" thinking that actually indicates growth in moral reasoning. Jason and Peter's reliance on a morality informed by a tacit understanding of reciprocity represented a developmental shift from an earlier moral worldview in which they obeyed grownups in order to avoid punishment.

Context: Morality Paradigms

Antoine de Saint-Exupéry (1943/1971) began his beloved children's book *Le Petit Prince* with his childhood drawing, *dessin numero 1*, of a fearsome boa constrictor devouring an elephant. Saint-Exupéry attributes his career choice of aviation rather than art to the reaction of *les grandes personnes* (grownups) who interpreted his masterpiece as a quite *un*-fearsome hat. Undeterred by this cautionary tale, we begin the first chapter of this text with Elly's own *dessin numero 1* (see Figure 2.1).

The four theoretical paradigms, or models, presented in this artistically-challenged drawing (from the low-technology days before PowerPoint) all have important implications for how you understand and intervene with future clients and students. Given our focus on application, this theoretical overview stresses the paradigms' psychological rather than philosophical roots. Although moral theorists rely heavily on core philosophic ideas from works ranging from Aristotle, Plato, and Nietzsche to Baldwin, Mead, Dewey, and Rawls and Habermas, space limitations preclude a substantive

DOI: 10.4324/9780429295461-3

Figure 2.1 Morality Paradigms.

discussion of those thinkers (Lapsley, 1996, and Reed, 1997, provide two
fine discussions of the philosophical roots of moral theory).

   Gielen (as cited in Kuhmerker, 1991) points out that the major moral
theories make radically different assumptions about the nature of morality,
thus giving rise to either irrational, culture-bound conceptions or rational,
nonrelativistic ones. In other words, some theories assume and stress the
primary role of emotions and societal rules while others assume and stress
the primary role of the independent intellect. Freud and the behaviorists
(and, we would add, many evolutionary psychologists, see Chapter 5) assume that morality is basically irrational and represents humans' adjustments

or adaptations to their environments and/or the rules and expectations of society. In contrast, cognitive developmentalists such as Kohlberg and Piaget focus on conscious, rational decision-making that can rise above societal conventions. Before examining individual thinkers' ideas in some depth, we take a brief look at each perspective.

Psychoanalysis

Morality is best thought of as control of socially unacceptable impulses, especially sexual and aggressive ones, by a personality structure that Freud (1923) **called the super-ego.** The super-ego uses guilt, shame, and inferiority to keep unacceptable influences in check. In this conception, the super-ego or conscience contains the internalized rules of a culture as transmitted by parents. The standard cartoon convention of angels and devils whispering contrasting advice into the characters' ears exemplifies the psychoanalytic tension between biological urges (the id) and the constraints of culture (the super-ego). If you are spending this evening diligently reading about morality instead of running naked through the streets, Freud would say that you have the stern, internalized voices of your parents to thank!

Behaviorism

Bandura's social learning theory has been particularly influential in the field of morality. Briefly, from this perspective, morality can be thought of as a set of learned habits, attitudes, and values dependent on the social environment and reinforcement contingencies (Kuhmerker, 1991). Did you give blood at a blood drive recently? Chances are that someone in your family or friendship group was also a donor, and you observed the positive responses to their altruistic act. There is a good reason that the Red Cross always puts stickers on the chests of donors saying: "Be nice to me, I gave blood today." Social learning precepts don't get much more obvious!

Cognitive Developmental

This paradigm proposes that people construct morality through active engagement in their social world. For Kohlberg (1984), morality is the development of universal and increasingly more complex and adequate stages of moral thinking. For later thinkers, morality is better understood as the development of a wider range of strategies or schemas for solving moral problems. Imagine that a 3-year-old, a 6-year-old, a 13-year-old, and a 21-year-old are playing *Candy Land,* a classic young children's board game in which you roll dice and advance to the Candy Castle or slide back into the Gum Drop Mountain. Now imagine that the 3-year-old rolls a 2 and cheerfully moves her little gingerbread man marker 6 spaces ahead to reach an attractive gum drop. Who will be driven completely crazy by this action? Who will accept the move good-naturedly but perhaps gently explain the rule about moving a piece the number of spaces corresponding to the die? (And who will be so socially mortified at playing a game of *Candy Land* that she or he does not care how *anyone* moves so long as the game ends with merciful swiftness?) Welcome to the world of cognitive development.

Evolutionary/Biological

Morality arises from a genetic predisposition to certain social emotions and behaviors that have evolved through natural selection because they increased the ability of our ancestors to survive, mate, and get their genes into the next generation. For example, many of you have at one time or another helped a friend move. You probably feel reasonably certain that if you were ever to need help with a move of your own, you could call on that friend. Current theorists would see the roots of your behavior in your chimpanzee ancestors' propensity to share grubs with chimps that have shared grubs with them in the past. In scarce times, the sharers upped their chance of surviving and so a genetic bias towards reciprocity emerged.

In this chapter, we examine two early attempts to understand the development of morality. Although both Freud's and Piaget's theories are no longer deemed adequate explanations of complex moral functioning, all later theories take them into account in some way, whether as a foundation from which to build ideas or as an edifice to be challenged and supplanted.

Freud and Morality: A Charitable View

> The tension between the harsh super-ego and the ego that is subjected to it is called by us the sense of guilt; it expresses itself as a need for punishment. Civilization, therefore, obtains mastery over the individual's dangerous desire for aggression by weakening and disarming it and by setting up an agency within him to watch over it, like a garrison in a conquered city.
>
> (Freud, 1930, pp. 123–124)

It may seem strange to begin our discussion of moral development theory with a discussion of Sigmund Freud in a field originally dominated by cognitive-developmental accounts and later by a range of biological, evolutionary, and cultural explanations. Although Freud's psychoanalytic theory had tremendous influence in the early years of the 20th century, many of his ideas have not stood up well to rigorous testing. Hogan and Emler (1995) begin their largely sympathetic treatment of Freud's work with the observation that his writings "are not well-respected today in academic psychology and, in a real sense, that is as it should be" (p. 210). However, we concur with their argument that "although many aspects of psychoanalysis *are factually wrong,* many of its assumptions and implications are quite insightful and we forget them at our peril" (p. 210).

Anyone who has taken an upper-division class in psychology or a graduate class in the helping fields is likely to have been exposed to Freud's basic model of personality—the id, the ego, and the super-ego (Freud, 1923, 1930). Rather than rehash the summary and surface treatment many of you have read in multiple formats, we concentrate on modern thinkers who have examined morality from a psychoanalytic framework. We believe you will be pleasantly surprised to see that neoanalytic thinkers provide some provocative insights with important implications for parents and professionals.

These newer ideas were not, however, evident in the first comprehensive moral development textbook (Lickona, 1976). In that book, psychiatrist James Gilligan laid out the classic psychoanalytic position that morality *represses* individuals. For Gilligan (1976), Freud's theory marked the beginning of the scientific rather than philosophical investigation of morality:

> A psychoanalytic theory of moral experience sees morality as a force antagonistic to life and to love, a force causing illness and death— neurosis and psychosis, homicide and suicide. I see morality as a necessary but immature form of affective and cognitive development, so that fixation at the moral stage represents developmental retardation, or immaturity, and regression to it represents psychopathology.
>
> (p. 145)

Here, morality is viewed as being motivated by shame and guilt and may be contrasted with the goal of psychoanalysis—a level of healthy functioning in which individuals are motivated by the positive desire to love. Ethics tends to *tell* people what to do; psychoanalysis aims at *asking* people what they *want* to do. The analyst hopes to give patients the intellectual framework to address life's big questions: "How to live and what to do" (Lickona, 1976, p. 145).

Researchers in the cognitive-developmental tradition are fond of presenting respondents with a hypothetical moral dilemma about a man named Heinz who has to decide whether it is right to steal a drug to save his dying wife. Gilligan suggests that a psychoanalyst would ask Heinz why he's hung up on what he *should* do—is he avoiding looking at what he *wants* to do? Analysts would view Heinz's moralizing as a defense mechanism. Rather than worrying about the adequacy of patients' justice reasoning, the goal of psychoanalysis is to help patients make honest assessments of what they want to do and the realistic costs of those choices.

We suspect that many readers find themselves uncomfortable with a conception of morality that sees conscience as the root of mental illness. Yet we have all experienced moments in adult life when we find ourselves feeling guilty about an action, such as leaving a whiny toddler with a spouse so that we can go off to do something we enjoy. We try to ignore the internal voice telling us how selfish we are—"Shouldn't I really be home watching the Paws Patrol video, again, rather than running off to see the latest *Avenger* movie?" If Freud is right, are all our good deeds just neurotic compliant reactions? Fortunately, many analysts have found ways to integrate a healthier conception of conscience into a Freudian framework.

Eli Sagan's 1988 book, *Freud, Women, and Morality: The Psychology of Good and Evil,* offers a compelling alternative vision. Like feminist Nancy Chodorow (1978), Sagan believes that morality has its roots in the care and attachment of the pre-Oedipal relationships of infancy and toddlerhood.

Sagan (1988) contrasts this perspective with Freud's belief that morality arises between the ages of 4 and 6 when children come to desire the opposite-sex parent and resent the same-sex one. For little boys, the Oedipal complex is resolved when fear that large, powerful dad may castrate them convinces them to drop their pursuit of mom. For little girls, the parallel Electra complex is resolved when little girls give up hopes of winning dad and decide to throw in their lot with mom. In both cases, the resolution of the complexes leads to the creation of the super-ego. The super-ego is created when children stop competing with their same-sex parents and instead incorporate them—especially their moral imperatives—into their own personalities. The super-ego can then function as the parents' agent. Cultural *oughts, shoulds,* and *shouldn'ts* now ring in the child's head as the voices of parental strictures:

"We always wash our hands before meals."

"If you can't say something nice, don't say anything at all."

"What goes on in this house stays in this house."

Sagan's (1988) major problem with Freud's conception is that although it posits that children swallow their parents whole—their nurturing, loving, encouraging, admirable parts *and* their punishing, detracting, aggressive, frightening ones—Freud actually writes **10 times** as much about the harsh, punitive aspects of the super-ego than he does about its loving, benevolent aspects. Like many modern readers, Sagan also disagrees with Freud's contention that women are incapable of the same degree of super-ego development as men. Because they do not have the threat of castration (and hence castration anxiety) to motivate the resolution of their Electra complexes, Freud (1923) believed that little girls' super-egos were never quite as strong as little boys'. Sagan argues that Freud's theory of morality fails to link nurturing and love with morality. Why? Sagan turns the tools of psychoanalysis on Freud himself and concludes that Freud repressed his own memory of a pre-Oedipal mother. In doing so, he repressed early experiences of love, identification, and idealization.

If the super-ego forms when young children incorporate their parents' norms, then the super-ego is profoundly dependent on the particular society the parents belong to. Sagan (1988) notes that in slave societies, the super-ego would legitimate slavery; in sexist societies, it would legitimate sexism; and, more specifically, in Armenia, Nazi Germany, and Rwanda, the super-ego could (and did) legitimate the horrors of genocide. He suggests, however, that while the super-ego may indeed be an amoral structure that swallows whole the norms of a prevailing culture, the conscience, in contrast, can differentiate moral from amoral attributes. Classic Freudian theory does not allow us to progress beyond the morality of our parents and culture. But people *do* triumph over the inadequacies of their particular families and the prejudices of their particular culture.

Sagan (1988) lays out an explicit summary of Freud's model for moral development:

A little boy masturbates.

A parent (usually the mother) threatens that the father or doctor will cut off his penis (not an uncommon parental threat in Freud's time).

The little boy cannot believe this!

Eventually he sees a naked girl and becomes a believer. He gives up all hope of doing in dad and seducing mom.

He introjects the authoritarian parents into his ego and forms the nucleus of the super-ego "which takes over the severity of the father and perpetuates his prohibition against incest" (p. 75).

The process both preserves and paralyzes the little boy's penis and moves him into Freud's stage of latency.

Sagan's alternative model posits a three-stage model of healthy conscience development:

1. The more adequately a child is loved and nurtured in infancy and early childhood, the greater chance she or he will develop a sound conscience.
2. Children show two types of identification in their early years:
   a. Identification with their nurturer, which leads to the "universal human inclination… to give back love for love received" (p. 160); and
   b. Identification with their comforters, which later allows them to identify with victims and feel pity and compassion.
3. Children's desire to give back love and nurturance eventually generalizes to others beyond their families. This step is dependent on

the development of the abilities to generalize and abstract described by Piaget (1932/1997) as the formal operations stage. A mature adult conscience is the end product of this stage.

In summary, Freud lost his way because he ignored children's powerful need for reciprocity—to return nurturance for nurturance given (Sagan, 1988). He saw them controlled only by punishment and fear of loss of love. He forgot that children also want to please the people they love. With Sagan, we would argue that identification with the nurturer is a much better candidate for the core foundation of moral development than fear of a castrating father.

In moving from Gilligan and Sagan to Hogan and Emler's (1995) model of moral development, we shift from the traditional psychoanalytic focus on the child and the family to consider the child's development within the wider society. The psychoanalytic perspective stresses how children and their families develop in particular times and places. Hogan and Emler's analysis provides a useful model for helping professionals in that it salvages important Freudian insights and integrates them with Mead (1934) and Durkheim's (1961) sociological conceptions and Erikson's (1968) psychosocial theory.

In the psychoanalytic model, moral development is conceptualized as a by-product of personality. Children develop through a process of three major transformations in their relationships with social groups:

1. As Freud (1923) noted, in early childhood, children's identification with their parents helps them develop respect for authority.
2. Drawing on George Herbert Mead's work, Hogan and Emler (1995) posit a second transformation in middle childhood or early adolescence. Developing role-taking and perspective-taking skills result in identification with the social group and a growing responsiveness to other's expectations.
3. Finally, in late adolescence or early adulthood, taking on adult roles helps individuals to develop a personal sense of identity and articulate justifications for accepting the rules of chosen groups or institutions.

Hogan and Emler (1995) accept Freud's evolutionary perspective that civilizations must somehow control human's evolutionarily pre-attuned selfishness. They argue that his definition of morality as the rules or conventions of an individual's society is not naïve relativism but rather a valid analysis of how conventional moralities arise of necessity to regulate the universal human instincts of sex and aggression that have such potential to disrupt any society. Given these realities, it should be no surprise that what society asks of us—the super-ego's control of the id's desires—leads to "painful renunciations" (p. 213). So, although Freud argues that societies (and their agents, the super-ego) are of necessity repressive and the principle cause of neurosis, he held that a just society "is one in which everyone suffers equally" (p. 213).

Although this may seem at first blush a relativistic perspective, a deeper understanding of Freud uncovers a more complex vision. Yes, humans are by nature selfish, aggressive, and lustful. Societies have no choice but to develop rules and consequences to keep these instincts in check. The moral person must comply with society's rules because the alternative is chaos. However (and this is a major "however"), Freud believed in a moral obligation to pursue self-awareness. Without self-awareness, which he believed the process of psychoanalysis could deliver, people are at the mercy of their instincts. When we gain self-understanding and come to acknowledge and integrate the animal side of our nature, we can then *choose* to follow society's rules because we now understand how necessary they are.

Current Evaluation of Freud's Theory

Although the ideas of psychoanalysis remain important in Western culture, they have faced serious and legitimate scientific criticism and no longer play a significant role in most contemporary conceptions of moral development. In the following sections, we summarize a few of the most central challenges. Interestingly, however, recent findings from neuroscience suggest that Freud's observation of tensions between components he called the id, ego, and super-ego may actually have a basis in brain systems. In further support of Freud's focus on early childhood experiences, Narvaez and Vaydich (2008) noted mounting evidence for lifelong effects of parenting on brain formation and later emotional regulation (see Table 2.1).

Table 2.1 Strengths and Challenges of Freud's Theory

Strengths include:
- Stress on the importance of early attachment and other childhood experiences for later adult functioning.
- Attention to the tension between rational conscious thoughts and "unconscious," more emotional forces that foreshadowed current dual-processing theories.
- Concepts of internalization, identification, and introjection (Kramer, 2006).

Challenges include:
- Lack of testable hypotheses.
- Gender bias.
- Overreliance on case studies.
- Developed his theories from observations of a clinical sample and his own self-analysis rather than a random sample of a normative population.
- Frequently distorted or ignored data that challenged his ideas (e.g., Esterson, 2001; Kramer, 2006).
- Inadequate evidence to support his theory of psychosexual stages, children's incestuous desires, or the Oedipal and Electra complexes (Kramer, 2006; Weiten, 2016).

Applications of Psychoanalytic Theory

Despite well-justified skepticism about many aspects of Freudian theory itself, what might helping professionals want to take away from a psycho-analytic perspective on morality? If we accept that love is the great teacher (e.g., Sagan, 1988) and that legitimate respect for authority arises from identification with parents (Damon, 1988; Hogan & Emler, 1995), then it should become a societal priority both to promote responsive parenting and to provide alternative caring adults for children who are not getting or did not get responsive parenting.

Consider the case of children whose parents have not been there for them either literally (e.g., biological fathers who play no role in their children's lives) or emotionally (e.g., parents whose own problems with substance abuse or mental illness interfere with their parenting). The pro-fessional literature in education and therapy is replete with examples of abandoned or neglected children struggling with a wide range of problems that frequently include problems with authority and rules and lack of conscience.

In cases like this, it is not uncommon to see helping professionals turning to the commonsense strategy of trying to provide alternative parental fig-ures. Big Brother/Big Sister programs, concerned extended family mem-bers, mentors, teachers, and counselors have all attempted to provide caring adult guidance for children adrift. Older adolescents are sometimes steered into the military, where the drill sergeants provide a crash course in rules and discipline. In connecting children with caring and/or consistent adults, concerned helpers seem to be using the Freudian idea that children develop respect for authority through identification with parents or parental figures. These connections also reflect a commitment to Sagan's (1988) key concept that, in the end, **love is the great teacher.** When biological parents fail to adequately serve as loving teachers and society's agents, then alternative agents must be found.

Piaget and His Marbles

> It is of paramount importance during this… interrogatory to play your part in a simple spirit and to let the child feel a certain superiority at the game (while not omitting to show by an occasional good shot that you are not a complete duffer).
>
> (Piaget, 1932/1997, p. 24)

In 1932, Jean Piaget (1896–1980), one of the great intellectuals of the 20th century, published a delightful study of children's moral develop-ment. *The Moral Judgment of the Child* begins with Piaget's oft-cited de-finition: **"All morality consists of a system of rules and the essence of morality is to be sought for in the respect which the individual**

acquires for these rules" (p. 13). The book describes his exploration of developmental changes in children's respect for rules using methods such as asking children about the rules of the game of marbles or to respond to questions about short moral stories. Although most of us learned about Piaget's theories of cognitive and moral development as classic *stage* theories, we argue (with, e.g., Chapman, 1988; Gibbs, 1995; Lapsley, 1996) that this conception does a disservice to his actual, more nuanced conception of *phases* of development.

This section's opening quotation captures the creative spirit underlying Piaget's innovative methods and respectful engagement with children. Unfortunately, his methodological creativity, conceptual complexity, and many lovely little caveats tend to be missing from the standard presentations of his work in introductory or developmental psychology textbooks. We attempt to lay out some of his basic ideas in a manner that is more faithful to his actual writings and then provide a brief discussion of current critiques and reconceptualization's of his work.

Freudian theory gave us a perspective of morality as self-control (of the id by the ego) and conformity to socially acceptable standards and rules (enforced by the super-ego). But the quality of interpersonal behavior is not simply a function of the adoption of proscriptive rules and restrictions. Morality is much more than "thou shalt nots." Of equal importance, and the focus of Piaget's, and later Kohlberg's, interests are social actions based on prescriptive moral rules or standards of what individuals *should* do.

Piaget's theory of moral judgment parallels and builds upon his earlier theory of cognitive development from 1928. As a brief refresher, remember that this famous theory posits that children's thinking moves through ever more complex sequences as children mature and encounter a widening range of social experiences.

Piaget's Conception of Cognitive Development

Sensorimotor "Thought" (used from birth to about age 2)— Characterized by a developing ability to coordinate sensory input with motor actions. Children learn about the objects in their world through acting on them (e.g., looking, grabbing, mouthing). **The major accomplishment of this phase is *object permanence*, the understanding that things exist even when they disappear.**

Preoperational Thought (approximately from ages 2 to 7)— Characterized by an improving ability to use mental images but still hampered by the tendency for *centration,* a tendency to focus on one salient or obvious feature of a problem or situation and to neglect other important features. You may remember being more pleased with a present that came in a big box, regardless of its value when you were a young child. Another limitation of thought in this period is a tendency towards egocentrism, defined by Piaget (1932/1997) as the child believing "himself to be sharing the point of view of the world at large" while unaware that "he is really still shut up in his own point of view" (p. 36). Elly remembers being 5 years old and terrified to tell her father that she had broken a cellar window playing baseball. It took her years to understand that being a baseball player himself, as well as a good dad who understood the skill limitations of a kindergartener, he saw no necessity to punish her. She couldn't put herself in his shoes yet and could not even imagine that he could see her in any way other than as the naughty child she saw herself to be.

Concrete Operational Thought (ages 7 to 11)—Characterized by the child's ability to perform operations such as reversibility and decentration on images of tangible, concrete objects and happenings. For example, a child can sort a pile of shapes into triangles and circles and tell you that there are more triangles than circles. The child using concrete operational thought can answer correctly the question that befuddles the typical child using preoperational thought: "Are there more triangles or more shapes?" **Piaget identified the major cognitive achievement of concrete operations as** *conservation,* **or the understanding that physical quantities remain constant even when they change shape or appearance.**

Formal Operational Thought (begins about age 11)—Characterized by the ability to use operations on abstract as well as concrete objects. You can have lively and meaningful conversations with teens about abstract topics like justice and duty. Children also become more systematic in their thinking. We begin to ask a lot more of older children both in school and home settings, correctly assessing that they can now envision the consequences of their actions and so should be held more accountable for them. (If, at 14, Elly had been practicing with a hardball a few feet from a window, her father would not have been at all so forgiving.) **In this final phase, children's thinking thus becomes more logical, systematic, and abstract** (Elkind & Flavell, 1969; Flavell, 1963; Flavell, 1982; Flavell et al., 2002; Piaget 1936; Piaget, 1960).

In Piaget's foreword to one of the first works introducing his research to US scholars (Flavell, 1963), he described how Professor Flavell's goal was difficult "not only because I had written too much in the course of tackling too many different problems... but above all because I am not an easy author" (p. vii). Piaget saw the principle source of problems as arising from the fact that he was a naturalist and biologist by training, with a primary interest in epistemology, not psychology. In his own words, "my most central concern has been to determine the contributions of the person's activities and the limiting aspects of the object in the process of acquiring knowledge... those who read my work often find themselves confused" (p. vii). Most thinkers who have grappled with Piaget's work would agree (see e.g., Chapman, 1988; Lapsley, 1996). As Flavell noted in his introduction, Piaget's theory and research are scattered across more than 25 books and 150 articles (some of near-book length). Many are not translated from French to English and, no matter the language, all are difficult to read and comprehend.

Before moving from cognition to morality, we should review four terms central to Piaget's (1932/1997) ideas about development. Piaget observed that children constructed *schemas,* or generalized knowledge structures about things and events. You can think of schemas as the building blocks of thinking and knowledge. For example, we have a schema about what mothers are like, another about how to act in a classroom, yet another about what should happen when we meet a new person. Piaget believed that thinking changed in two major ways: *assimilation,* which occurs when people incorporate new information into their existing schemas, and *accommodation,* which occurs when people must adjust their schemas to new information.

Let's consider the greeting schema. One hallmark of neurotic people is that they tend to have ineffective or annoying schemas. When asked, "How are you?" the healthy individual knows to give a response such as "Fine, thanks, and you?" rather than "I'm so depressed, nobody ever seems to care about my rashes, my dismal love life, and my sadistic boss." However when someone has a "poor me" schema, he or she frequently takes in information and makes it fit into that structure. In working with people like our aforementioned lovelorn example, therapists frequently push their clients to construct new, healthier schemas—to accommodate.

For Piaget, the mechanism of *equilibration* explains how children shift states of thought. Assimilation and accommodation result in cognitive changes that frequently result in disequilibrium as children try to understand the world. The phases of cognitive and moral development represent points of equilibrium arising from children's active exploration of their world.

Using the operational definition of morality as a system of rules, and building upon his ideas of cognitive development, Piaget began his study of morality by interviewing children of different ages about their conceptions of and respect for the rules of the common (at the time) childhood game of marbles. He assumed that, just as cognitive development proceeded through specific sequences, so too should moral reasoning move forward in phases related to the growing complexity in the child's cognitive capacity. He borrowed Freud's method of the clinical interview and added his own twist by using structured questions. Reading his results, one sees both the scientific standardization of questions and the creative ability to follow a child's reasoning by using perceptive prompts and clarifying questions.

The Moral Judgment of the Child (Piaget, 1932/1997) is divided into four major sections. In the first, "The Rules of the Game," Piaget describes the protocol for the marbles study and provides numerous examples of the answers of children of different ages:

> The experimenter speaks more or less as follows. "Here are some marbles.... You must show me how to play. When I was little I used to play a lot, but now I've quite forgotten how to.... Let's play together. You'll teach me the rules and I'll play with you."
>
> (p. 24)

As the child and interviewer are playing, the interviewer asks a series of questions, such as whether he can invent a new rule, whether new rules could lead to new games, and which rules are fairest. Piaget found that very young children thought they were playing the game but handled the marbles with little to no regard for formal rules. From about ages 2 to 5, children began to imitate the rules they saw others use but still played very egocentrically. They might play together but did not use unifying rules. Between ages 7 and 8, children he interviewed began to try to win and became interested in using standard rules. Yet they tended to have inconsistent versions of rules. It was only between ages 11 and 12 that children appeared to have codified the rules and described them with a great deal of concordance. In Gabain's 1997 translation of Piaget's work, the discussion of these changes uses the word *stages* consistently. However, as Piaget summarized the section, he added one of the many caveats that are sprinkled through his work and undermine the traditional understanding of his work as describing stages: "After having done our utmost to show that child thought differs from adult thought not only in degree but in its very nature, we confess that we no longer know precisely what is meant by these terms" (p. 84). He notes that sometimes features of children's thinking appear in adults and sometimes, especially when the children are co-operating with equals, features of adult thinking appear in children: **"There is an adult in every child and a child in every adult"** (p. 85).

Piaget's most important finding was the existence of two moralities in childhood. In the second section of his book, "Adult Constraint and Moral Realism," he described the type of thinking characteristic of early school-age thinking. Piaget uses two analogous terms for the thinking in this phase: *moral realism* and the *morality of constraint.* Described as the *stage of heteronomous morality* in most textbooks, moral realism is characterized by the child's belief that any action that shows obedience to adult authority is good. In addition, children reason using the letter rather than the spirit of the law and evaluate actions by their objective outcomes rather than by their underlying motives. Rules tend to come from the outside for younger children. They obey because of external adult constraints rather than any inner resolve or true conscience. Piaget (1932/1997) believed that children's thinking until the ages of 7 and 8 showed a great deal of subordination of justice to adult authority, but during the ages from 8 to 11 showed progress towards "equalitarianism" (p. 315):

The morality of constraint is that of duty pure and simple and of heteronomy. The child accepts from the adult a certain number of commands to which it must submit whatever the circumstances may be. Right is what conforms with these commands; wrong is what fails to do so.

(p. 335)

Piaget's (1932/1997) third section, "Cooperation and the Development of the Idea of Justice," describes thinking during the developmental period that begins around ages 11 and 12, when children move into a genuine feeling of equality with others. Most undergraduate textbooks describe this period as the **stage of autonomous morality**. Piaget frequently refers to it as the **morality of cooperation,** "whose guiding principle is solidarity and which puts the primary emphasis on autonomy of conscience, on intentionality, and consequently on subjective responsibility" (p. 335).

The book ends with an extensive discussion that argues for the supremacy of Piaget's research-based theory of morality over those of Durkheim, Baldwin, Falconet, and Bovet. Modern readers may be unfamiliar with some or all of these thinkers but should find Piaget's lively treatment of the intellectual ideas of the time an engaging exercise.

We hope that you have noticed how careful we are being to avoid using the word *stage*. Piaget (1932/1997) himself is quite clear about the matter in work from 1960 in which he states, "There are no general stages" (p. 14). His research had shown him that children sometimes used different types of thinking across different content domains. Lapsley's (1996) excellent analysis of Piaget's theory makes abundantly clear that Piaget's "stages" of cognitive development were meant to describe some of the formal properties of children's thinking, not the children themselves.

Interviews with Discipline Leaders: Daniel Lapsley Ph.D. (Professor and Chairperson Department of Psychology Notre Dame University)

Dan Lapsley's research focuses on various topics in adolescent social cognitive and personality development including work on adolescent invulnerability and risk behavior; narcissism; separation-individuation; self, ego, and identity development; and college adjustment. He also studies the moral dimensions of personality and other topics in moral psychology and has written on moral identity and moral and character education. As you can see in the following excerpts from his work while admiring the foundational work of Piaget, Lapsley's more recent work explores the importance of a complex conception of moral development rooted in the formation of the moral personality.

> Piaget taught us many things not the least is that what we see in the world depends upon our understanding and this insight will continue to pay dividends in the study of many areas of moral psychology.
>
> (D. Lapsley, personal communication, September 27, 2012)

> And yet to speak of an apotheosis that is now past, and of an era in moral psychology that is post-Kohlberg is to suggest that something has happened to the status of moral stage theory... that the topic is more a matter of faint historical interest than a source of animated research activity (Lapsley, 2006, p. 38).... This suggests that the formation of moral identity is the clear goal of both moral and identity development too, just as it is for the moral self, and that the trajectories of moral and self-identity development are ideally conjoined in the moral personality.
>
> (Lapsley, 2006, p. 60)

Because most of us learn better, no matter our cognitive sophistication, when we can approach abstract ideas through familiar, concrete examples, let us attempt to provide one that may make this distinction a bit clearer. Imagine that a child exhibits a sore throat and a fever. Her doctor takes a throat swab, and the culture reveals that a streptococcus bacterial infection is the underlying structure causing the external symptoms of fever and sore throat. The child is not the disease but the child *has* the disease, so she manifests its symptoms. Analogously, a child is not concrete operational but the thinking structure he or she uses in a particular situation may be concrete operational. Just as we say a child ill with strep exhibits a sore throat, we can say that a child using concrete operational thought will exhibit conservation.

As we turn to Piaget's theory of moral development, we refer to the same sort of model. Contrary to the hard stage theory of development we see in Kohlberg, Piaget's *phases* (his preferred term) of moral development describe how a child understands social-moral situations. They do not imply a general stage of development characterized by functional unity. As cited by Michael Chapman (1988), Piaget makes quite clear the following:

> Nowhere have I seen structural unity, at no stage in the development of the child.... And if there is no structural unity, there are no general stages that permit fixed correspondences, verifiable in all domains, and between all functions.
>
> (pp. 346–347)

Piaget's Phase Theory of Moral Development

Piaget described children as **premoral** until the ages of 3 and 4. In his view, very young children do not truly understand rules and, hence, cannot make judgments about violations of rules. Preschoolers play in idiosyncratic ways and frequently invent their own rules or change rules at will. They conduct games according to their own private fantasies and desires.

As children mature, they begin using Piaget's first actual phase of moral reasoning, called alternately **heteronomous morality, the morality of constraint,** or **moral realism.** This type of reasoning corresponds to preoperational thinking. Piaget observed that young children, from approximately ages 3 to 6, tend to be moral absolutists. They see rules as handed down by authorities (e.g., parents, teachers, police) and thus are fixed, sacred, immutable, and absolute. Ideas about right and wrong are inflexible and justice is subordinate to adult authority. To test this concept, Piaget (1932/1997) told children pairs of stories about childhood moral transgressions:

> The little girl had a friend who had a cage and a bird. She thought this was too unkind. So she took the cage and let the bird out—[another] little girl stole a sweet and ate it.— Are they both equally naughty or is one of them naughtier than the other?
>
> (p. 132)

He found that, in general, as children got older they are less likely to judge actions by their material consequences (the cage is bigger, so the first girl is naughtier). Instead, they take intentions into account. Once again, however, in the original text, Piaget (1932/1997) was careful to point out that the "two attitudes may co-exist at the same age and even in the same child, but broadly speaking, they do not synchronize" (p. 133). Piaget found that young children focused on consequences more than intentions although he admits that they were often aware of the intentions.

In his research, Piaget frequently encountered children in this phase who exhibited a conception of *imminent justice,* or the notion that breaking rules or disobeying authority will surely result in punishment. For example, when I (Elly) was about 4, my mother put down ant poison around some of the door frames of our house and told me, "Don't touch this—it's a bad poison." When she left the room, I put my finger out and touched it. For the next year or so, I lay in bed every night resignedly waiting to die.

About the age of 11, the children Piaget studied began to use more thinking that exhibits **autonomous morality** (also described by him as **moral relativism,** and **the morality of reciprocity**). Years of social interactions, especially with their peers, have helped children develop an idea of the need for reciprocity in interactions. Older children believe that everyone has an equal right to justice. They come to realize that rules are statements of convention and can be changed by consensus or agreement. They now reject blind obedience to authority and see moral rules as products of cooperation, reciprocity, and interaction among peers. Their moral judgments show more flexibility and take into consideration the circumstances of an individual's action as well as the actor's point of view, emotions, and feelings.

For example, Piaget told children a story about a mother who had one obedient daughter and one disobedient daughter. She liked the obedient one best and gave her the biggest piece of cake. Children were asked, "What do you think of that?" Of 6- to 9-year-olds, 70% thought the mother had done a good thing. Only 40% of 10- to 13-year-olds agreed (Piaget, 1932/1997). Instead, their comments revealed a developing conception of justice as evidenced in the responses of 10-year-olds Pres and The:

> Pres (10; 0): "*The mother ought to have loved the other one and been kind to her, then perhaps she would have become more obedient.*— Is it fair to give more to the obedient one?—*No.*"

> The (10; 7): "*She ought to have given them both the same amount.*— Why?—*Because they were her daughters, she ought to have loved them both the same.*"

(p. 265)

Piaget believed that the transition from heteronomous to autonomous thinking schemas was a joint function of children's greater cognitive capacity and their more extensive social experiences. With maturity, children's cognition manifests two important changes:

1   A decline in egocentrism.
2   An increase in the ability to take roles and assume another's perspective.

While young children are prone to center attention on salient features that capture their attention (**centration**), older children are capable of **decentration**—an ability to attend to multiple features of social reality. Gibbs (1995) makes the important point that the features in social situations that are often most salient to younger children are their own "claims, needs or desires" (p. 40). In contrast, older children can often put themselves in another's shoes without an adult reminding them, "How would you feel if...?"

Current Evaluation of Piaget's Theory

There is no doubt that Piaget's contribution to developmental psychology has been enormous. After decades of research, however, some parts of this theory stand up better than others. Today, most developmentalists believe that children's thinking is more like a loosely connected set of systems than

Table 2.2 Strengths and Challenges of Piaget's Theory

Strengths include:
- Important concepts such as assimilation, accommodation, schemas, and conservation.
- The view of the child as active constructor of knowledge.
- Creative methods for observing children.
- The idea is that we can structure environments slightly above the child's current level to foster development.

Criticisms include:
- Piaget underestimated children's competence in some areas (e.g., egocentrism)—babies and young children are more competent than his theory predicted.
- He overestimated children's competence in others (e.g., formal operations)—many teens and adults do not use much formal operational thinking at all.
- Evidence suggests that stages are not unitary structures (however, note that Piaget himself cheerfully acknowledged this point).
- He underestimated the role of culture and education in fostering or retarding cognitive and moral development (Flavell et al., 2002; Santrock, 2018).

one general cognitive system (Flavell et al., 2002). Research has shown that performance is often domain specific. Children may, for instance, show more advanced strategies when solving math problems than they do in solving interpersonal ones. Thus, contemporary developmental researchers are more likely to look at how "attention, memory capacity, expertise, problem-solving strategies... and social supports" (p. 9) influence performance on cognitive tasks. Coming from his strong biological background, Piaget tended to view children's cognition "as a specific form of biological *adaptation* of a complex organism to a complex environment" (p. 5). That was, and remains, a brilliant and important frame for understanding cognition and moral judgment. As Flavell et al. (2002) note, Piaget's theory is so central to cognitive psychology that most of us have *assimilated* it so thoroughly that we are in danger of failing to notice how often we filter new information through Piagetian spectacles (see Table 2.2).

Applications and Implications for Helping Professionals

Teachers, parents, counselors, and social workers are most effective when they can put themselves into the shoes of the student/child/client with whom they are working. Piaget's theory helps us understand that, in general, as children get older, they move through phases from more primitive to more evolved thinking. They progress "from an external morality of physical appearance and consequences, to a pragmatic morality of tit-for-tat reciprocity, and finally to a more internal or autonomous morality entailing consideration of psychological contexts and ideal reciprocity" (Gibbs, 1995, p. 31).

Piaget was a researcher, not a clinician, but he did offer one bit of practical advice. He believed that parents could (although they rarely did) help their children develop into the phase of autonomous morality by being more egalitarian and less authoritarian. It would not be until decades after the publication of *The Moral Judgment of the Child* that Lawrence Kohlberg and others (e.g., DeVries & Zan, 1994; Hayes, 1991; Power et al., 1989) explored some of the practical applications of Piaget's cognitive developmental approach to morality for educational settings. These applications are discussed in some detail in Part II, but first we examine how Lawrence Kohlberg (and, later, James Rest) built upon Piaget's ideas to develop one of the best-known and most heuristic theories in 20th-century psychology.

Discussion Questions

1   In what ways do you think your current moral values were shaped by fear of parental punishment and in what ways by identification with one or both parents?
2   Consider how your schemas for how relationships work have changed across development. Did your schema for the ideal romantic partner change significantly from your early to your late teens? In what ways?

Additional Resources

- This site will help you situate Freud's work on morality within his broader ideas and theory: https://www.iep.utm.edu/freud/
- For a brief biography of Piaget with some interesting links to thinkers who influenced him as well as those he influenced: http://www.intelltheory.com/piaget.shtml

3 From Stages to Schemas: Kohlberg and Rest

There is probably not an introductory or developmental psychology text-book on the market today that does not devote a section to Lawrence Kohlberg's (1927–1987) influential six stages of moral development. Texts generally follow a brief overview of his theory, with discussions such as "Kohlberg's Critics" or "Evaluating Kohlberg's Theory." As was the case with Piaget's theories of cognitive and moral development, after an initial period of intense work within the Kohlbergian paradigm, many theorists and researchers began to challenge his assumptions, methods, and adherence to the primacy of moral cognition over other components of morality. You will read brief synopses of these challenges in this chapter and Chapter 4.

James Rest's Neo-Kohlbergian approach, while known less well than Kohlberg's famous stage theory, emerged from a careful and thorough analysis of decades of research using the Defining Issues Test (DIT), a re-cognition measure of development in moral reasoning. Rest's colleagues from the Minnesota Group believe that their approach "has been a pro-gressive force in the field, promoting change in both theory and mea-surement and also serving as a stabilizing force by reaffirming Kohlberg's basic view that moral judgements are both cognitive and developmental" (Thoma, 2002, p. 225).

Most of the theorists in the upcoming chapters raise serious concerns about the strong focus on moral reasoning in Piaget's, Kohlberg's, and Rest's early cognitive-developmental accounts. Our stance, however, is that the conception of developmental growth in cognitive complexity at the heart of all three theories continues to have important practical value for applications across the helping professions.

Kohlberg's Universal Theory of Structural Stages

As a moral educator I was... asked to lecture to the staff of my old... school. When I arrived, I saw a number of my old teachers in the audience looking at me with disbelief. They remembered me as a high-school boy who was always on probation for smoking, drinking, and visiting the girls in a nearby school. In this regard I was not vastly

DOI: 10.4324/9780429295461-4

different from many of my... friends who felt little responsibility for rules about which we had no say. The rules I violated were to me rules of arbitrary convention rather than rules of justice or concern for the rights and welfare of other persons.

(Kohlberg, 1986, p. 4)

Before exploring the applications of Kohlberg's theory, it is necessary to understand and evaluate it. We begin with a brief portrait of the man behind the theory and the innovative dissertation study that gave rise to it.

Kohlberg the Man

The center of Kohlberg's vision, a universal justice-centered morality, is not surprising given his powerful life experiences at the end of World War II. After serving two years in the Merchant Marines, 20-year-old Kohlberg signed on as an engineer on a ship smuggling Jewish refugees, many fresh from the horrors of the concentration camps, to Palestine. The British captured the ship and the crew was (ironically) interned in a British concentration camp on Cyprus. The crew was rescued and eventually made it to Palestine, where Kohlberg briefly experienced life on a Jewish kibbutz. These events left him with an almost visceral need to address the horrors of the Holocaust. Because he was a man of the mind, he turned to philosophy and psychology to give, in the words of his colleague Gil Noam, "reality to the often-empty slogan of 'Never Again'" (Fowler et al., 1988, p. 40).

Kohlberg dedicated his life to articulating and applying a universal theory of the development of moral reasoning. As philosopher Don Reed (1997) has noted, Kohlberg devoted more than 30 years to answering the question at the heart of his project: "How do we foster justice and respond to injustice without arbitrarily imposing our own culture-laden ideals?" (p. 56). Kohlberg's project began with a groundbreaking dissertation study that is all too frequently criticized with no consideration of the contexts of its time.

The Dissertation: Kohlberg's Original Study of Moral Development

Lawrence Kohlberg's 1958 University of Chicago dissertation represents the founding document of modern moral development. Kohlberg not only staked out a claim for moral development as a distinct field with a distinct theory, methods, and domain, but also moved away from Piaget's biological focus to an emphasis on social theories in the tradition of Dewey, Mead, and Durkheim (Puka, 1994).

Kohlberg constructed a design that compared the moral reasoning of fourth-, seventh-, and tenth-grade boys who were social isolates versus social integrates and upper-middle class versus lower middle class. Today, his interest in how being a social isolate or social integrate influences moral reasoning has been almost forgotten (Vozzola, 1996). Instead, people remember one feature of the sample design: the absence of female participants (Gilligan, 1982). The obvious care given to every detail of sample selection argues against the interpretation that this lacuna represents a deliberate bias of the researcher. In fact, in a preliminary paper based on his research for a biography of Kohlberg, Reed (1994) noted that Helen Koch, Kohlberg's dissertation mentor, advised him to work with boys because of Piaget's finding that boys tended to be more responsive subjects than girls for this sort of research. Reed further argues that the dissertation study represented a "politically and personally meaningful response to Nazi atrocities. He [Kohlberg] was going to address fundamental issues of social justice and directly help people at the same time" (p. 3). Helen Koch introduced the young prodigy to the works of Mead, Dewey, and Piaget. Kohlberg integrated these ideas into a theory whose breadth, originality, and importance were almost unprecedented in a doctoral study.

Beyond its historical significance, Kohlberg's dissertation contains many ideas relevant to moral development today. The early document foreshadows his future interest in the promise of moral education. "Yet the understanding of the moral educator is not that of the permissive therapist; it is an understanding which leads to higher demands as well as to forgiveness" (Puka, 1994, p. 367).

Kohlberg's Structural Stage Theory of Moral Development

Building on Piaget's work, Kohlberg posited a developmental paradigm of invariant, sequential, deep-structural stages of moral judgment. Kohlberg's work, however, extended Piaget's two *phases* to six, later modified to five, invariant *stages* of moral development across the lifespan. **Each of his stages represented an increasingly adequate logical structure for reasoning about rules, roles, and institutions.** A key concept of the theory holds that stage progression entails the development of logically richer and ever-more inclusive reciprocity that can be used to solve moral problems or dilemmas. At the pinnacle of moral reasoning, postconventional judgments, reciprocity involves the balancing of the rights and responsibilities of all concerned parties and arises from an attitude of mutual respect and commitment to universal principles. **Justice** represents the central notion in Kohlberg's theory, and each of his successive stages embodies justice for a larger body of people (Colby & Kohlberg, 1987; Kohlberg, 1976, 1981, 1984; Lickona, 1976).

Kohlberg revised his six stages several times over the years and thus readers of primary and secondary literature in moral development will note differences in terminology and definitions in tables summarizing the stages. The brief tables found in various texts and articles have sometimes resulted in confusion and "inventive interpretations" (Rest & Narvaez, 1994, p. 5). In the interest of clarity and simplicity, we use Rest and Narvaez's (1994) conception of the stages as conceptions of how best to organize cooperation (Table 3.1).

Table 3.1 Six Stages in the Concept of Cooperation

Stage 1	The morality of obedience: Do what you're told.
Stage 2	The morality of instrumental egoism and simple exchange: Let's make a deal.
Stage 3	The morality of interpersonal concordance: Be considerate, nice, and kind: you'll make friends.
Stage 4	The morality of law and duty to the social order: Everyone in society is obligated to and protected by the law.
Stage 5	The morality of consensus-building procedures: You are obligated by the arrangements that are agreed to by due process procedures.
Stage 6	The morality of nonarbitrary social cooperation: Morality is defined by how rational and impartial people would ideally organize cooperation.

Level I: Preconventional Morality

Kohlberg's research identified three levels and six stages of moral reasoning. At the first level, **preconventional morality,** generally seen at about ages 4–10, judgments are based on proximal and generally superior sources of authority. The standards of judging right and wrong are external rather than internal.

Stage 1, The Morality of Obedience

At the first stage of the preconventional level, which Kohlberg called the **punishment and obedience orientation,** children rely on the physical consequences of actions to decide if they are right or wrong. Hence, children behave morally because adults have greater power. They are acutely aware of the perceptually salient features of adults' larger size and greater strength. The social perspective of the stage is rooted in children's egocentric point of view. They do not consider other's interests or re-cognize that they may differ from their own. Often, children seem to confuse an authority's perspective with their own.

Elly remembers well the way we would tell on each other in first grade if someone did not line their math papers in exact accordance with the tea-cher's instructions. Not only did we feel morally obligated to "tell" on the miscreants, but we also felt morally outraged at their transgressions. "Miss Ivins said to make the boxes every two inches and you made your lines at three—I'm telling!"

Stage 2, The Morality of Instrumental Egoism and Simple Exchange

In the second stage of this level, **individualism, instrumental purpose, and exchange** (to use Kohlberg's more convoluted title), children judge actions from a concrete, individualistic perspective. They become aware that all people have their own interests to pursue and that these may conflict. Therefore, the right course of action is relative. Concern for others tends to be limited to children's own needs and is often expressed in "you scratch my back, I'll scratch yours" interactions.

For example, during my (Elly's) childhood in the late 1950s, playing with Barbie dolls was a major social activity for girls. One day, I packed up my Barbie carrying case with Barbie and her collection of slinky evening gowns and little plastic shoes and biked over to my third-grade friend Donna's house for an afternoon of play. My great-aunt had sewed a lovely purple velvet evening coat for my Barbie and Donna asked to borrow it. Well-trained oldest daughter that I was, I agreed and asked if I could use Donna's Barbie convertible. Donna responded, "Sorry, my mother doesn't allow me to share that." The next day, I returned and Donna again asked to borrow the velvet coat. I told her I was sorry but my mother didn't allow me to share it. Donna quickly decided that I could use the convertible, I responded by lending the coat, and all backs were not only well scratched but also well dressed!

Level II: Conventional Morality

At Kohlberg's next level, **conventional morality,** found across widely varying age ranges, judgments based on external standards and consequences gradually give way to judgments based on the rules or norms of people's group. Individuals come to internalize the definitions of right and wrong of their particular reference group.

Stage 3, The Morality of Interpersonal Concordance

For children at Kohlberg's Stage 3 of Level 2, **mutual interpersonal expectations, relationships, and interpersonal conformity,** the social perspective shifts to that of the individual in relationship with other individuals. Early conventional thinkers come to an awareness of shared "feelings, agreements, and expectations which take primacy over individual interests" (Kohlberg, 1976, p. 34). However, they do not yet consider a generalized systems perspective. Growing cognitive complexity is evident, though, in that judgments now take into account and place high value on the principles of trust, loyalty, gratitude, and maintaining relationships.

Stage 3's moral perspective is especially evident in the moral rationales of adolescents at the high school level. Teachers and administrators are often frustrated at watching an adolescent show caring and empathic behavior towards a lacrosse teammate and then turn around and mercilessly tease a fellow student from the Goth clique.

Stage 4, The Morality of Law and Duty to the Social Order

As adolescents' physical and social environments expand, so too does their conception of the source of norms. At Kohlberg's Stage 4, **social system and conscience** (also called **law and order**), people focus on duty, respect for authority, and obedience to laws and rules. Stage 4 thinkers differentiate the societal point of view from interpersonal agreement or motives. A person can now take the view of the system that defines and generates rules and roles. The Stage 4 individual considers individual relations in terms of their place in a larger system.

During my (Elly's) doctoral internship at the Scarsdale A-School, an alternative high school that incorporated many of Kohlberg's ideas into its philosophy and methods, I often observed the weekly community meetings. I was particularly fascinated by a weeks-long debate on whether A-School students should vote to "own" the school system's drug policy. Although most of the students began with a range of rather conventional and fairly unsophisticated arguments against accepting an obligation to uphold the rules (e.g., "Isn't it a free country?"), the arguments of students using an interesting mix of Stage 3 ("We can't be much of a community for each other if we come to school stoned") and Stage 4 reasoning eventually won the day: "The fact of the matter is that this is a school system rule and whether we 'own' it or not, we are going to be held to it. It makes a lot more sense to be responsible and say we accept that it's a rule made for the good of everyone than to act like idiots and say we have some right that other students in town don't."

Level III: Postconventional Morality

As with Piaget's theory, Kohlberg's theory (e.g., 1976, 1984) holds that the development of moral reasoning rests upon the development of cognitive capacities. Kohlberg believed that cognitive growth was a necessary but not sufficient condition for growth in moral reasoning. The transition to Level 3, principled or **postconventional morality,** occurs when a person is cognitively able to conceptualize considerations of justice, individual rights, and contracts. Individual judgments are now determined by self-chosen, internal principles rather than accepted from external authorities.

Stage 5, The Morality Of Consensus-building Procedures

During Stage 5, which Kohlberg (1976) called the **social contract orientation,** rules and laws continue to be respected as a means of ensuring fairness. However, the postconventional reasoner understands that there are situations in which the rules must be changed or even ignored. A prior-to-society perspective characterizes thinking at this stage and manifests itself in an awareness of values and rights having priority over social relationships and contracts. Stage 5 individuals integrate perspectives by formal mechanisms such as contracts, impartiality, and due process, although when conflicts arise between moral and legal points of view they find them difficult to resolve.

For example, the rise of the Black Lives Matter movement in the USA and around the globe has led many people to re-examine the morality of allowing historical statues honoring individuals who were slave holders, racists, or imperialists to stand in public places. In the summer of 2020, people pulled down and/or vandalized many statues and called for the removal of many more. For a Stage 5 thinker, the morality of removing the statues may be justified but the lack of a consensual and thoughtful process for their removal makes many deeply uncomfortable.

Stage 6, The Morality of Nonarbitrary Social Cooperation

The endpoint of Kohlberg's developmental sequence posits the sixth stage of **universal ethical principles orientation.** At this stage, individuals base their judgments on fundamental and universal ethical principles, such as justice, reciprocity, and respect. Stage 6 thinking is characterized by taking the perspective "of any rational individual recognizing the nature of morality or the fact that persons are ends in themselves and must be treated as such" (Kohlberg, 1976, p. 35). Research evidence supporting the evidence of Stage 6 has been mixed, and Kohlberg eventually dropped the stage from consideration in assessment (Colby & Kohlberg, 1987; Lapsley, 2006).

Although Kohlberg had originally evaluated some of his research participants at Stage 6, his later writings tended to claim that only rare historical individuals such as Jesus, the Buddha, Gandhi, and Martin Luther King, Jr. exemplified such reasoning. Kohlberg continued to argue, however, that Stage 6 was important philosophically and logically to anchor his theory. Our own evaluation would be that many moral exemplars (e.g., Colby & Damon, 1992) exhibit mixes of both Stage 5 and Stage 6 thinking but, as we shall see when we examine Rest's Four Component Model, the limitations of Kohlberg's central focus on moral reasoning may account for his difficulty in defining and assessing a Stage 6.

Current Evaluations of Kohlberg's Theory

Philosophers of science have set several criteria for a good theory, including elegance or simplicity, comprehensiveness, and heuristic value. At first glance, Kohlberg's theory seems both elegant *and* comprehensive; and clearly his ideas have been some of the most heuristic in psychology. In the words of Fowler et al. (1988): "No other contemporary scholar, in my experience, has drawn to himself so able and extensive a group of colleagues and friends as did Larry Kohlberg" (p. 1).

In 2008, the *Journal of Moral Education* (Reed, 2008) put out a special issue on the occasion of the 50th anniversary of Kohlberg's 1958 dissertation study. In his foreword, Elliot Turiel (2008) noted both Kohlberg's profound influence on the field of moral development and the strengths and challenges of his body of work. The intent of the special issue was to build upon Kohlberg's work and present current attempts to construct a more comprehensive and integrated model of moral functioning. In 2009, Gibbs et al. countered with a critique of the special issue, charging that the essays inadequately represented developmental themes, especially Kohlberg and Piaget's "key concept of development as the construction of a deeper and more adequate understanding not reducible to particular socialization practices or cultural contexts" (p. 271).

More recently, on the 25th anniversary of Kohlberg's death, Zizek et al. (2015) edited a volume revisiting and critically examining his theory in light of current movements such as neurocognitive and emotion-centered approaches. Schrader's (2015) thoughtful and comprehensive introductory chapter attempts to shed light on both Kohlberg's contributions and shortcomings. While acknowledging the legitimate challenges raised by brain research, evolutionary and intuitive theories of morality, Schrader believes Kohlberg's ideas continue to have value for the field.

> If we attend carefully to the richness and complexity of his work we come to see that Kohlberg, along with Jean Piaget, John Dewey, and William James before him, intuited and mapped the future exploration of moral psychology that he could never have addressed alone.
>
> (p. 22)

In the following section, we attempt to summarize the literature on Kohlberg's theory and research by noting several points that seem most relevant to the helping professions.

Unfortunately, the elegance and simplicity of Kohlberg's vision of a morality of universal justice and the primacy of Kantian formalism left him vulnerable to a host of thoughtful critics who have argued that his focus on justice limits the comprehensiveness of his theory. Critics have addressed possible challenges in his developmental research methods and results as well as allegations of possible gender and cultural bias (see Table 3.2)

Perhaps one of the most critical questions concerns whether the stages of moral reasoning Kohlberg described have a logical relationship to differences in moral behavior (Blasi, 1980; Thoma, 1994). We argue in the next section that Rest's more comprehensive Four Component Model can help to explain at least part of the puzzling gap between moral thinking and moral action.

Applications and Implications for Helping Professionals

As did Piaget's theory, Kohlberg's conception of developmental progression in the complexity of people's thinking and their ability to put themselves in

Table 3.2 Strengths and Challenges of Kohlberg's Theory

Strengths include:

- Simplicity and comprehensiveness: Differences in moral reasoning across development and cultures are explained by six qualitatively different sequential stages that are very useful in evaluating a client's or student's current functioning.
- Heuristic value: Many of the major researchers and theorists in the field today began their work directly with Kohlberg or by testing his ideas. The initial Just Community school interventions encouraged myriad other research-based social-emotional programs.
- His theory provides a compelling explanation for how, across development, people construct deeper and more adequate conceptions of right and wrong that are not simply reliant on their socialization or culture.
- By describing structure rather than content, the theory provides a strong challenge to moral relativism as well as criteria for evaluating why some opinions, arguments, and positions are "better" or more adequate than others.

Criticisms include:

- Kohlberg placed too much emphasis on moral reasoning.
- He relied too heavily on measures using hypothetical dilemmas.
- He could not provide an adequate explanation of the gap between moral reasoning and moral action.
- His claim of universal structures of morality cannot account for "fundamentally different rationalities pertaining to conceptions of self and social relations that can differ by cultural frameworks" (Turiel, 2008, p. 284).
- His theory is biased against females and the "different voice" of women and girls (e.g., Gilligan, 1982). (Note: This challenge is addressed in detail in Chapter 4.)

---

other's shoes is enormously helpful in understanding the perspective of a student or client whose behavior might otherwise make little sense to us.

For example, Elly was once working as a therapist with a family whose 3-year-old had been inappropriately fondled by a babysitter. The family was very loving and supportive of the child and tried to help her by telling her what a bad person the babysitter was. The child then became very upset and shouted, "She's not bad!" When Elly explained to the family that a concrete thinker has trouble conceptualizing what might have felt like pleasurable stroking as "bad," they were able to switch their support to statements such as, "It is a rule that we don't touch people on parts of the body covered by a bathing suit. You need to tell mommy or daddy if that happens and we will be sure the person follows the rule." Very young children find it quite appropriate that big people make and enforce the rules; thus the parents' reframed statements helped her feel safe without feeling damaged.

Kohlberg's theory has also given rise to numerous school-based interventions that attempted to promote a positive moral climate that nurtured democratic functioning, a caring community, and more complex moral reasoning. In upcoming chapters, we explore these interventions with special emphasis on his Just Community model. We will give special attention to recent evaluations of Kohlberg's legacy for education written by expert practitioners Ann Higgins-D'Alessandro (2015) and Wolfgang Althof (2015).

Most helping professionals today work from a whole-child or whole-person perspective that involves not only people's thinking, but also their emotions, strengths and challenges, goals, and environmental contexts. Although many of Kohlberg's concepts can be quite useful in working with clients or students, the focus on moral reasoning limits their application to more holistic application models. However, one of Kohlberg's students, James Rest, proposed a more complex model that better meets the comprehensiveness criteria for a good theory.

James Rest and the Minnesota Group: From Stages to Schemas

> While Piaget's impact on psychology is and has been tremendous, doubts have been raised about his stage concept and his use of logical formalism to model cognitive processes. Were Kohlberg alive today, he might well be open to altered views... Kohlberg embraced Piaget because Piaget was the most profound and defensible theory of the human mind available at the time. If we find new theories of learning and cognition that are more profound and more defensible, we should adapt these new approaches.
>
> (Rest, 1991, p. 203)

James Rest met Lawrence Kohlberg at the University of Chicago and followed him to Harvard as a postdoctoral student. Although he began his work in moral psychology in the Kohlbergian tradition, his own work in developing a *comprehension* measure of moral judgment, the **Defining Issues Test** or **DIT** (see following DIT discussion), led him to question the Kohlberg group's reliance on the **Moral Judgment Interview,** a *spontaneous production* measure of moral stages (Rest et al., 1999; Thoma, 2002).

Rest continued his studies of moral comprehension at the University of Minnesota but became increasingly convinced that moral functioning could not be adequately explained by a narrow focus on moral reasoning. During the 1980s, as he worked on a major review of morality for the *Handbook of Child Psychology,* he developed a Four Component Model of moral behavior that is now widely accepted in the field (Thoma, 2006).

In 1988, Rest was diagnosed with Machado-Joseph's disease, a degenerative disease of the nervous system that had killed both his mother and uncle before him. However, until his death in 1999, he continued an active and generative scholarly regimen that culminated in yet another reconceptualization of the moral domain, a Neo-Kohlbergian approach that focused on schemas, or generalized knowledge structures, rather than stages (Rest et al., 1999).

From Stages... The Defining Issues Test (DIT)

During his postdoctoral studies, James Rest developed an objective multiple-choice test, now called the **DIT I,** that indexes moral development, or maturity, based upon recognition of, and preference for, 72 moral considerations or arguments. The test is based on the premise that people at different stages of development will have different interpretations of moral dilemmas, or critical issues in the dilemmas, and of what is right and fair in particular situations. Answers revealing differences in the way dilemmas are defined are taken to measure the person's underlying tendency to organize moral experiences.

The long form of the test presents participants with six hypothetical dilemmas, which are followed by a list of issues in the form of questions or arguments a person might consider in solving each dilemma. Scores are traditionally reported in the form of a P-score that indexes the person's preference for principled or postconventional reasoning. The test, widely used for moral development research, has been updated and revised and is currently available in a computerized iteration, the DIT II, that provides additional information about moral functioning across several new scales. Recently, Hyemin Han and colleagues have developed and validated a modified version of the DIT (the **behavioral DIT; bDIT**) that uses reaction time to assess a person's preference for principled reasoning (Choi et al., 2019; Han et al., 2020).

... To Components: The Four Component Model of Morality

Although not as widely known as Kohlberg's theory, Rest's Four Component Model offers perhaps the most adequately dimensionalized and compelling conception of moral reasoning and its place in the wider domain of morality (Rest, 1983, 1986). His particular theoretical orientation towards the deeply social nature of morality may provide the best conceptual model for framing questions about clients' or students' moral behavior. For Rest (1986), the term *morality* refers to a particular type of social value, "that having to do with how humans cooperate and coordinate their activities in the service of furthering human welfare, and how they adjudicate conflicts among individual interests" (p. 3). Rest, as did Kohlberg, viewed morality as arising from the fact that people live together and perform actions that affect each other. He proposed that understanding the end point—the moral behavior of individuals—involved understanding a four component model involving four basic psychological processes:

1. **Moral sensitivity**—The individual must be able to interpret a particular situation in terms of possible courses of action, determine who could be affected by these possible courses, and understand how the affected parties would regard the effects. For example, when Elly was a teenager, she thought nothing of exceeding the speed limit when she thought no police were in the vicinity. However, when as an adult, she learned she was pregnant with her first child, she experienced an "aha" moment that other cars were full of people, some with babies,

whose lives were endangered by speeding drivers. She "saw" the moral nature of obeying traffic laws for the first time—an issue she had never considered before in light of anything except a Kohlberg Stage 1 concern with not getting a ticket.

2. **Moral judgment**—The individual must be able to make judgments about which of the possible courses of action is morally right and thus make a decision about what one ought to do in a particular situation. This component concerns the domain of moral reasoning described in such detail in Kohlberg's theory. For example, members of the US Congress, in considering responses to then-President Trump's 2021 incitement of a mob of followers to insurrection, had to wrestle with both moral ("What is a just consequence for sedition?") and practical ("Will my vote to impeach lose me support from Trump's followers?") issues as they decided whether to call for the president's impeachment.

3. **Moral motivation**—The individual must "give priority to moral values above other personal values" (Rest, 1986, p. 3), such as a desire for material possessions or a commitment to group norms and, hence, decide to do what is morally right. We believe this is the most problematic of Rest's components. It seems to violate the ordinary language use of the term *motivation*. We agree that people might indeed be sensitive to an issue and know the right thing to do but not move to moral action unless they are motivated to do so. However, in our experience, **empathy and faith commitment are two powerful motivators of moral action.** Motivation may indeed result in prioritizing doing the right thing over practical concerns, but we see motivation itself, rather than prioritization, as the key element of the third component.

4. **Moral character**—The individual must have "sufficient perseverance, ego strength, and implementation skills" (Rest, 1986, p. 3) to follow through on his or her intentions. When Elly asked her undergraduate students to describe times in middle school, high school, and college when they knew the right thing to do but did not do it, a common theme of the responses about middle school was that they saw someone being teased or bullied but did nothing about it. Young adolescents, many still insecure and desperately sensitive about the judgment of peers, frequently lack the ego strength or assertiveness skills to stand up for an unpopular child.

... *To Schemas: Rest's Neo-Kohlbergian Approach to Moral Thinking*

In 1999, Rest and his colleagues further elaborated on the Four Component Model and integrated [then] current research from the cognitive sciences into what they called a Neo-Kohlbergian approach to theory and research. The team used four core ideas from Kohlberg's work to guide their research:

1. An emphasis on cognition as the best way to understand how people make sense of the world;
2. The assumption that individuals self-construct basic categories of morality like justice rather than passively absorbing them from the culture;
3. The proposition that people's moral judgments *develop* from more simple to more complex;
4. The shift from conventional to postconventional thinking as adolescents and young adults become aware of the systems of their society (e.g., laws, institutions, roles) and develop concerns about the systems' morality rather than simply concerning themselves with interpersonal morality.

The team came to regard Kohlberg's theory as addressing moral issues such as free speech and due process in the "macro-morality" of society's laws and institutions. However, much of moral life takes place at the micro-morality level of interpersonal relationships with particular others or "generally acting in a decent, responsible, empathic way in one's daily dealings with others" (Rest et al., 1999, p. 2). Rest and his colleagues hoped to overcome the limitations of the Kohlberg approach by

- holding onto core assumptions and ideas that had stood the test of decades of research,
- expanding the narrow domain of moral judgment to the Four Component Model, and
- integrating conceptions from social cognition research such as schema theory.

The Neo-Kohlbergian approach conceptualized the DIT as a measure that tapped moral schemas relying on implicit processes and tacit knowledge that social cognition research had shown to underlie much of human decision making:

> [The] last 5 years have seen a number of significant changes to the DIT and the theory of moral development it claims to measure. It is now proposed that the DIT measures the default schema by which individuals interpret moral issues... [It] is now more aligned with modern schema theory than Kohlberg's stage theory.
>
> (Thoma, 2006, p. 87)

In later chapters, we examine the issue of implicit processing in some detail but suffice it to say that Rest and his Minnesota team played a major role in moving the field of moral development from a focus on universal stages of moral thinking to a new era of research on the multifaceted nature of morality that conceptualizes moral reasoning as **an ability to draw on multiple schemas of varying complexity.**

Interviews with Discipline Leaders: Stephen J. Thoma, Ph.D. (Professor Emeritus and former Program Coordinator, Department of Educational Studies in Psychology, Research Methodology, and Counseling, University of Alabama)

Steve Thoma has written widely on the use of the Defining Issues Test. His research interests have included personality and social development in late adolescence and youth, as well as moral judgment development. Below are Steve's to responses to two questions about his current thinking about the Four Component Model (FCM).

Have conceptions of the FCM changed over time? The Four Component Model was developed to both describe the processes that lead to moral action and to stimulate new measures. Not surprisingly, over time and with new information changes have been made to the model. For instance, Component II [moral judgment] has been revamped to better organize the various processes and in so doing make clearer how one identifies what one ought to do. Similarly, Component III [moral motivation] has been reinterpreted based on work that focuses on moral identity development. Rest always described the model as a work in progress and current reinterpretations of the model suggest he was right.

Is cognition prioritized? The FCM does prioritize cognitive and developmental processes in part because these aspects of moral functioning lend themselves to instruction and, to a lesser extent, measurement development. This is not to say that emotional processes are absent from the model. From its earliest inception, Rest noted the role of intuition and emotions as influences of moral action—particularly in promoting moral motivation. The trick from our perspective is to identify the interactive nature of these many influences and to show how they work together to promote moral motivation.

(S. Thoma, personal communication, January 17, 2013)

Although we are ending this section on Rest's (1991) work with his work on the Neo-Kohlbergian approach, his spirit of adapting "new theories of learning and cognition that are more profound and more defensible" (p. 203) continues to permeate the work of his colleagues (see Table 3.3). Muriel Bebeau (2014) has developed numerous measures and an evidence-based guide for ethics instruction for professionals based on the

Table 3.3 Strengths and Challenges of Rest's Theory

Strengths include:
- Comprehensiveness
- Strong research base
- Integration of research across broad areas of psychology

Criticisms include:
- Research continued to privilege moral thinking, in part because of a lack of reliable and valid widely accepted measures of the other three components
- Theoretical ideas relied heavily on DIT research

Four-Component Model of Morality. Darcia Narvaez, in particular, has gone on to continually update and expand her theoretical and research work in response to advances in cognition, neuroscience, and evolutionary psychology and we will examine her work in depth in Chapter 5.

Applications and Implications for Helping Professionals

At the most general level, Rest's ideas are enormously helpful in under-standing the "default" schemas that students or clients tend to rely on in their habitual, often unexamined, moral responses to people and situations. For example, the stress of repeated academic failures may cause a high school student with a learning disability to regress toward rather dualistic preconventional thinking about teachers who try to challenge her to push forward: "All they ever do is give me C minuses and Ds—why should I try to please them?" Understanding the level and content of moral schemas can allow teachers and therapists to develop lessons and interventions that promote moral growth and address cognitive distortions.

More specifically, the Four Component Model has been used as a theoretical base for an innovative, research-based middle school curriculum (Narvaez et al., 2009). Using a developmental novice-to-expert model, Narvaez and colleagues developed four activity booklets with detailed goals, objectives, and lesson ideas for moral sensitivity, judgment, motivation, and action.

In later chapters, we revisit many of these ideas as we examine the neurobiology of morality and specific moral education interventions. At this point, the most important summary point for helping professionals to take away is that the relatively weak relationship between moral reasoning and moral behavior can be best explained by understanding that a complex interaction of multiple components, arising from both learning and bio-logical hardwiring, underlies moral actions. Deficits in any of the four components can leave our clients/students/patients vulnerable to mala-daptive decisions and behavior. Relatedly, as John Gibbs (2010) has de-monstrated so convincingly in his work with delinquents, interventions that target only one component of morality will be far less effective than comprehensive, theory, and research-based programs.

Discussion Questions

1. Did you find yourself wondering where you might fall in terms of Kohlberg's moral stages? Do you think you tend to rely primarily on reasoning from one stage, or are you more of a "layer cake" of stages whose thinking often changes because of the "pull" of a specific situation?

2. Think about a recent experience in your life in which you helped someone. What do you think motivated you to do so? Was it more of a cognitive prioritizing of moral concerns as Rest describes or a more emotional cause like empathy or faith?

Additional Resources

- For a thoughtful assessment of Kohlberg's legacy, see: https://www.moraledk12.org/lawrence-kohlberg

- Zizek et al.'s (2015) *Kohlberg Revisited* can provide graduate students with a useful and insightful collection of essays by leaders in the field of moral development, many of whom worked directly with Kohlberg himself.

- Students or professionals interested in ordering or learning more about the Defining Issues Test should visit the Center for the Study of Ethical Development webpage: https://ethicaldevelopment.ua.edu/

4   Theoretical Challenges to Classic Cognitive Developmental Models

The first three chapters went into great detail laying out classic theories that have had a significant influence on moral development research and applications. Although the field has moved beyond these foundational theories in many ways (with the exception of a continuing reliance on the Four Component Model), all current theories react to the classic ones in some way. Thus, current concepts make sense only if you have a deep and thorough understanding of the ideas they challenge or build upon.

In this chapter, we look at three major theoretical challenges to the ideas of Freud, Piaget, Kohlberg, and Rest: the ethic of care, domain theory, and moral self/personality theory. After a brief overview of the key points of the next round of influential theories, we lay out some ways in which these ideas can enrich your understanding of the future students, clients, or patients with whom you will work.

Feminist Challenge: Gilligan's and Noddings's Ethic of Care

Thomas Kuhn (1970) famously defined **paradigms** as "universally recognized scientific achievements that for a time provide model problems and solutions to a community of practitioners" (p. 62). For most of the years between the publication of Lawrence Kohlberg's 1958 dissertation and his untimely death in 1987, "his work and ideas united an international web of scholars in the field of moral education… [who]… produced an explosion of research confirming, challenging, and ultimately stretching the limits of Kohlberg's paradigm" (Vozzola, 1991, p. 22). A major challenge to Kohlberg's theory of a rational, constructivist theory rooted in the core concept of justice came with the publication of Carol Gilligan's (1982) widely read *In a Different Voice,* that articulated a competing paradigm, the ethic of care. In that book and subsequent works (e.g., Gilligan & Wiggins, 1987), Gilligan explored the question of whether, in leaving out females at the stage of theory building, major theories by developmentalists such as Piaget, Kohlberg, Erikson, and Vaillant reflected core biases arising from using all male research samples.

DOI: 10.4324/9780429295461-5

Theories are very much shaped by the times in which they arise and the Ethic of Care provides a prime example of how cultural narratives influence scientific inquiry. In the early 1980s, as the feminist movement gained prominence in society and the academy, Gilligan's competing paradigm captured the imagination of many scholars.

What Did Gilligan Actually Say?

> I have studied identity and moral development by listening to the ways in which people speak about themselves and about conflicts and choices they face... The strong feelings and the judgments often made by girls and women about being excluded, left out, and abandoned, as well as the desperate actions girls and women often take in the face of detachment, indifference or lack of concern—may reflect an awareness on some level of the disjunction between women's lives and Western culture.
>
> (Gilligan et al., 1988, pp. vii–viii, xi)

As with Piaget, Gilligan's ideas evolved across time but several key points come through consistently in her best-known works (Gilligan, 1982; Gilligan & Wiggins, 1987; Gilligan et al., 1988):

- Gilligan contended that developmental theories, most specifically Kohlberg's theory of moral development, are biased against women and that Kohlberg's early scoring method unfairly relegated women's culturally constructed orientation towards maintaining relationships to lower stage scores.
- Gilligan argued that Kohlberg's ethic of justice and rights focused too narrowly on separation and principles. She suggested the need to broaden the moral domain to include an orientation towards care that focuses on issues of relationship, connection, responsibility, and avoiding harm (Gilligan, 1982; Gilligan et al., 1988).
- Although Gilligan's earlier writings seemed to stress that males preferred and chose the more abstract voice of rights and justice, and that females preferred and chose the more contextual "different voice" of care, she later tempered this position and acknowledged that both males and females think rationally and feel compassion. Gilligan and Wiggins (1987) expressed no surprise at comprehensive analyses (e.g., Thoma, 1986; Walker, 1984) that found no gender differences in moral reasoning when samples were controlled for education. However, she noted persistent sex differences in moral behavior, resulting in our prisons being filled with males and our child care centers staffed with females.

Current Status of Gilligan's Care Ethic

Today, there is general agreement that her claims overreached her evidence and that despite the common sense appeal of her accessible and well-written books, she was often guilty of generalizing from small samples and disregarding contradictory evidence. Broughton (1983) reviewed some of her interview data and found evidence of cherry picking—for example, pulling out quotes from a male participant who used justice language but ignoring his equally eloquent use of care reasoning later in the interview. However, a recent study using functional magnetic resonance imaging (fMRI) identified significantly different neural networks involved in care versus justice moral cognitions (Cáceda et al., 2011) that suggests a biological underpinning for some of the differences in reasoning care that scholars observed.

We would argue that, in the end, rather than the justice/care debate resulting in a Kuhnian scientific revolution in which one research paradigm overthrows an earlier one, Gilligan's challenge moved the field to a spiral of Hegelian thesis, antithesis, and synthesis that has widened the moral domain (Vozzola, 1996). When one paradigm (or a new one) dominates the field, it shapes both the nature of the inquiry and the interpretation of the results. For many years, Kohlberg and colleagues used hypothetical moral dilemmas to assess moral reasoning and test the tenets of his theory longitudinally and cross culturally. In contrast, Gilligan and colleagues examined real-world dilemmas and interviews to better hear the voices of girls and women. Both paradigms have proven heuristic and generated excitement across a wide range of scholars and disciplines. Today, mixed-method studies integrating methods from both paradigms are so common that they go almost unnoticed. Most of us have integrated into our understanding and research both Kohlberg's conceptions of (a) increasing levels of cognitive and moral complexity and (b) decentering across development; as well as Gilligan's stress on the importance of seeing moral reasoning as occurring within complex relationships and situations.

While agreeing that Gilligan's comprehensive claim of sex differences overstepped her actual data, Sherblom's (2008) highly sympathetic analysis of the legacy of the care challenge holds that it had "an evolutionary effect on the field, helping… to create more philosophically inclusive and psychologically realistic conceptions of moral engagement in the moment and moral development across time" (p. 81). Walker and Frimer (2009) acknowledge that Gilligan and other care theorists have contributed to the field with their "broadening emphasis on care, response and interdependence; with the caution to better represent the experiences of females in psychological theories; and with the methodological innovation of… personally generated, real-life moral dilemmas" (pp. 53–54). However, they adamantly disagree with Sherblom's positive evaluation of Gilligan's work and legacy and hold that most of the primary claims of the care perspective have been empirically discredited. The best evidence to date suggests that rather than there being some gendered moral orientation, individuals are inconsistent in their moral orientations, "even within the limited context of real-life dilemmas" (p. 65). Nor has Gilligan's allegation of bias against women or people with a care orientation in Kohlberg's model held up. Numerous subsequent analyses found either no difference or a slight bias in favor of women (e.g., Jaffe & Hyde, 2000; Walker, 1989).

Our sense is that most contemporary moral development scholars (e.g., You et al., 2011) agree with Walker's (2006) call that it is time to set aside the issues of gender differences and gender bias in Kohlberg's theory. We now know that educational level is profoundly more important than gender for explaining differences in moral reasoning complexity. We know that we need to attend to the "pull" of certain types of dilemma and situational demands on our moral judgments and behaviors. Both Kohlberg's elegant stage theory and Gilligan's eloquent voice theory arose in a time of focus on moral reasoning. Today, our models of moral functioning have become much more comprehensive and often a bit overwhelming in their attempts to integrate new empirical findings from cognitive science, evolutionary theory, and neuroscience. But that is a story for a later chapter. Let us first take a brief look at another prominent care theorist before turning to the domain challenge.

Nel Noddings's Care Ethic

> On the one hand, as citizens of a liberal democracy, we are committed to the free exercise of religion. On the other we are also committed to gender equality. Can we permit girls to be schooled in such a way that they never gain the critical thinking skills needed to make an autonomous decision about their roles in society?... Without denying our moral commitment to gender equality we should try to keep the lines of communication open. Without coercing, we should keep trying to persuade.
>
> (Noddings, 2005, p. 126)

One credo of developmentalism holds that "We become what we do." Kohlberg's love of philosophy infused his theoretical work with a rational centrality that gives it both its great strength and great weakness. Gilligan's strong arts background (literature and dance) primed her to attend to issues of voice and positionality. Respected philosopher Nel Noddings brings a more practice-oriented background to work in care ethics: She is a mother of 10 and former elementary math teacher and school administrator. Noddings's early experiences with caring teachers led to a lifelong interest in the relations between students and teachers (Smith, 2020).

We personally like Noddings's work much better than Gilligan's but, although Noddings is much respected in the field, her work has not had the same level of broad societal impact that Gilligan's has. It may be that her proposals for creating classrooms modeled on families simply came at a time when the United States was leaving behind the experimental spirit of the 1960s and 1970s and entering an era of accountability and high-stakes testing (e.g., the infamous US No Child Left Behind laws). In any case, we did want you to see at least a brief overview of her feminist approach to ethics and moral education.

Noddings's (1992) definition of care is rooted in relation; she defines a caring relation as "a connection or encounter between two human beings" (p. 5). This encounter is not a one-way street—both parties must contribute something, or the connection will be broken and caring cannot occur. Most centrally, Noddings (2002) argued that care is a basic life process. Both men and women often express "natural caring" (p. 2), a receptive, related, and engrossed state of being in relation with roots in their own experiences of being cared for.

She also provides a helpful distinction between caring about and caring for (Noddings, 1984). Most of us would probably say that we care about the hungry among us and might even send checks to our local food banks at holiday time. However, there are clear limits to both our attentiveness and engagement. In contrast, when we have been cared for ourselves, we learn both to care for and then, in a larger sense, care about, others. When we care for a hungry person, we are more willing to engage with that person face-to-face, perhaps serving at a soup kitchen or delivering meals to him or her regularly at home. Noddings's care theory sees the roots of a sense of justice in caring about. (It cannot be right that in a country of such wealth, there are children going to bed hungry at night.)

Part of why we like Noddings's work so much is that she consistently links her theory to concrete implications for practice and social policy. Given that the home functions as the major educator for care, she argued that all children should "live in a home that has at least adequate material resources and attentive love" and that "schools should include education for home life in their curriculum" (Noddings, 2002, p. 289). We also particularly appreciate her own twist on the "We become what we do" credo: "If we want to produce people who will care for another, then it makes sense to give students practice in caring and reflection on that practice" (O'Toole, 1998, p. 191).

In sum, then, Nel Noddings provides us with a vision of parenting and education grounded in what she believes to be a natural moral attitude. At the end of this chapter, we reflect a bit on the dark side of her positive vision—the challenges helping professionals face when they deal with clients coming to us from (and often going back to) uncaring homes and schools.

Social Cognitive Domain Theory: Turiel, Nucci, and Smetana

What is morality? Is it the same thing as social rules? Is morality different for religious children?... Is morality universal or does it change from one culture to another?… Are there some things that people do that should be up to them and not controlled by social rules? How do these personal and private things relate to morality?

(Nucci, 2009, p. 5)

Grand stage theories such as Kohlberg's offer clear and testable models. That is one of their great strengths, but it also leaves them vulnerable to challenges as researchers discover **anomalies**—findings that do not fit the theory's predictions. So, despite agreeing on the central importance of moral judgments and seeing a developmental progression in such reasoning, researchers such as Elliot Turiel, Larry Nucci, and Judith Smetana came to see serious problems with Kohlberg's map of the moral domain. Although domain theory generally holds to the basic tenets of the cognitive-developmental tradition, their findings caused them to call out, "Whoa!—There has been a major error in seeing social conventional reasoning as a **stage** in the developmental process towards greater moral complexity." For students wanting to explore this tradition in depth, Killen and Smetana's 2014 *Handbook of Moral Development* provides many excellent essays by researchers using a domain approach, especially Smetana et al.'s (2015) explanation of the social domain approach to children's moral and social judgments—material covered in more depth in our new chapter on early moral socialization.

All children have to figure out how to navigate their complex social worlds. For example, the expectations and rules in preschool ("We never talk without raising our hand first") may come as a rude shock to a cherished only child whose parents have delighted in her lively verbal behavior. The child has to construct many situational and conditional schemas. For example, "At home it's OK to shout out a great idea, but at school we raise our hands and take turns." She also has to figure out if some rules always hold no matter where, no matter with whom: "We **never** hit" (Smetana, 2006).

Through a clever research program using structured questions about children's understanding of the social order, researchers such as Nucci, Turiel, Smetana, and others discovered that children as young as five distinguish between practical/personal, moral, and social conventional **domains.** How did they figure this out? They began by giving children scenarios (e.g., "Some people want to wear a religious head covering to a public school," or "A woman had an old national flag she didn't need any more and wanted to tear it up to use for cleaning rags.") They then asked a series of questions, including some variation on these general core queries:

- Is it right or wrong to do that?
- Why or why not?
- What if there were no rules against doing _____. Would it still be wrong?
- What if there was a country where it was OK to do _____? Would it then be wrong to do it?

Response patterns suggested that when harm of some kind is involved, children generally see the actions as wrong, wrong even without rules prohibiting it, and wrong even in a country that permitted it. However, if the actions appeared to be simply a violation of social consensus or an edict from an authority, children were more likely to qualify the situations under which it would be wrong and those under which it might be acceptable. Nucci (2009) argues that we can tease out the universal aspects of morality if we distinguish the moral from the social conventional domain.

Let's look now at how these domains are defined and how they might play out in interactions between young people and adults. Synthesizing the ideas of the original domain theorist, Turiel, Smetana offers a crisp overview that reflects the current conceptualization of theory.

> Domain theory… [views] morality as one of several strands of children's developing social knowledge…. Thus, concerns with justice, welfare and rights—all **moral** issues—coexist with concerns about authority, tradition, and social norms (viewed as **social-conventional** issues) and concerns with privacy, bodily integrity and control, and a delimited set of choices and preferences (described **as personal** issues). Domain theory proposes that each of these constitutes an organized system or **domain,** of social knowledge that arises from children's experiences of different types of regularities in the social environment (Turiel, 1993, 1998). Smetana, 2006, p. 120)

Let's now lay out some explicit definitions and examples:

1. **Moral domain**—Issues are categorized into this domain on the basis of the child's perception of actions' effects on people (the harm or benefit they cause), not because there is some rule about doing or not doing the action (Nucci, 2009). For example, mean-spirited social media posts will be seen by many teens as a moral concern.
2. **Social conventional domain**—Actions and issues sorted into this second domain are only right or wrong if there is a rule or norm. As a norm or rule can be changed by social consensus, social conventions are arbitrary (Nucci, 2009). When Elly was a high school student, girls' skirts had to reach the middle of their knees. In 1968, she was sent to the principal's office because her very fashionable new paisley skirt touched the top of her knee, not the middle. Like many young women at that cusp of the miniskirt era, it seemed very clear to her that this was an arbitrary and unjust rule just begging to be broken.
3. **Personal domain**—Some behaviors and choices affect only the individual rather than others, and we tend to see these aspects of our social life as "personal matters of privacy and discretion" (Nucci, 2009, p. 25). So the personal domain is not about right or wrong but about our sense of self—the friends we choose, the music we listen to,

the way we wear our hats. Interestingly, in an age of widespread social media use, many young people are now eagerly sharing their personal domains in ways that often violate the social conventions of other generations (and sometimes the privacy of their peers). To give another example from Elly's life, she has long been known among her friends as someone who falls asleep at 9 P.M. (even doing so in the midst of college parties in her dorm room) as well as a very moderate drinker. One night when she was in her 20s, she fell asleep in a beanbag chair in one of those embarrassing mouth-open snoring poses. Her friends thought it would be hilarious to prop a large bottle of Bailey's Irish cream in her hand and snap a photo. And it *was* hilarious because they put the photo in their album, gave her a copy, and that was the end of it. Today she would **not** be amused to see that photo posted on Instagram, Snapchat or Facebook and become an Internet sensation. (Drunken Youth of Formerly Respected Professor of Morality!)

You are probably already noticing that it's not quite as neat and simple as the category definitions suggest. And the domain theorists would agree with you. How we categorize events into domains is influenced by development, education, and culture. We revisit the culture question in later chapters, so we defer comments on cultural influence until then. But let's take one more incident "snatched from the 60s."

On a typical hazy, hot, and humid summer day in 1967, Elly was a high school student with an afternoon dentist appointment. She was wearing shorts and a t-shirt and all set to leave when her mother (born in Europe and raised in Indonesia as the daughter of a high-ranking Dutch army officer) told her she needed to change to a skirt for the appointment. Cue the eye roll. Her personal domain just came up against her mother's social conventional one and, after a lot of heated argument (on her part) and unmovable firmness (on her mom's), she changed into the #$%#@ skirt and went to the dentist.

Little did she know how absolutely typical she was. As children develop, they begin to argue with parents about issues that parents see as moral or important social conventions (e.g., respect, manners, dressing appropriately) and that children see as "mere" social conventions or a matter of personal choice. For example, many teens do not see that sneaking around violates trust (a moral issue for parents). They see it as getting around an arbitrary rule ("My parents are SOOOOO unreasonable about my curfew"). We believe that a combination of teens' predominant use of reasoning at Kohlberg's moral judgment Stage 3 ("Good people help their friends") and their tacit perception that sharing homework is an issue in the personal rather than moral domain might explain why they often do not see cheating as a big deal.

Moral Personality Theory and Research

People are often drawn to the teaching and helping professions because of a deep interest in people, especially their personalities and core life stories. Even a radical behaviorist like B. F. Skinner (1948) argued his philosophical case most persuasively through the use of story in his novel *Walden Two*. For an excellent overview of cutting-edge work on the moral self, we highly recommend a volume of essays from a conference on moral personality held at Notre Dame University (Lapsley & Narvaez, 2004) and a 2019 interdisciplinary issue of the *Journal of Moral Development* (Narvaez & Snow, 2019a) that explores new research in the area of self, motivation and virtue studies. In the later work, Narvaez and Snow (2019b) argue for a view in which the moral self is conceptualized as "the possessor of both character and personality with moral character the bearer of moral character traits or moral virtues, and the personality the bearer of personality traits" (p.1).

However, in the brief space available in this chapter, we present only two of the influential theorists and researchers who have examined the role of personality in moral development: Gus Blasi, who focuses on the moral self, and Dan P. McAdams, who focuses on how we construct that self through stories and life myths.

Blasi and the Moral Self as a Bridge Between the Judgment/ Action Gap

> At least in three respects I can say that I have been fortunate in my career: I came to psychology with an interest in a field, moral development and functioning, that is of crucial importance beyond the confines of academic psychology; over 20 years ago I raised for myself the question of the relations between morality and personality at a time when the field of moral psychology needed to expand its concern in that direction; finally, I found a congenial group of colleagues and friends that share my interest.
>
> (Blasi, 2004, p. 335)

The field of moral development has long grappled with the implications of research evidence demonstrating a gap between measured level of moral judgment complexity and actual moral behavior or actions. Gus Blasi's (1980) classic review of the problem called attention to moral reasoning's very modest contribution (accounting for only 10% of the variance) to moral action. Clearly, the field needed a more comprehensive explanatory model and, in a Festschrift for Blasi, editors Lapsley and Narvaez (2004) argue that we now have one: "Blasi's 'self-model' is now the standard explanation for the relation between moral cognition and moral behavior (p. vii)."

The Festschrift opens with Lawrence Walker's (2004) clear and succinct outline of the self-model. Where Kohlberg identified justice as the central explanatory principle for moral functioning, Blasi sees the concept of moral identity as "better able to integrate moral cognition and moral personality within a framework that better explicates moral behavior" (p. 2). The self-model proposes three components of moral functioning:

1. **The moral self**—Or, the extent to which moral considerations and values are central to an individual's self-identity. Clearly, individuals differ widely in the extent to which their personal goals are consistent with their moral goals and understanding.

2. **A sense of personal responsibility for moral action**—It may be that our sense of moral obligation to act on our moral judgments is rooted in early developmental processes of attachment. Thus, the origins of moral responsibility may arise from close personal relationships in which we observe and learn about empathy, guilt, and commitment (p. 3).

3. **Psychological self-consistency**—Our deeply felt motive to be seen by ourselves and others as a good and moral person can result in either self-consistency between our beliefs and actions or the rationalizations and defense mechanisms described by Freud.

Like the domain theorists, Blasi holds fast to the centrality of the rational core of morality. Reasons help us to create meaning and to determine truth. For Blasi (e.g., 2004, 2009), self-identity is, at least partially, constructed through moral reasoning. However, although he has argued consistently that "understanding is the essence of morality" (Blasi, 2004, p. 338), he stresses that he uses the term in the sense of everyday language rather than in Kohlberg's theoretical construction. He noted that, in the real world, people distinguish praiseworthy from merely admirable moral actions on the basis of them being worthy of admiration, intentional, and arising from moral motives.

Like Walker, we see the heart of Blasi's vision in his conception of an emerging **self-identity** in which moral principles and values become increasingly integrated and central for one's true self. Adolescents and emerging adults often *explore* aspects of their selves but, according to Blasi (2004), many adults eventually *organize* self-aspects into a hierarchy in which "the person... acknowledges that a few aspects of himself or herself are the center or the essence of his or her being" (p. 342). At this point, people become motivated to maintain and stay true to their moral selves through intentionally and consistently acting on core moral values.

The group of active researchers represented in Lapsley and Narvaez's (2004) and Narvaez and Lapsley's (2009) influential edited volumes on moral self and moral identity continue to, in Blasi's (2004) words, "engage in serious discussions and debate" (p. 335) on his ideas. Their work also contributes to an emerging theory of a moral self as an explanatory mechanism not only for gaps between moral reasoning and moral behavior, but also for understanding why we become the people that we do. Indeed, Hertz and Krettenauer's (2016) recent meta-analysis showed that moral identity predicts moral behavior while Patrick et al. (2018) found that moral identity may be a mediator that bridges the judgment action gap among teens and appears to play a key explanatory role in their engagement and prosocial behaviors.

Some of the most important recent work on the moral self has been carried out by Lawrence Walker and colleagues. Walker's (2020) research with moral exemplars also demonstrates that moral character explains engagement in moral action, over and above moral reasoning. He believes that research on exemplars reveals "what is humanly attainable and sustainable" (p. 382) as well allowing the field to use the understanding of the "characterological dynamics involved in moral excellence...to devise effective intervention programs" (p. 383). Moral exemplars with mature moral character can be distinguished by (a) moral and faith development or "epistemic development" (p. 388), (b) significant early relationships, early exposure to the needs of others and optimistic tone, and (c) instrumental use of agency in the service of communion (Walker, 2020).

We turn now to a researcher whose work explores how we discover ourselves through creating personal myths.

Dan P. McAdams and the "Stories We Live By"

> If you want to know me, then you must know my story, For my story defines who I am. And if *I* want to know *myself*, To gain insight into the meaning of my own life, then I, too, must come to know my own story.
> (McAdams, 1993, p. 11)

What exactly is a *moral* personality? It depends on what aspect of personality you are talking about—be it dispositional traits, characteristic adaptations, or life stories (McAdams, 2009, p. 13). McAdams (1993) claims that "identity is a life story... a personal myth that an individual begins working on in late adolescence and young *adulthood in order to provide his or her life with unity or purpose*" (p. 5). McAdams's research suggests that people come to know themselves by creating, both consciously and unconsciously, "a heroic story of the self" (p. 11). He believes that the types of main characters people script into their self-defining stories—"the warrior, the sage, the lover, the caregiver... the survivor" (p. 13)—determine our identities. Stories of discontent in the early years can signal problems in finding direction and meaning in the years to come. At midlife, people sometimes strive to bring opposing parts of the story into harmony and to develop a generativity myth that attempts to link the personal story to the collective stories of the broader society.

McAdams (1993) believes that the first two years of life "leave us with a set of unconscious and nonverbal 'attitudes' about self, other, and world, and about how the three relate to each other" (p. 47). These attitudes set the "narrative tone" for the myths we construct in adulthood. Drawing on Erikson's psychosocial theory, he posits that these early years leave securely attached infants with a legacy of hope. They have learned that their needs will be met by caring others. Such children, and later adults, adopt an optimistic narrative tone based on their early life experiences that the world is trustworthy, predictable, knowable, and good. In contrast, insecurely attached infants have learned that the world is often "capricious and unpredictable, narratives take unforeseen turns, and stories are bound to have unhappy endings" (p. 47). Their early experiences lead them to develop a pessimistic narrative tone in which wishes go unmet.

Yet McAdams (1993) does not argue for a simple correspondence between life history and narrative tone. Rather, he believes that our constructed life stories or personal myths "involve an imaginative reconstruction of the past in light of an envisioned future" (p. 53). However, early experiences of attachment do appear to influence very basic attitudes about the intentions of others and how the world works.

How Might These Theoretical Challenges Apply to the Helping Professions?

One of the main points we have taken away from Gilligan's work is to integrate the ideas of voice, relationship, and positionality into our understanding of people's moral complexity and understanding. The key critical thinking questions we teach our students can apply equally well to counseling and teaching:

- Who's speaking? (Where is the person in terms of cognitive and moral development? Race? Class? Gender?)
- Who's the audience? (For helping professionals: What is the nature of the relationship? Is this an interaction among equals or do issues of status and power influence the speaker?)
- What's put in? (What is the person choosing to share with us? What issues, words, narratives recur? How are cultural norms shaping the narrative?)
- What's left out? (Few young people share the tough things in their lives with adults unless there is a strong, trusting relationship. Sometimes the student or client feels ashamed. At other times, things are left out because of a simple lack of knowledge that they might be important.)

We find the critical reactions to Gilligan's work to be enormously important for helping us to notice the crucial importance of education and significant life experiences for fostering complex moral reasoning. By knowing a person's age and level of education, we can get a good fix on the sorts of schemas he or she calls on to understand the world and other people. For instance, we know that most college students are capable of understanding and using reasoning at Kohlberg's Stages 4 and 5. We know that most elementary and junior high students use a lot of Stage 2 "tit for tat" thinking.

We also owe Carol Gilligan (and Jim Rest) sincere thanks for pushing us to notice that reasoning is not necessarily the central factor in moral behavior. Both those scholars who accepted the care ethic and those who challenged it began to attend to the emotional and relational issues that make real-world morality so very messy (see Table 4.1). Knowing how you answer the Heinz dilemma is useful for assessing your moral understanding, but we discovered it often didn't have much predictive power for what you would actually do if your own spouse were dying and you had a chance to steal a life-saving drug.

Nel Noddings's ideas about using the family as a model for classrooms not only provide a model for educators interested in creating caring environments, but also call us to renew our efforts to care for and about children (e.g., Noddings, 2008). Helping professionals in the trenches see all too clearly the damage done when care is not taught or caught.

Table 4.1 Key Concepts of Theoretical Challenges

Theory	Theorists	Key Concepts
Ethic of Care	**Carol Gilligan** **Nel Noddings**	The moral domain needs to move beyond a focus on moral reasoning about hypothetical justice dilemmas and attend to issues of relationship, care, and connection in real-world dilemmas.
Domain Theory	**Elliot Turiel** **Larry Nucci** **Judith Smetana**	Even very young children distinguish between moral, practical/personal, and social conventional domains. Social conventional reasoning is not a stage but a category.
Personality/Self/ Identity Theories	**Gus Blasi** **Dan P. McAdams**	As we mature, we construct a self in which moral concerns and understanding play a major or minor role in motivating our moral actions. One way in which we construct that self appears to be through creating personal narratives.

Especially in the United States, we are enamored of egalitarian, one-size-fits-all solutions to societal problems. But most professionals work at the more micro level of individual students and clients and know the deep value of another developmental credo: "For which child/person, under which circumstances?" Character education workbooks might provide a valuable tool for quiet, responsible children. However, your lively class clown may need some room to move and a hands-on task (being a buddy for a special needs student in gym class) to get the lesson about caring across. And the child from a violent home who has been taking his anger out on classmates may need an intensive, individualized program of support to heal and grow.

In the 1980s, the early childhood education program in Winona, Minnesota, developed an intervention that exemplifies best practice in designing a targeted program. The program provided parenting classes in which some participants had been ordered by the court to attend because of charges of abusing or neglecting their children. The perceptive program director was struck by the remark of one such parent—"I hear the other parents talk about their kids and I feel so in the dark—I have absolutely no idea what a healthy family feels like." The director set up a special group "Parenting in the Dark" for parents with their own histories of family of origin abuse, neglect, alcoholism, or mental illness. She created a safe place to **care for** these wounded parents where they could learn to care for their own children without the shame of comparing themselves with parents who seemed so effortlessly to love and engage with their children.

While care ethics **widened** the moral domain, domain theory attempts to **redefine** the landscape into multiple domains. We have found domain conceptions a particularly useful lens through which to understand client/family and student/educator interactions. Domain theory can help us to respond to cultural or developmental clashes with useful insights into the roots of those clashes.

Let's take the example we used earlier about cheating. Differences in how teachers and administrators see copying homework (as a moral issue of cheating) versus how young people often see it (as a personal domain issue of sharing with a buddy) provide a clear example of the usefulness of getting a fix on how a student or client is perceiving his or her social world. One of the most helpful resources we have found for taking the research-based findings of domain theory into classroom practice is Larry Nucci's (2009) *Nice Is Not Enough: Facilitating Moral Development*.

In terms of counseling practice, you will often see domain issues underlying family conflict and disrupting healthy developmental negotiations and renegotiations of family rules. Depending on the age and cognitive ability of the client/student, it may be quite productive to "give psychology away" and share a bit about the findings of the domain approach. Moral development rests on both cognitive development and role-taking ability, so "nudges" to consider alternative perspectives may be effective: "Some people see being on time as a matter of manners, some people as personal choice. Have you ever noticed that sort of difference in how you and your dad see things?"

In our experience, however, it is even more helpful to share this information with adults such as parents, teachers, and administrators. Better developmental understanding of a young person often helps the adult to craft more appropriate responses (and sometimes even to get a private chuckle out of a comment or action). Just be very sure that if you are working with a concrete thinker, you caution him or her to **use** the knowledge and not toss it around as one more weapon in the conflict. "Oh, you young people just don't know enough yet to understand that this is a moral issue!" The important message you want to share is the need to **choose your battles** in the personal and social conventional domains but to **hold the line on the true moral issues** that involve harm or potential harm: "No, I'm not allowing you to spend a week at the beach with the guys in your older brother's fraternity. I know you're a good kid, and your continuing to act in responsible ways will make it easy for me to see you do something like this when you are in college yourself."

Moving to the applications of personality theories, Blasi's theory of a developing moral self offers parents, teachers, and counselors a wise and complex perspective on moral functioning, understanding, and personality. Blasi's (2004) central ideas include the following: (a) moral competencies must be understood in the context of the overall personality system; (b) for actions to be moral, they must be guided by moral intentions; and (c) we must conceptualize a personality type that is specifically motivated by morality. He acknowledges, however, that the moral self may only become fully constructed and integrated in adulthood. Thus, we should not be surprised when we encounter bright teens who can talk the talk of complex moral reasoning but often do not walk the walk of corresponding moral actions. It may be that they have not yet constructed a mature self-identity, an "agentic I," to pull disparate aspects of their selves into a congruent whole.

Relatedly, in getting to know a client and the schemas underlying her or his life story, McAdams's work can provide rich guidelines for questions that tap into deep and meaningful life events as well as the mythic components of the characters and plot of the overarching narrative. McAdams's integration of insights across psychological paradigms (e.g., Erikson, Jung, Horney, Piaget) infuses his work with a deeply developmental perspective on the ever-evolving self and personal myth.

And so, if the moral self is indeed a story-telling self, then the process of telling our stories to another—especially a skilled counselor—holds great promise for clients' growth and healing. One way of thinking about counseling is as a dialogue in which the counselor facilitates conversations that help clients to identify and examine the stories or schemas that underlie their sense of self and motivate their behaviors. Often, a therapeutic breakthrough occurs when a client is able to reframe old, dysfunctional stories in healthier ways. And if the counselor is particularly interested in helping a client to develop a sense of meaning and a moral compass, McAdams's (1993) paradigm offers a rich resource:

> In the context of an evolving personal myth, an adult constructs and seeks to live out a generativity script, specifying what he or she plans to do in the future in order to have a legacy of the self. [It]... is an inner narration of the adult's own awareness of where efforts to be generative fit into his or her own personal story, into contemporary society and the social world he or she inhabits.
>
> (p. 240)

In Chapter 10, we explore ideas about an evolving/emerging/developing self in much more detail, and I think you will see even more clearly how theoretical insights underlie real-world applications. Halstead's work on assessing client core issues provides an especially relevant example of developmental practice.

Discussion Questions

1. McAdams (1993) and his colleagues ask their participants to talk about eight key events in their lives using the definition of a key event as "a specific happening, a critical incident, a significant episode in your past set in a particular time and place... that stands out for some reason" (p. 258). Can you remember a key event that has shaped your ideas about the kind of person you want to be?
2. Give two examples of how your thinking about the personal, social conventional, and moral domains has changed over time in terms of specific concepts such as cheating, school honor codes, manners, privacy, respect, homework, curfews, sexual encounters/relationships, alcohol/drug use, and so on.

Additional Resources

*   As, once again, space constraints dictate limiting this chapter to a few short examples from complex and valuable perspectives, we hope those of you interested in exploring you own life stories will follow up in more detail by going to the original source. McAdams's chapter on "Exploring Your Myth" explains the process and questions used in conducting a life history interview. Students may also be interested in seeing how McAdams applied his theory to an analysis of "The Mind of Donald Trump" based on observations of Trump's life narrative prior to winning the presidency.

- McAdams, D. P. (1993). *The stories we live by: Personal myths and the making of the self.* Guilford.
- https://www.theatlantic.com/magazine/archive/2016/06/the-mind-of-donald-trump/480771/

- Educators interested in learning more about moral development from the domain theory perspective will find Larry Nucci's website "Domain Based Moral Education" a valuable resource: https://www.moraledk12.org/

5 The Rise of Theories from Neuroscience and Evolutionary Perspectives

A Time Between Paradigms

Elly worked on the first edition of this book for over a decade and accumulated several large file cabinets of articles, a wall full of books, and many a plan (later discarded) for writing this chapter on new theories. For the second edition, Amie did the heavy lifting of researching the latest research and theories. We then put our heads together to make sense of the changes we see in the field. The first four chapters were relatively easy to write, despite the painful task of ignoring so many fascinating conversations in the field and leaving out many important thinkers in order to keep the text focused and brief. We hope that, in this age of Google, TED talks, and rich online databases, readers with special interests in the topics we introduce in this text delve deep into additional resources.

One of the most important goals of this book has been to present the most **current** theoretical ideas guiding work in the field, especially those that have direct implications for the work of helping professionals. Human Development texts tend to stop at coverage of Freud's, Piaget's, Kohlberg's, Gilligan's and now Haidt's theories, and that leaves practitioners and future practitioners at a real disadvantage. You often learn concepts and ideas beyond which the field has long ago moved.

The problem, as we see it, is that we are in a messy time of competing paradigms that makes it very hard to pull out the sort of grand theories (see e.g., Reed, 2008, 2009; Reed & Stoermer, 2008) that guided productive research and practice for so many years. However, we do sense a contender for a new sort of grand theory gradually emerging and, at the end of this chapter, we attempt to explain why. At present, however, the field encompasses some thinkers who have moved beyond Kohlberg but still maintain a special interest in the study of moral reasoning (e.g., John Gibbs, Larry Nucci, Elliot Turiel, Steve Thoma), as well as researchers from the Care tradition (e.g., Sharon Lamb, Mark Tappan, Lynn Michel Brown) who have gone on to do productive work across a range of topics, including sex education, the moral use of stories, and the marketing of girlhood. Others, especially Darcia Narvaez, Dan Lapsley, Dennis Krebs,

DOI: 10.4324/9780429295461-6

Hyemin Han and Jonathan Haidt (among many others), have attempted to link new ideas from evolutionary psychology and/or neuroscience to moral development. We see the latter group as gradually shaping and defining a new paradigm. We'll defer until Chapter 7 our discussion of Jensen's (2020b) argument that the field has moved from paradigms to plurality.

To give you a sense of the directions and issues of this new generation of theoretical challenges, we briefly address the importance of new tools and ideas from neuroscience and evolutionary psychology, summarize an attempt to sketch out an integrated model of moral functioning, give an example of one of those integrated theories, and end with an evaluation of the controversial new contender for a "grand" theory.

The Rise of Theories from a Neuroscience or Evolutionary Perspective

> We may wonder with Darwin how exactly to divide the credit for morality between natural selection, culture and learning, but suspect like him that, especially at the later stages of the evolution of morality, culture and learning, both individual and social, had the larger roles... Still, as Noam Chomsky says, "it certainly seems reasonable to speculate that the moral and ethical system acquired by the child owes much to some 'innate human faculty' and is 'rooted in our nature'" (Chomsky, 1988, p. 153).
>
> (Katz, 2000, p. ix)

Let's sketch out some of the basic premises and research methods used to explore these new perspectives on morality. Very basically, the argument goes that the evolved human brain now has a set of biases or propensities, which have been selected over time because they contributed to our ability to survive, mate, and get our genes into the next generation. For example, what began as a simple perceptual bias to attend to changes in stimulus intensity that might signal either threat or opportunity in our physical environments now underlies our tendency to spring to attention when a commercial comes on that is louder or brighter or faster than the program that preceded it. Similarly, evolutionary theorists believe we developed certain *moral biases* that allowed our ancestors to be more successful at staying alive and attracting mates. So, while we believe we are deciding to do the right thing because of free will, it may be more likely that we have innate, quick, emotional responses guiding our moral decisions and actions that we only later rationalize consciously.

How would you test such a hypothesis? Well, there have been various strands of research but let's begin with studies using the basic strategy of observation. Some researchers have studied (a) people living in conditions fairly similar to our hunter-gatherer ancestors as well as (b) our close primate cousins for clues to the evolutionary origins of morality. Others have used fMRI scans of people deliberating about moral issues, while still others have studied people playing a game called "The Prisoner's Dilemma," in which your choices to cooperate, act selfishly, or punish the other can be observed and quantified. There are many fine and accessible books on the market about the evolutionary origins of morality (e.g., de Waal, 1996; Katz, 2000; Krebs, 2011; Ridley, 1996; Wright, 1994), and we hope interested readers explore these topics further on their own.

For our purposes, we simply give you a sample of the sorts of findings emerging from research grounded in evolutionary theory. We are especially impressed with the work of renowned primatologist Frans de Waal (2018), who has been observing the behaviors of groups of chimpanzees and other primates for decades. He concludes (Flack & de Waal, 2000) that while the foundations of morality may indeed be built on emotional reactions, morality itself is also influenced by our ability to *evaluate* the situations giving rise to our emotional reactions. It is probably also tempered by our understanding of possible consequences (to ourselves and others) of behavioral responses to our emotional reactions. He sketches out morality as a process that begins in emotional and intuitive responses but plays out through cognitive evaluations that, in both human and animal societies, have been shaped by the group or culture's "social contracts" (p. 21).

In short, our primate origins have given us specific moral tendencies and capacities, of which, the four most important are as follows:

1. **Sympathy-related tendencies,** such as attachment, succulence and emotional contagion, cognitive empathy, and the learned adjustment to the needs of the disabled or injured
2. **Norm-related tendencies**, such as prescriptive social rules, the internalization of rules, and anticipation of punishment
3. **Reciprocity tendencies**, including concepts of giving, trading, and revenge, and aggression toward violators of reciprocity norms (interested readers may also want to see Brosnan and de Waal, 2014)
4. **Getting-along tendencies** to maintain good relationships, avoid conflict, and (sometimes) negotiate (adapted from Flack and de Waal, 2000, p. 22)

Another important evolutionary thinker, Dennis Krebs (2000, 2011, 2020), came out of, and then moved beyond, the Kohlbergian cognitive-developmental tradition. He sees evolutionary theory as a sort of broad tent that can encompass psychodynamic, social learning, cognitive developmental, dual-processing, and cultural perspectives on morality. All approaches in some way explore how experience interacts with evolved human brains. Evolutionary theory explains that brains evolved specific structures and predispositions or biases because those structures and predispositions gave people who had them advantages for natural selection. In Krebs's account, we developed morality because we (and our primate kin) are social beings. We need each other to survive, and that means we had to develop ways to get along. Thus, Krebs argues that the "fittest" developed respect for legitimate authority, learned to resist the temptation to gain at others' expense, stood up for their group or tribe, played fair, and honored social contracts.

We will skip over the line of neuroscience research that has been putting people into fMRI scanners and seeing what happens when participants consider the "Trolley problem" (Would you save five people by pulling a switch and rerouting the trolley to hit one person? versus Would you push one "large" person off a bridge to stop the trolley from killing five people?) Suffice it to say, different parts of our brains light up when we consider the two possible solutions and one of the choices is emotionally unpalatable. You can guess which. Although we are starting to make some very interesting and important strides in understanding the neural underpinnings of moral decisions and emotions; at the present time, we know more about specific structures activated than we do about the incredibly complex interactions among structures and systems. Recent evaluations of prior fMRI studies raise questions about small sample size and changes in participant readings from day to day under identical conditions as well as incorrect analyses and interpretations (Elliott et al., 2020; Renault, 2020)

As we learn more, we are going to get much closer to understanding the "what" and "how" of the moral schemas we construct and use. For example, Hyemin Han is a prolific young scholar whose use of fMRI and focus on the neuroscientific underpinnings of morality may help to propel the field forward. In 2017, he conducted a meta-analysis of 43 fMRI studies of morality and used Rest's 4 component model to contextualize the findings. Engagement with moral tasks lit up interrelated areas of the brain associated with the default mode network (a brain network associated with self-related processes, such as thinking about yourself or daydreaming), but within the default mode, moral judgment and moral sensitivity lit up different brain areas.

Interviews with Discipline Leaders: Hyemin Han, Ph.D. (Associate Professor in Educational Psychology and Neuroscience at the University of Alabama)

In addition to his position at the University of Alabama, Hyemin Han is a collaborator with the Center for the Study of Ethical Development, previously directed by James Rest and Steve Thoma. Hyemin describes his research as connected to one unified goal: "the pursuit of students' flourishing," and specifically aims to collect scientific evidence with multiple methods including traditional survey methods, interviews, as well as behavioral and neuroimaging experiments.

We asked Hyemin to choose one finding from his work that he was most proud of. Hyemin's choice of his 2017 *Frontiers in Psychology* article,

"Attainable and Relevant Moral Exemplars are More Effective than Exemplars in Promoting Voluntary Service Engagement," illustrates his deep desire to use knowledge in psychology and neuroscience to facilitate moral education. Han and colleagues tested students in both a lab setting and a school setting and found that a moral education intervention involving attainable and relevant moral exemplars worked better to promote prosocial behavior than historical moral exemplars. In discussing his pride in this article, Han pointed out its interdisciplinary and applied nature, noting: "It is interdisciplinary and it has potential contributions to real education. It is not an abstract fMRI study but did the real thing in a classroom based on neuroscience…This study can provide a bridge between neuroscience, education, and psychology" (H. Han, personal communication, 11/8/2019).

In addition to this cutting-edge neuroscience research, other intriguing recent attempts to propose broad and comprehensive theories of how biology and/or evolution have shaped morality include Tomasello's (2019) Theory of Ontogeny and Wrangham's (2019) explanation of what he calls **the goodness paradox**—humans' unique evolutionary path to becoming *both* virtuous and violent. Tomasello takes a neo-Vygotskian approach to new findings in **evolutionary developmental biology** (Evo-Devo) to explain how we are biologically prepared to engage in the unique forms of moral engagement with which our culture presents us. Wrangham explores a variety of fascinating comparative studies of our closest human relatives (chimps and bonobos) and 3-year-old human children. Among his provocative arguments is that in our evolutionary history, fear of execution by coalitions of males stands at the root of prosocial behavior and morality.

In a 2008 special issue of the *Journal of Moral Education,* Turiel's foreword framed the swing of the pendulum to biological explanations of morality as a reversion to exactly the kind of reductionist explanations Kohlberg's theory had been designed to overcome. Turiel cautioned against neuroscientists' propensity to ignore conscious processes and epistemological considerations in their rush to show how moral decisions are "emotionally and genetically based and determined by non-conscious processes" (p. 286). However, the biological train has very much left the station, and our sense is that people in the rationalist tradition are probably going to have to jump on board and, at minimum, integrate their ideas with the new biological research.

Toward an Integrated Model of Moral Functioning (and Its Critics)

In 2008, philosopher Don Reed edited the aforementioned special issue of the *Journal of Moral Education* in honor of the 50th anniversary of Lawrence

Kohlberg's 1958 doctoral dissertation. In his foreword to the issue, in addition to cautioning about the rush to biological explanations, Elliot Turiel (2008) argued that, although Kohlberg was often criticized for his focus on the primacy of moral reasoning in any integrated theory of moral functioning, he also understood that a comprehensive theory needed to explain the relationship between the development of moral thought, moral conduct, and moral emotions.

Reed (2008) envisioned the special issue as a prospective look forward rather than a commemorative look backward. In the process, Reed and Stoermer (2008) saw a core idea emerge: "The field lacks a single comprehensive model of moral functioning. Such a model would have to integrate accounts from multiple levels of analysis of organ system, organism and organized group functioning" (p. 418). The design for the issue solicited papers from top scholars representing multiple levels of analysis from neuroscience to personality and culture. Reed and Stoermer identified several key points and themes that ran through the issue's offerings:

- The field is in a **time between paradigms,** but there is consensus that an analysis of moral reasoning alone will be entirely insufficient to explain moral functioning.
- Researchers have become aware of the **central importance of early experience** and nurturing practices for optimal moral development.
- We now know that **both implicit/tacit processes and explicit/ deliberative processes** (sometimes called **System 1 Thinking** and **System 2 Thinking**) influence our moral decisions and actions.
- **Concerns about the judgment action gap,** a term for the fact that research finds only weak correlations between moral reasoning complexity and moral behavior, remain. Frimer and Walker (2008) believe that a better understanding of the centrality people give to their **moral self** may be the key to bridging this gap.
- Many authors addressed the mediating role of **culture and cultural discourses** in cognitive processing and moral functioning. Even writers stressing the role of brain functioning acknowledged that we make sense of our world through the lens of culture.
- Perhaps the most controversial point in Reed's summary comes with his argument that the field has moved beyond the "naïve universalisms" of modernism and should be ready to accept **the not-so-menacing specter of postmodernism and moral relativism** (Adapted from Reed & Stoermer, 2008, pp. 419–425).

In short, Reed and the authors in the special issue were saying, "Things are getting very complicated, and it's time we develop a more comprehensive or integrated model of moral functioning." However, not everyone agreed with the prominence of cultural pluralism and biologically rooted explanations advanced by issue authors. John Gibbs and colleagues (Gibbs et al., 2009) believe the issue neglected core cognitive-developmental concepts that have stood the test of time and research. Specifically, these critics argue for the continued usefulness of the Kohlbergian and Piagetian "concept of development as the construction of a deeper or more adequate understanding not reducible to particular socialization practices or cultural contexts" (p. 271).

Dual Processing Theories of Morality

One of the most important issues identified in this "time between paradigms" is the growing understanding of a phenomenon William James described a century ago: Humans process ideas and events using two different systems. Before looking at any specific new theories, let us give you a very brief overview of the two systems posited to operate when you make a moral decision (or any decision for that matter).

System 1 Thinking (Kahneman, 2003, 2013) describes a form of cognition that developed earlier in evolutionary time and provided our ancestors with an automatic, fast, and unconscious process for making quick decisions and taking decisive actions. Such processing had an obvious evolutionary advantage. In a harsh world full of danger and predators, he who hesitates might literally find himself lost (or lunch). Kahneman explains System 1 Thinking as intuitive, emotional, implicit, and experiential. However, this type of thinking has been criticized as being prone to the kinds of mental shortcuts or **heuristics** (part of why it's so fast!) that can lead to biased thinking. For example, let's say you are a staunch Republican and you end up on a long plane trip with a seatmate reading a book that clearly identifies her as an equally staunch Democrat. In today's hostile political climate, you're likely to take a quick and largely unconscious dislike to your seatmate and quickly plug in your iPod earbuds.

System 2 Thinking (Kahneman, 2003, 2013) developed later in human history and, in contrast to System 1 thinking, tends to be controlled, slow, and conscious. Other characteristics include being rational, analytic, explicit, and rule based. System 2 allows us to consider possibilities and probabilities—that's part of what slows it down. It has the capacity to monitor and, at times, override the quicker, emotional decisions of System 1. For example, if you catch yourself making a snap (and dismissive) judgment of someone just because of the book she is reading, you might catch yourself and say, "Boy, I'm acting just like the kind of closed-minded people I so dislike." You might still put in your earbuds, but it will be in a spirit of rational tolerance rather than irrational disgust. Denton and Krebs (2017) and Krebs (2020) argue that evidence supporting dual-process models of moral decision-making can be interpreted through an evolutionary developmental framework, with emotional-intuitive reasoning (e.g., Haidt, 2012, who we will talk about shortly), arising from older parts of the brain we share with all animals, and more rational reasoning (e.g., Kohlbergian stage theories) consistent with more recently evolved brain structures that change as children grow.

Narvaez's Triune Ethics Meta-Theory

To better understand exactly what people are talking about in terms of more comprehensive and integrated theories, we briefly summarize one of the most thoughtful attempts to construct a comprehensive theory that integrates research from multiple disciplines (e.g., Narvaez, 2008, 2010, 2011, 2014, 2016; Narvaez & Vaydich, 2008).

> Both the rationalist and the intuitionist paradigms provide incomplete views. Rationalism neglects implicit processes, narrowing morality to a small slice of human behavior. Intuitionism ignores the complexities of moral functioning that rely also on complex interplays between reasoning, intuition and other factors.
>
> (Narvaez, 2010, p. 164)

In an acclaimed, thought-provoking and integrative book, *Neurobiology and the Development of Human Morality: Evolution, Culture, and Wisdom*, respected moral development researcher Darcia Narvaez (2014) drew on her extensive reading and research across a dizzying array of fields (including, but probably not limited to, anthropology, evolutionary systems, moral psychology, moral philosophy, neuroscience, developmental psychology, and clinical psychology) to illustrate how she has come to believe that theories of moral development must acknowledge the neurobiological roots of morality. She proposed a complex and thoughtful theory she calls **Triune Ethics Meta-Theory** that we outline for you in the following sections. Although this theory is an impressive and compelling accomplishment, it does not seem to be attracting the level of acceptance of some of the theoretical projects she worked on in the past (e.g., the Four Component Model or Neo-Kohlbergian schema theory). After laying out both **Triune Ethics Meta-Theory** and Haidt's Moral Foundation Theory, we hazard a hypothesis as to why one model seems to be generating much more interest and acceptance than the other.

Triune Ethics Meta-Theory posits that humans have three distinct moral systems (rooted in global brain states) that influence both individual and group behavior (Narvaez, 2008; 2014; 2016). The meta-theory describes how neurobiological systems are shaped by early experience leading to better or worse self-regulation and capacities for sociomorality, identifiable in one's situational or dispositional ethics: Self-Protectionism and Engagement refer to face-to-face relations; Imagination refers to imagining possibilities outside the present moment (see Table 5.1).

The Ethic of Security (Narvaez, 2008), associated with structures in some of the oldest portions of our brain, often functions as our default

Table 5.1 Triune Ethics Meta-Theory: Ethics, Neurobiological Underpinnings, and Characteristics

Ethic of Self-Protection	Hard-wired set of survival systems integrated with stress response. Can be conditioned in early months and years of life by undercare or trauma.	When individual feels threat, will shift into dominance (social oppositionalism) or submission (social withdrawal).
Ethic of Engagement	Rooted in mammalian emotional systems related to play, care and empathy that promote intimacy, harmony, and sociality.	Active when individuals feel safe, have developed social skills and social pleasure from early life caregiver interactions (secure attachment).
Ethic of Imagination	Dependent on more recently evolved brain parts especially the prefrontal cortex.	Active when using abstracting capabilities which make it possible for humans to step back from the present moment. Can be fueled by self-protectionism (vicious imagination) or engagement (communal imagination), or emotionally and relationally detached (detached imagination).

(Adapted from Narvaez, 2008, pp. 95–119).

system when we are stressed, frightened, or angry. You can think of this moral mindset as a survival system that helps us respond to perceived physical or psychological threats by activating our stress systems in a similar way to the physiological response of fight or flight. For example, the massacre of 20 young children at Sandy Hook Elementary School in 2012 activated the ethic of security for many people. However, for people oriented to dominance by their early experiences, the activated mindset led to calls to protect gun rights ("Guns don't kill people, mentally ill people kill people.") Others, coming out of a different set of interactions with caregivers and others, responded to the perceived threat with calls for very different solutions: "We can only protect society by strengthening gun control laws and procedures."

The Ethic of Self-Protection (Narvaez, 2008, 2014, 2016), associated with structures in some of the oldest portions of our brain linked to survival, can be triggered when we are threatened, frightened, or angry. When the stress response kicks in, blood flow shifts to facilitate self-protectionism physiologically, changing perception and affordances (action possibilities). In chronically threatening environments such as situations of neglectful or traumatic early care, a self-protective mindset can become a habitual personality trait. When stress becomes reactive, a self-protectionism mindset will be activated frequently, making it difficult to be open-minded or open-hearted and we will be oriented to dominance-submission relations. For example, imagine someone bumping into you. If you are in a protectionist mindset, like aggressive individuals typically are, you will assume it was on purpose and take offense. If you are in the next mindset, engagement, you take it as an accident, and are likely to forgive the offender.

The **Ethic of Engagement** refers to relational, flexible attunement to the other in the moment. It is fostered in early childhood from attuned caregiving, which shapes neurobiological systems (like the stress response) to work in a healthy manner and to provide deep social experiences. Children who form secure attachments through responsive and appropriate nurturing are literally forming self-regulatory and social skills oriented towards prosocial and peaceful interactions. Narvaez (e.g., 2014, 2016) has written extensively about the importance of early childhood experiences, specifically, a set of key characteristics she calls the **evolved developmental niche** (EDN), including warm, responsive caregiving, breastfeeding on demand, outdoor play, cuddling, and relationships with multiple supportive adults. These develop healthy neurobiological underpinnings for moral functioning: "Child rearing has profound effects on brain functioning that can last a lifetime. The quality of early care shapes the functioning of multiple systems, from neurotransmitters, to immunity and stress response, to moral imagination" (Narvaez, 2011, p. 31).

Narvaez and colleague's recent research showed significant relationships between early caregiving (specifically provision of the EDN) and sociomoral outcomes including empathy, self-regulation, and concern for doing wrong, across US (Narvaez, 2016) and Chinese samples (Narvaez et al., 2013) of parents of 3- to 5-year-olds. Similarly, the EDN has been positively associated with Social Thriving, a sense of skillful enjoyment of being with others that is characteristic of the Engagement Ethic, across US, Chinese, and Swiss samples of 3- to 5-year-old children (Narvaez et al., 2019). In a retrospective survey of adults, Narvaez et al. (2016) found further evidence linking EDN-consistent care in childhood with the Ethic of Engagement in adulthood, and EDN-inconsistent care to self-protection and the Ethic of Self-Protection.

Finally, the **Ethic of Imagination** is rooted primarily in more recently evolved parts of the brain and, most specifically, in the prefrontal cortex (Narvaez, 2008, 2014, 2016). This ethic allows a person to move beyond the present moment, or override particular impulses, to consider the big picture of future consequences and possible outcomes. When the engagement ethic's empathy and prosociality drive imagination, it fosters **Communal Imagination**. When the self-protectionist ethic guides imagination, the result is **Vicious Imagination** (control of others). **Detached Imagination** occurs when the person is emotionally and relationally detached (e.g., hypothetical). You may be noticing that the Ethic of Imagination sounds a lot like the moral version of Kahneman's System 2 Thinking (2003, 2013), and we would agree. It should also sound a lot like the kind of reasoning studied by Piaget and Kohlberg—because it is! However, Narvaez argues that Communal Imagination, an integration of abstraction and inclusive empathy and perspective taking, is our species' primary heritage. Narvaez further argues that the "ability to think outside the present moment and about future possibilities" (p. 34), rooted in the development of the prefrontal cortex, is profoundly influenced by early childhood care and experiences. She worries that poor or traumatic early experiences have long-term and serious consequences such as deficits in prosocial emotionality, which leave the adult self at risk of dominance by the more primitive Ethic of Self-Protection and its brother, Vicious Imagination.

In contrast, children nurtured by responsive caregivers in healthy environments develop a moral understanding by actively participating in social interactions. At the earliest stages of life, moral learning is embodied through the experience of having one's basic needs met (Narvaez, 2018). Expanding opportunities for give and take teach reciprocity and fairness in a way no book or lecture ever could. Narvaez (2011) proposes that the child's moral identity is slowly co-constructed with their caregivers and others through multiple interactions in the real world. But she fears that all too few children get the early experiences needed for optimal growth because the modern world has abandoned the evolved child-rearing practices most appropriate to human flourishing. She worries about modern child-rearing practices designed to make life easier for busy parents rather than for developing children.

We began our theoretical explorations with Freud's psychoanalytic theory and his insistence on the importance of early childhood experiences and here we are, a century later, hearing a top researcher conclude, "Child rearing has profound effects on brain functioning that can last a lifetime" (Narvaez, 2011, p. 31). These are sobering but, perhaps, *potentially* optimistic conclusions, especially if a child or young adult receives strong nurturing later in life.

Dilemma of the Day

Before you begin the next section, take a few minutes to think about your answers to a set of scenarios Jonathan Haidt used in research testing a hypothesis that intuitions played a larger role than reason in people's moral decisions. The following exercise was developed from methods used to explore **domain theory** (Chapter 4) as well as specific questions developed by Haidt (2012). Elly's moral development class usually begins with a discussion of a "Dilemma of the Day—Ripped from the Headlines." As you might imagine, using this exercise when exploring Haidt's leads to quite lively discussions! (Your professor may want to use this as a pair/share in-class exercise.)

Dilemmas of the Day—From Domain and Moral Dumbfounding Research

Questions: Ask after each scenario: *"So what do you think about this?"*

1. *Would it be wrong to... have sex with the chicken?/Eat the family dog?/Have sexual intercourse with a sibling?/Use the flag as a rag?*
2. *Why?*
3. *Would it be wrong to... in another country?*
4. *Would it be wrong to... if there were no rules about it?*

1. A man goes to the supermarket once a week and buys a chicken. But before cooking the chicken, he has sexual intercourse with it. Then he cooks it and eats it.
2. A car kills a family's dog in front of their house. They had heard that dog meat was delicious, so they cut up the dog's body and cooked it and ate it for dinner. Nobody saw them do this.
3. Siblings Julie and Mark are traveling together in France during summer college vacation. One night, they are staying alone in a cabin by a beach and decide it would be interesting and fun to try making love. (At the least, it would be a new experience for both.) Julie is on the pill but Mark uses a condom just to be safe. They both enjoy it but decide not to do it again. They keep that night as a special secret between them, which makes them feel even closer.
4. A woman finds an old American flag in her closet and tears it up to use for cleaning rags (Haidt, 2012).

Haidt's Moral Foundations Theory

Liberals can't understand why conservatives appear to be so unmoved by the concerns of people protesting systemic racism. Conservatives can't understand how liberals appear so unmoved by obvious threats to personal liberty like the requirement to wear masks in public spaces during a pandemic. Traditionalists in Iran are disgusted by the immoral dress of Western women, and Westerners are disgusted by the repressive dress requirements in Iran. How can morality vary so widely by culture yet paradoxically exhibit so many recurring patterns and similarities? Jonathan Haidt has emerged as the voice of a group of social and cultural psychologists who believe they have discovered the answer to these paradoxes.

In brief, the theory [Moral Foundations] proposes that **six (or more) innate and universally available psychological systems are the foundations of "intuitive ethics."** Each *culture* then *constructs virtues, narratives, and institutions* on top of these foundations, thereby creating the unique moralities we see around the world, and conflicting within nations too.

(Iyer et al., 2019)

In his widely reviewed and discussed book *The Righteous Mind: Why Good People Are Divided by Politics and Religion,* Haidt (2012) made a series of bold assertions about morality:

- Intuition, not reason, drives our moral judgments.
- Morality both binds us and blinds us.
- Evolution has etched into our brains a set of psychological foundations that underlie the virtues seen in cultures around the world.
- Although all humans are prewired with the same six foundations, cultures teach us which ones to prioritize and prize.
- Liberals in the Western world respond strongly only to care/harm and fairness/cheating but their WEIRD perspective (Western, Educated, Industrial, Rich, Democratic) is at odds with not only conservatives but also with most of the rest of the world.
- Conservatives and people in more traditional societies feel the pull of all six foundations, with the specific strength of the tug of each ultimately set by learning and culture (Haidt, 2012; Iyer et al., 2019; Jacobs, 2012; Parry, 2012).

Haidt believes that morality developed in humans because it helped us solve adaptive challenges. Working together in groups helped our group survival and thus phenomena like religions in which we circle around sacred objects or ideas and gain a sense of self-transcendence have endured across time and cultures. Our sense of morality binds us to our tribe or group but it can also blind us to the needs of others.

He also believes that his own research (e.g., Haidt, 2001, 2012) demonstrates convincingly that it is our "emotional dog" wagging our "rational tails" and not the other way around. His recent work uses the metaphor of *intuition* (a word he now wishes he had used instead of *emotion*) as an elephant and reason as the rider. The rider thinks she or he is in charge but it is actually the large, strong elephant that is making *most* decisions. He supports this belief by pointing to the findings when he asked people to respond to the aforementioned moral scenarios. He found that even though there was no actual harm done to either the animals or the humans (remember, the chicken and dog were already dead, and the siblings used a condom) many people evidenced **moral dumbfounding,** or a sense that they knew it was wrong but they really couldn't describe why. He found respondents often had an intuitive "eww" response that they then attempted to rationalize. Although Haidt presents a convincing argument, you should note that many thinkers believe his intuitionism overlooks the important role of reason in everyday life (e.g., Haste, 2013; Jacobs, 2012; Maxwell & Narvaez, 2013; Narvaez, 2010).

Although we side with those critics who believe Haidt overstates his case for the primacy of intuition, we find his argument for prewired moral foundations and their evolutionary roots a compelling one. Very briefly, Haidt reviews some of the key adaptive challenges faced by early humans and attempts to see how solutions evolved that eventually prewired our brain systems to respond intuitively to core adaptive issues he calls *moral foundations* (see Table 5.2).

Let's take a closer look at Haidt's most recent descriptions of the foundations of human morality but defer for now an in-depth look at criticisms of his arguments (Haidt, 2012; Iyer et al., 2019; Jacobs, 2012; Parry, 2012). Recall that the primary goal of evolution is for individuals (and species) to survive, mate, and get their genes into the next generation. Many people assume that evolution means we are evolving toward some goal or better model. That is not so. Rather, the evolutionary theory holds that mutations that arise and provide an adaptive advantage for an organism in a specific environment will be selected and passed on.

Table 5.2 Haidt's Moral Foundations Theory: Evolutionary Challenges and Modern Manifestations

Moral Foundation	Adaptive Evolutionary Challenge	Modern Manifestations
Care/Harm	How to care for vulnerable children?	Underlies our virtues of kindness, gentleness, and nurturance
Fairness/ Cheating	How to reap rewards of cooperation without getting exploited?	Underlies virtues of justice, rights, and autonomy
Liberty/ Oppression	How can we avoid domination by bullies & tyrants?	Underlies egalitarianism of Left and "Don't tread on me" of conservatives
Loyalty/Betrayal	How to form and maintain coalitions?	Underlies virtues of patriotism and self-sacrifice for the group
Authority/ Subversion	How to form beneficial relationships within social hierarchies?	Underlies virtues of leadership, followership, and respect for traditions
Sanctity/ Degradation	How to survive in a world filled with parasites & pathogens?	Underlies striving for less carnal, more noble, body-is-a-temple ideas

Adapted from Haidt (2012) and Iyer et al. (2019).

The Six Foundations of Morality

Care/Harm

A primary adaptive challenge for early humans involved the need to care for vulnerable infants and children. Haidt (2012) believes that our mammalian attachment systems, originally triggered by the distress or needs of our own children, currently respond to any person or animal (or even cartoon character) in distress. We developed the ability to feel and be distressed by the pain of others as well as to feel compassion for them, because such feelings contributed to the survival of both individuals and groups. The contemporary virtues rooted in our ancient systems include empathy, caring, and kindness.

Fairness/Cheating

This foundation arose from the need to reap the benefits of two-way partnerships. The adaptive challenges faced by our primate ancestors as well as early humans led to the selection of the tendency for reciprocal altruism. Humans became especially sensitive to cheating, cooperation, and deception because doing so was adaptive. This tendency to notice and appreciate fairness and to be enraged by cheating lies at the root of our contemporary ideas of trustworthiness as well as "justice, rights, and autonomy" (Haidt, 2012, p. 125).

Liberty/Oppression

Haidt and his colleagues eventually divided his original fairness foundation into two parts to accommodate findings that emotions about fairness/cheating were triggered not only by the need for cooperation but also by

> feelings of reactance and resentment people feel toward those who dominate them and restrict their liberty.... The hatred of bullies and dominators motivates people to come together, in solidarity, to oppose or take down the oppressor.
>
> (Iyer et al., 2019)

Loyalty/Betrayal

Humans spent most of their evolutionary history in tribes where we needed to form cohesive but flexible coalitions. With scarce resources for survival available in our early environments, it was important to be able to count on "our tribe" for both protection and production. Religious ceremonies, sporting events, and war all tend to promote a self-transcendent feeling of oneness with the group that Haidt (2012) argues had great evolutionary benefits for our species. We feel pride when our group does well and rage when we learn of traitors. Haidt (2012) and Iyer et al. (2019) see this foundation underlying virtues such as patriotism and sacrifice for the group. We would add that the need to sometimes form "shifting" coalitions is also evident in political compromises (and backstabbing).

Authority/Subversion

If you have ever watched a nature special about chimpanzees, you probably witnessed the importance of hierarchy for primate groups. According to Haidt (2012, Iyer et al., 2019), this long history of hierarchical societal interactions (e.g., dominant alpha males, submission gestures) underlies our moral virtues of obedience, leadership, and followership. He also sees it contributing to human's deference to legitimate authority and respect for traditions.

Sanctity/Degradation

The most problematic foundation for most liberals was originally shaped by our highly adaptive innate disgust towards things that might sicken, kill, or contaminate us (e.g., dead bodies, ulcerating rashes, rotted food). Haidt (2012) argues that this intuitive response to pathogens in our physical world now underlies religious (as well as secular humanist) ideals of living in nobler, less carnal ways. For instance, Christian, Muslim, and Hindu religions all hold some version of the idea that the body is a temple that can be debased or desecrated when we act immorally. Cultures set down rules and norms for which actions are noble (moral) and which are degrading. In traditional societies, these rules often encompass a wider swatch of daily life—not only sexual practices but also food, dress, and mandatory rituals. If you want a contemporary real-life example of how cultures specifically shape objects of disgusts, think about the difference between how cool and sophisticated smoking appeared in the 1940s, 1950s, and 1960s and how dirty and polluting it appears to many people today. In the past decade, many Western countries have observed a sea change in attitudes about gay marriage that also exemplifies how the same activity (homosexuality) that once triggered the sanctity/degradation foundation now triggers the fairness one, especially for young people.

In sum, Haidt (2012) holds that the first principle of moral psychology should read: "Intuitions come first, strategic reasoning second" (p. 315). Its second principle should be "There's more to morality than harm and fairness" (p. 315). He hopes that his work can help people to understand that there can be no "one true morality for all people, times, and places" (p. 316). His third major principle argues that morality both binds and blinds because humans evolved as both selfish chimps (90%) through individual selection and as groupish "bees" (10%) through group selection. Although we would quibble with his specific percentages (what evidence supports them?), we agree with his proposal that although humans often act like selfish chimps, we also have the capacity to transcend that selfishness and become part of a whole that could conceivably work together towards common goals.

Haidt's Moral Foundations Theory and research have been applied across countless diverse areas of study including social psychology, politics, economics, the law, healthcare, and public health. During the COVID-19 pandemic, global public health experts explained that vaccinations were the most effective way to control the deadly virus. In earlier findings directly relevant to the pandemic, Jacobs (2019) shared results of Rossen et al.'s (2019) research findings that parental vaccine hesitancy and rejection were related to high scores on the liberty foundation. Jacobs and Rosen et al. reason that vaccine persuasion campaigns focusing on coercion could spark moral outrage for these parents, while more effective communication strategies preserve parental autonomy and potentially "emphasize why vaccines are so crucial, to your child and to society as a whole—while conceding that parents have the final choice" (Jacobs, 2019, p. 2).

For Haidt (2012), we're divided by politics and religion

> because our minds are designed for groupish righteousness. We are deeply intuitive creatures whose gut feelings drive our strategic reasoning. This makes it difficult—but not impossible—to connect with those who live in other matrices, which are often built on different configurations of the available moral foundations.
>
> (p. 318)

We do not doubt the sincerity of Haidt's hope that people reading his book will be more open to understanding people "who live in other matrices." It's an admirable goal, albeit one that can seem wildly optimistic in this age of increasing global and national divisions, resentments and hatred.

Current Evaluation of Haidt's Theory

In the *Journal of Moral Education* Special Issue on Haidt and Moral Foundations Theory's "significance for theory, research, and practice in moral development and education" (Maxwell & Narvaez, 2013, p. 271), Maxwell and Narvaez (2013) concluded that the jury was still out. We would argue that in the time since this publication, Haidt's theory has been enormously influential in social psychology, igniting interest in researching morality (Vozzola, 2017) and propelling him to one of the top 25 living psychologists ("The Best Schools," 2019). His theory has challenged key assumptions of the cognitive-developmental paradigm that dominated moral development and education for decades, reminding people of the importance of intuition in moral decision-making.

Despite its heuristic value, Haidt's theory does not address *how* people grow in morality or reach their highest potential, limiting its application to moral education. As Gibbs (2019) explained, Haidt's theory focuses on our (often) self-centered intuitions, but he does not explain how we can sur-mount them, except for trying to understand those who are unlike our-selves. As Maxwell and Narvaez (2013) noted, "condoning and celebrating intuitions regardless of their source—many can be naïve or prejudiced ra-ther than well educated—is like celebrating children's preference for candy instead of educating their palates to enjoy healthy foods" (p. 278). As Gibbs (2019) reminded us, "A comprehensive and valid theory of moral psy-chology is one that represents the developmentally mature and admirable at least as well as the commonplace and immature or even venal aspects of human reason, development, and social behavior" (p. 39).

Is a New Paradigm Emerging?

Moral philosopher Don Reed (1994), once gave a talk at a moral education conference whose central point ran something along the lines of "What if everybody is right?" And our own take on the important contributions of new research in neuroscience and evolutionary perspectives might use that same title. Well, yes, a lot of moral decisions and behavior seem rooted in our biological predispositions. This should not be surprising—we are biological beings.

It is equally unsurprising that those biological moral predispositions unfold and are shaped through interactions with the world. So, each child, a won-derful blend of common humanity and her or his own uniqueness, begins to grow and develop in a specific family, in a specific neighborhood, in a specific culture, at a specific time. The universal experience of early attachment ap-pears to provide the roots for our capacities for empathy, sympathy, and love. Like our primate ancestors, we are social creatures who learn about concepts of fairness and rules through our interactions with others.

You probably noticed these common observations running through this chapter's sample of current theories. Is perhaps some consensus emerging? If so, might we be coming out of this time between paradigms and beginning to accept a new one? Although an analysis of numbers of citations (Vozzola, 2017) might suggest that Haidt's Moral Foundations Theory has emerged as the dominant one for the coming decades, we take seriously the criticism that: "A moral psychology that emphasizes human foibles or worse, and punts on remedial treatment or moral education, fails seriously short of adequate paradigm status" (Gibbs, 2019, p.41).

Philosophers of science rate theories using several criteria, such as com-prehensiveness, elegance (simplicity), testability, and heuristic value (gen-erating new research). Moral Foundations Theory certainly claims to explain a lot of things, not least of which is the important question of why human beings are so deeply divided by religion and politics. And yet, it is simple and easy to understand—six foundations defined in ordinary language. Haidt has produced a significant body of research in support of the theory and lays out clearly what he is doing and why. That has indeed led to an explosion of interest and further research that meets the heuristic value criteria.

In contrast, although Narvaez's theory offers a model that is particularly comprehensive and well-grounded in both theory and research, perhaps its very complexity and comprehensiveness have worked against it. Although Narvaez compellingly pulls together many strands of scholarship, her theory can be more difficult to comprehend without a background in the disciplines from which she pulls her ideas. While Triune Ethics Meta-Theory may not have garnered the number of citations that Moral Foundations Theory has, Narvaez and colleagues' recent strong body of research testing the application of her theoretical assumptions now provides evidence for its heuristic as well as testability value.

Thus, the observation that a new paradigm is emerging is not to say that Haidt's theory (or evolutionary theory in general) has not faced serious and substantive criticism. However, we shall save that discussion for Chapter 8. What we can say is that Haidt and colleagues have proposed and promoted a compelling theory that has generated both excitement and resistance.

Implications of Current Theories for Practitioners

New research and theory emerging from biological and evolutionary perspectives suggest that practitioners can no longer rely on a simple model of stages of moral reasoning if they wish to understand the moral beliefs and behavior of students and clients. We've reviewed some exciting new ideas about morality's biological underpinnings, but what exactly does all this mean for real-life applications?

For one thing, these new theories call us to be aware of how often people respond to situations with intuitions rather than with reason. Our implicit mind makes a lot of our decisions, as Kahneman and Tversky (1973) showed, so it is vital to train up our intuitions appropriately. Good enough mothering/nurturing in early life (evolved nest) shapes the foundations of our moral intuitions well, leading to capacities for and a predisposition for an engagement ethic (Narvaez, 2014). Poor early nurturing (and corporal punishment) leads to a disposition for self-protection (and missing social skills). According to Narvaez, what Haidt misses is the shaping of intuitions, and the difference between the intuitions of experts and novices. When we are in a situation, intuitions operate so quickly that we are unaware of how they shape our perceptions, thinking preferences and affordances (D. Narvaez, personal communication, September 16, 2020).

We believe (as do many other critics) that Haidt overreaches his laboratory data and ignores the large body of research on ways in which **both** intuition and reasoning inform mature moral functioning (Narvaez, 2010). In fact, a key goal of educating young people or working with clients in therapy is to help them identify emotional and intuitive responses or ideas that cannot stand up to the light of reason. We attempt to inculcate the habit of moral reflection—for example, catching oneself when one reacts to a practice with disgust just because it is different or strange.

Professional or future professionals reading this text will need to grapple with the ethical question of just how far we should go in accepting the sort of tolerance that Haidt proposes towards the myriad patterns of cultural foundations. Although we may agree that the evolutionary history behind sanctity/degradation foundation's disgust impulse makes sense in terms of keeping us away from pathogens, shouldn't it be deeply worrisome that it now plays out in "noxious beliefs such as the tendency to consciously or unconsciously equate illegal aliens with contamination" (Jacobs, 2012, p. 70)? Jacobs finds the "rhetorical somersaults" in Haidt's attempts to be fair to all sides ultimately unconvincing, especially with respect to sanctity/degradation. As he notes, some sacralizing impulses have led to attempts to preserve the environment, while others have led to centuries of warfare and violence. Ultimately, if we have our students' and clients' best interests at heart, it may be our ethical obligation to help them understand why feeling they are so very right and others are so very wrong may be getting in the way of not only their own thriving and flourishing but also of the larger social good for their communities and the planet.

Discussion Questions

1. Review Haidt's Moral Foundations Theory and give yourself a score of 1–5 for how important each foundation is for you with 1 being "not important at all" and 5 being "extremely important." Now consider the political figure with whom you most profoundly disagree. Think about his or her position about a controversial issue such as gay marriage or immigration or gun control. See if you can construct a similar rating on the moral foundations for this figure. How useful do you find Haidt's ideas for understanding the differences in your perspectives?

2. If Narvaez is right about the long-term neurological damage done by not only abusive, but also simply inadequate, parenting, what implications might this have for maternal and paternal work policies?

Additional Resources

- Many of you have probably already discovered the wealth of stimulating ideas shared in the growing series of online TED (Technology, Entertainment, & Design) Talks. Here are two with particular relevance to this chapter. The first link gives you a little background on primatologist Frans de Waal (2011) and has the link to his video talk "Moral Behavior in Animals" in the lower left-hand corner. This short video (TED talks generally come in at under 17 minutes) is a wonderful introduction to primate morality. What's not to love about footage of clever chimps conning each other or bonobos making connections in that special bonobo way? (If you don't know what we're talking about here, Google *bonobos*—primates who have found a rather unique way to solve conflicts!) https://www.ted.com/speakers/frans_de_waal

- The second link gives you a more detailed version of Jonathan Haidt's ideas as well as a sense of why he's become the rock star of moral development theories. Haidt's (2008) talk on the moral roots of liberals and conservatives got a lot of attention during recent US elections. Does he convince you or do you have questions about his arguments? https://www.ted.com/talks/jonathan_haidt_the_moral_roots_of_liberals_and_conservatives?language=en
- To follow Narvaez's work on the important implications of Triune Ethics Meta-Theory for child rearing and family policies, explore this website: https://evolvednest.org/

You may want to ask your own parents about the child-rearing methods that they used with you.

- For some fascinating videos of children and apes performing tasks in the studies cited by Tomasello, visit http:/www.becoming-human.org/ (username: *developmental*; password: *psychology*)
- For an accessible overview of challenges to brain scan findings, see: https://www.eurekalert.org/pub_releases/2020-06/du-sob060320.php

6 The Origins of Morality and Prosocial Behavior in Early Childhood

Amie K. Senland

Researching the moral lives of infants, as well as early childhood prosocial behavior, has become increasingly popular, as researchers have progressively drawn from and integrated evolutionary, neurobiological, and intuitivist perspectives on development (see Chapter 5) (Eisenberg et al., 2015; Eisenberg & Spinrad, 2014; Wynn & Bloom, 2013). Prior researchers such as Hoffman (2000), whose theory of empathy development we discuss in more depth in Chapter 11, have investigated morality, specifically empathy, in infants. However, Hoffman argued that even though children are born with a biological predisposition toward empathy, they do not experience empathic concern until their second year, and they do not develop genuine morality until later in childhood (Smetana, 2018b). As Smetana (2018b, p. 210) noted:

> *The novel aspect of the current emphasis on early moral development is that claims are being made about the advanced moral capacities of infants and young children* [emphasis added]. Some of these assertions have been controversial; for instance, surprising findings based on experimental studies of infants have led to bold and widely publicized assertions about "moral babies". [Bloom's (2010) term]

The intense interest in this topic over the past decade is illustrated by the dedication of at least four recent special issues of various journals including Brownell's (2013) special edition of *Infancy* (Early Development of Prosocial Behavior), Smetana's (2018a) special edition of *Human Development* (Early Moral Development), Warneken and Hepach's (2018) special edition of *Current Opinion in Psychology* (Early Prosocial Development), and Lucca et al.'s (2019) research topic in *Frontiers in Psychology* (Early Moral Cognition and Behavior).

Definitional Issues

At the broad level, **prosocial behavior** is defined as "voluntary actions intended to benefit others" (Eisenberg et al., 2015, p. 610). Considering a

DOI: 10.4324/9780429295461-7

person can be motivated to act prosocially for various reasons including concern for others, commitment to moral values, *or* external rewards, researchers have reserved the more narrow term **altruism** to refer to "a prosocial behavior motivated by concern for another and, for some theorists, by internalized moral concerns or internalized moral values" (Eisenberg & Spinrad, 2014, p. 18). **Empathy** "an affective response that stems from the apprehension or comprehension of another's emotional state… which is identical or quite similar to what the other person is feeling or would be expected to feel" (Eisenberg et al., 2015, p. 611) contributes to prosocial behavior, but empathy is related to one's *feelings and thoughts* about a person or situation, while prosocial behavior relates to one's *actions* in response to that individual or circumstance.

Padilla-Walker and Carlo (2014) effectively argue in *Multidimensionality of Prosocial Behavior* that there is a research problem with studying prosocial behavior as a global, unidimensional construct, which has been the predominant way of conceptualizing prosocial behavior. They also discuss the benefits of a more nuanced multidimensional approach that considers various types of prosocial behaviors (e.g., sharing, helping, cooperation; spontaneous versus compliant, costly versus less costly), predictors of prosocial behavior, targets of prosocial behavior (e.g., in-group versus outgroup; parents versus siblings versus extended family), and change over time/age differences in prosocial behavior. These advantages include helping us to explain why different types of prosocial behavior often show a little relationship with each other and to develop a more complex understanding of which prosocial behaviors are most related to morality. Eisenberg and Spinrad (2014) provide a useful example; spontaneous, costly prosocial behaviors (e.g., sharing a favorite toy with a peer) are more positively related to children's prosocial moral reasoning and behavior across time than compliant, low-cost prosocial behaviors (e.g., passing food at the table). A nuanced multidimensional approach is also useful for interventions, as we can target prosocial interventions toward those most conducive for morality and/or create separate program's for sharing versus helping (Padilla-Walker & Carlo, 2014).

As Dahl and Killen (2018) highlighted, initial research from the cognitive-developmental tradition (e.g., Kohlberg, Piaget, Turiel) focused on moral development in older children, adolescents, and adults. More recently, researchers such as Paul Bloom, Melanie Killen, Judith Smetana, and Kiley Hamlin, have explored early moral development in infants and toddlers. Much of the debate over early moral development focuses on whether morality is innate or inborn (e.g., Bloom, 2013; Hamlin, 2013; Warneken & Tomasello, 2009). Others argue for an interactionist approach, where morality is constructed through children's social interactions, and emphasize that we need a deeper understanding of *how* our relationships shape early morality and prosocial behavior (e.g., Dahl & Killen, 2018; Dahl, 2018, 2019; Smetana, 2018b; Turiel, 2018). We agree with Turiel

(2018) that evidence suggests that aspects of morality may emerge earlier than Piaget and Kohlberg theorized, but further research is needed to show how the capacities of infants and toddlers relate to those of older children and adults. Infants and toddlers may have "important precursors to morality" (Dahl & Killen, 2018, p. 2) but lack the more mature morality of older children. Potentially, early in development, nature or biological influences have more significance on morality, while later in development, nurture or learning can override biological preattuned moral dispositions. This suggests that both early responsive parenting and ongoing moral education are important to support optimal moral development.

Research on Early Morality and Fairness

The past decade has seen a profusion of research on early morality and fairness, and we will give you examples of some widely cited work. In *Just Babies: The Origins of Good and Evil*, Paul Bloom (2013) argues that babies are born moral, without any influence from the environment, and that this inborn moral sense has a strong connection to adult morality. Babies have an innate moral goodness that includes:

> a **moral sense**—some capacity to distinguish between kind and cruel actions... **empathy and compassion**—suffering at the pain of those around us and the wish to make this pain go away... a **rudimentary sense of fairness**—a tendency to favor equal divisions of resources... and a **rudimentary sense of justice**—a desire to see good actions rewarded and bad actions punished [emphasis added].
>
> (Bloom, 2013, p. 5)

Bloom (2013) and his colleague and wife, Karen Wynn, introduced a research technique at the Yale Cognition Center that became widely used in research on infants' moral sense (see Hamlin & Tan, 2020; Wynn & Bloom, 2013 for a review of these studies). Bloom's research used the habituation of looking-time method, where babies look longer at scenes that are unfamiliar and violate their expectations. He and his graduate student at the time (Kiley Hamlin) showed infants an animation where geometric figures helped or hindered each other. For example, a yellow square would go behind a red ball to help it up a hill by gently pushing it to the top of the hill or a green triangle would go in front of the red ball and hinder it by pushing it down the hill. Infants would then see the red ball approaching either the helper or the hinderer. Infants aged 9–12 months looked longer when the red ball approached the hinderer than the helper, suggesting that they anticipated the red ball would approach the helper. Hamlin et al. (2007) conducted a seminal follow-up study replicating these results with younger infants aged 6–10 months, which also demonstrated that these infants reached for the helper, suggesting a preference for the helper. Hamlin and

Tan (2020) argued that infants' innate moral sense may be evolutionarily advantageous as it could allow them to discern prosocial caregivers who will meet their needs and avoid those who might harm or abandon them.

A meta-analysis of 26 studies from the past decade confirmed that most infants (about 67%) aged 4–32 months choose prosocial over antisocial agents (Margoni & Surian, 2018). However, Margoni and Surian (2018) cautioned that many of the studies were from Hamlin's lab, and additional studies from independent laboratories were needed to draw conclusions. While infants may be biologically predisposed toward a moral sense (e.g., Bloom, 2013; Hamlin, 2013), the definition, measurement, and complexity of morality in infancy varies from later childhood and adulthood, highlighting the need for more, and hopefully longitudinal, research linking early moral capacities to subsequent moral functioning (Margoni & Surian, 2018; Turiel, 2018; Dahl & Killen, 2018).

In addition to infants' strong moral sense, Bloom (2013) also argued that "we are born with some sort of fairness instinct: We are born egalitarians" (p. 64). Prior research in the 1970s showed that young children aged seven (and later aged three) focused on equality of outcome (an **equality bias**) rather than equality of opportunity. More recent research suggests that this equality bias emerges even earlier in development. In a key study, Geraci and Surian (2011) showed 10- to 16-month-olds puppet shows where a lion or a bear provided disks to a donkey and a cow. The lion (or bear) either gave each animal one disk or one animal two disks and the other animal none. Toddlers were then asked, "Which one do you want? Pick it up" (p. 1015). The 16-month-olds chose the animal fairly distributing resources (the 10-month-olds chose at random).

Infants and toddlers also utilize fairness information to make decisions. Lucca et al. (2018) found that 13- to 17-month-old infants who watched one actor distribute resources fairly and another actor distribute resources unfairly later chose to socially engage with the actor who distributed resources fairly. While some (e.g., Bloom, 2013; Sloane et al., 2012) argue that an understanding of fairness is innate, a byproduct of evolution that is necessary for social interaction and cooperation, recent research by Ziv and Sommerville (2017) also supports the role of experience in developing fairness expectations, as sharing behavior and having siblings uniquely influenced fairness concerns for infants aged 9–15 months. Many of you may have had parents who frequently quoted the mantra "sharing is caring." However, note that these infants did not yet have enough language to understand this phrase.

Research on Prosocial Behavior

Prosocial development is a special subset of moral development that has seen an explosion of research in the past decade. A growing body of research suggests that basic forms of prosocial behavior (e.g., helping, sharing, and cooperation) develop early in life, perhaps earlier than previously thought (see Eisenberg et al., 2015; Laible & Karahuta, 2014 for a review). However, more longitudinal studies are necessary to understand how children develop from "being nice to being kind… [where they experience] a selfless concern for the welfare of others" (Malti & Dys, 2018, p. 45) and to understand which children, under which circumstances, make the transition to more advanced prosocial behavior. Consistent with Padilla-Walker and Carlo's (2014) emphasis on the importance of a multi-dimensional perspective on prosocial behavior, young children's ability to behave prosocially depends on the type of prosocial behavior. While sharing, cooperation, helping, empathy, and altruism partially overlap, researchers have especially studied helping and empathy.

Empathy and Instrumental Helping

Infants respond to the distress of others early in life, with newborn babies crying in response to the sound of other babies' cries, but there is debate over how early their responsiveness to others reflects empathic concern for others. While Hoffman (2000) argued that infants could not experience empathic concern for others until the second year of life, more recent research suggests that he may have underestimated their capacities. In an important review article summarizing evidence that infants experience empathic concern earlier than anticipated, Davidov et al. (2013) focused on a prior study (i.e., Roth-Hanania et al., 2011) to support their argument that 8- to 10-month-old infants demonstrated concern for others. The infants responded to maternal and peer distress with little self-distress but moderate amounts of affective empathy (e.g., facial expressions showing concern) and cognitive empathy (e.g., efforts to understand another's distress). Infants' affective and cognitive empathy predicted prosocial behavior during the second year of life.

Helping also emerges early in development, but its timing depends on the complexity of the helping, with **instrumental helping** (performing an action to help another person meet a goal) emerging first, followed by **empathic helping** (understanding another's negative emotional state and wanting to improve it), and finally **altruism** (being willing to help others without considering one's own interests) (Dahl & Paulus, 2019; Eisenberg & Spinrad, 2014; Svetlova et al., 2010). Warneken and Tomasello (2009) found that 14- to 18-month-old toddlers helped unfamiliar adults instrumentally (e.g., by picking up dropped clothespins so that the experimenter could finish hanging clothes on the line) without rewards or prompting. Svetlova et al. (2010) examined instrumental, empathic, and altruistic helping in 18- to 30-month-old infants and found a transition from instrumental to empathic helping in the late second to early third year. Both age groups helped instrumentally, but only by 30 months were toddlers able to consistently help without extensive prompting in more complex and subtle situations that required understanding another's emotional state (e.g., handing a hairclip to an experimenter who demonstrated frustration and distress at having hair in her eyes). Sharing one's own possessions (altruistic helping) was uncommon at both age groups; thus, Svetlova et al.'s results suggest helping behavior during toddlerhood is influenced by cognitive complexity, as well as the cost to oneself.

Sharing and Cooperation

While less is known about the developmental trajectory of sharing than helping, sharing may be the earliest developing prosocial behavior. By 8 months, infants enthusiastically share food with parents, and this behavior is normative by infants' first birthday, potentially motivated by infants' desires to socially engage with their caregivers (Laible & Karahuta, 2014). However, sharing is multifaceted, depending on the context and target of the behavior. Infants readily share with parents; however, during peer interactions, toddlers around 24 months will share during spontaneous play situations but otherwise, will generally only do so when requested by an adult (Laible & Karahuta, 2014). Preschoolers are also less likely to share than to engage in other prosocial behaviors, potentially due to the more cognitively complex and costly nature of sharing. Sharing may be caring, but it takes **a lot** of adult nudges to enforce this behavior! Not surprisingly, toddlers were more likely to share with other children who shared with them and when others' needs are made explicit, suggesting the potential importance of scaffolding (Laible & Karahuta, 2014). Cooperation also emerges early, with infants engaging in dyadic play involving turn-taking and responsiveness to others (e.g., Peek-a-boo), with scaffolding and support from adults. However, like sharing, cooperation with peers develops more slowly, occurring by the end of the second year (Laible & Karahuta, 2014).

Explanations for Why Children are Prosocial

As stated previously, much of the debate over early moral and prosocial development focuses on whether babies are born moral (e.g., Bloom, 2013; Hamlin, 2013; Warneken & Tomasello, 2009) or whether morality and prosocial behavior are constructed over time through our social relationships (e.g., Dahl & Killen, 2018; Svetlova et al., 2010). Similarly, researchers disagree on what motivates young children to be prosocial, whether it is socialization, happiness, intrinsic motivation, empathy, or desire for social interaction. Several studies suggest that toddlers act prosocially because it leads to happiness and "the warm glow of giving" (Aknin et al., 2012, p. 3) (Aknin et al., 2015; Aknin et al., 2018). For example, Aknin et al.'s (2012, 2015) experimental studies demonstrated that children 2–5 years old in two different cultures (North America versus a rural, isolated village in Vanuata) showed greater happiness when they gave treats to the puppet than when they received treats themselves, and that they experienced even more happiness when the giving was costly (e.g., when they had to give away their own candy as opposed to the experimenter's candy). Similarly, Hepach (2017) reviewed research that used increased pupil dilation to show that children's helping behavior is motivated by prosocial arousal to others' unfulfilled needs, suggesting that children's prosocial behavior is driven in-part by intrinsic motivation. We turn now to discuss the socio-cognitive and parenting/socialization factors that foster prosocial behavior, which may potentially build on (and interact with) children's preattuned biological dispositions, as well as intrinsic motivations, to lead to increasing individual differences in prosocial behavior.

Fostering Prosocial Behavior

Relationships between Moral Cognitions and Emotions and Prosocial Behavior

Cognitive development theories have emphasized several social cognitive mechanisms for explaining prosocial development including perspective-taking, justice-oriented moral reasoning, and Eisenberg's (1986) concept of **prosocial moral reasoning**, which is defined as: "decision-making re-garding helping opportunities when there is a conflict between one's own and others' psychological or physical needs in situations where there are no laws or formal social guidelines" (as cited in Carlo, Mestre, et al., 2010, p. 872). Other moral development theorists see empathy as the key mo-tivator of prosocial behavior (Hoffman, 2000).

Although this chapter's focus is on infancy and early childhood, we will need to look at some studies of older children and adults to get a sense of the probable lifespan trajectory of some of the concepts that we have been discussing, and why they are important. A lack of longitudinal studies necessitates this cross-sectional look at relevant research.

Both moral cognitions and moral emotions predict prosocial behavior but may not be enough to explain prosocial functioning. Recent research, with older children, indicates a modest, relatively consistent positive re-lationship between sympathy and empathy with prosocial behavior, across various types of measurements (e.g., self-reports, experiments, and phy-siological measures) and cultures (Eisenberg et al., 2013). In contrast, personal distress, a subtype of empathy referring to a negative self-focused response to another's emotional state, is unrelated to or negatively related to prosocial behavior (Eisenberg et al., 2013). Meta-analyses have also shown small but consistent positive relationships between perspective-taking and prosocial behavior (e.g., Carlo et al., 2010; Imuta et al., 2016). While additional longitudinal studies are needed, Carlo et al. (2010) examined children, who were on average, aged 12-years-old, across one year and found that moral cognitions (perspective-taking and prosocial moral reasoning), as well as moral emotions (sympathy) were positively related to each another, and predicted prosocial behavior. Consistent with Padilla-Walker and Carlo's (2014) argument that conceptualizing prosocial behavior from a multidimensional perspective generally leads to more nuanced results, prosocial moral reasoning has been shown to be positively linked to altruism, anonymous helping, costly helping, and spontaneous prosocial behavior, but not to compliant, low cost, or approval oriented prosocial behavior (for a review, see Eisenberg et al., 2015).

While *both* moral cognitions and moral emotions are crucial to acting prosocially, these constructs are only modestly associated with prosocial behavior. During adolescence and adulthood, **moral identity**—the extent to which someone considers moral values such as being helpful, compassionate, and cooperative as important components of one's self—has been increasingly studied as an internalized motive for prosocial action (Blasi, 1983; Patrick et al., 2018). While Patrick et al. (2018) found that moral identity and justice-oriented moral judgment both positively related to prosocial behavior in a sample of adolescents, moral identity was the stronger predictor. Moral identity served as a mediator between moral reasoning and prosocial behavior. However, Hertz and Krettenauer (2016) tempered the influence of moral identity in their meta-analysis, which showed that moral identity predicted prosocial behavior in adolescents and adults in Western cultures, but the impact was small, suggesting that it should be considered within the context of other variables such as moral judgment, perspective-taking, and moral emotions. As many of you learned in the first chapter of your introductory psychology texts, behavior is multiply determined.

Socialization, Specifically Parenting, and Prosocial Behavior

Some theorists (e.g., Bloom, 2013; Hamlin, 2013; Warneken & Tomasello, 2009) argue that infants would begin to help, share, and cooperate regardless of parental influence. While biology may hold more relevance in early than in later childhood, we believe that infants' active engagement in social interactions with their caregivers, as well as their caregivers' encouragement and support, also shape the emergence of prosocial behavior. We will discuss specific aspects of parenting that have been consistently linked to prosocial behavior.

1. **Parental Scaffolding**—Research suggests that caregiver scaffolding— prompts, support, encouragement, and explicit guidance about how to complete a task—increases infant helping, but the positive impact depends on age, with scaffolding potentially most useful when children are learning new skills (Dahl, 2018; Dahl et al., 2017; Dahl & Brownell, 2019). However, the use of concrete rewards (e.g., a prize or money)

may undermine intrinsic motivation to behave prosocially (e.g., Eisenberg et al., 2015; Spinrad & Gal, 2018).

2. **Parental Warmth, Sensitivity, and the Quality of the Parent–Child Relationship**—Parental warmth (caregivers' supportive, responsive, and loving interactions with their children) and sensitivity (caregivers' ability to accurately read and respond to a child's emotional and behavioral signals) have both been positively associated with prosocial behavior (Carlo et al., 2011; Eisenberg et al., 2015; Spinrad & Gal, 2018). Secure attachment, which is also associated with parental warmth and sensitivity, is also positively related to prosocial behavior (Eisenberg et al., 2015; Spinrad & Gal, 2018).

3. **Parental Inductions**—Inductions are a disciplinary strategy where parents try to provide a rationale for why a child needs to change his or her behavior, and attempt to increase perspective-taking by showing a child how his or her actions hurt others emotionally or led to other consequences (Eisenberg et al., 2015; Padilla-Walker & Memmott-Elison, 2020). While generally effective in increasing prosocial behavior, their impact may depend on age, socioeconomic status, tone, or overall discipline strategy—for example, inductions may be less effective if combined with power assertion, which is a discipline strategy designed to induce fear of punishment (Eisenberg et al., 2015).

4. **Emotion Socialization**—Parents who encourage their children to discuss their emotions, validate their children's emotions, and assist children in constructively resolving emotional situations are more likely to have children who behave prosocially (Eisenberg et al., 2015; Ornaghi et al., 2015; Spinrad & Gal, 2018). Receiving such support from parents likely increases children's emotional knowledge and ability to self-regulate (Spinrad & Gal, 2018). Thus, when a child is confronted with a situation that requires a prosocial response, he or she can respond with empathy rather than personal distress.

The Benefits of Prosocial Behavior: Social Competence, Academics, and Well-Being

Prosocial children have an advantage; prosocial behavior has been consistently linked to social competence (Spinrad & Eisenberg, 2017; Eisenberg et al., 2015), strongly linked to academic achievement (Carlo, 2013; Wentzel, 2015), and more recently linked to well-being (Carlo, 2013; Curry et al., 2018; Hui et al., 2020). A long-standing finding in the literature is that prosocial behavior is consistently linked to social competence. As discussed previously, perspective-taking fosters empathy and prosocial behavior, and being adept at these skills strengthens the quality of peer relationships (Spinrad & Eisenberg, 2017; Eisenberg et al., 2015). Prosocial children are typically popular and successful at developing supportive, high-quality relationships with others.

Perhaps unsurprisingly, children who are high on empathy and prosocial behavior also tend to be low on aggression (including bullying) (Spinrad & Eisenberg, 2017; Eisenberg et al., 2015). However, the relationship between the variables can be more nuanced than initially apparent. In a rare longitudinal study of prosocial behavior and aggression from birth to 7-years-old, Hay et al. (2021) found that during infancy (age 1.5-years-old), aggression and prosocial behavior were not related, but by 3-years-old, the constructs were related, and by 7-years-old, prosocial behavior also predicted lower callous-unemotional traits. Card et al.'s (2008) meta-analysis of 148 studies examining direct and indirect aggression during childhood and adolescence provided a unique insight into these general findings. Direct aggression (e.g., physical aggression) and indirect aggression (e.g., "behaviors that attack a victim's actual or perceived social relations with others, often (though not always) in a way that avoids direct confrontation" (p. 1186)) related to prosocial behavior in differential ways. While direct aggression was related to lower prosocial behavior, indirect aggression was related to **higher** prosocial behavior. Card et al. explained that children high in prosocial behavior could draw on such skills to drive the social support necessary to engage in the decidedly **un**-prosocial tactics of indirect aggression such as rumor spreading on social media.

More recently, researchers have also begun investigating the relationship between prosocial behavior and psychological and physical well-being, a topic we will return to in Chapter 10. Hui et al.'s (2020) meta-analysis of 201 studies showed a small but positive relationship between prosocial behavior and well-being in adults, with prosociality more strongly linked to psychological functioning compared to psychological malfunctioning or physical health. Similarly, Curry et al.'s (2018) meta-analysis of 27 experimental studies (primarily focused on college students) showed a small to moderate impact for interventions designed to investigate whether being kind to others fostered subjective well-being (happiness, satisfaction with life, and positive emotions).

Applications and Implications for Helping Professionals

Increased understanding about how to foster prosocial behavior, as well as the benefits of being prosocial, have inspired both school-based and parent-based interventions. Historically, schools have focused predominantly on academics and when social and emotional competencies have been addressed, the emphasis has predominantly been on decreasing aggression, bullying, and problem behavior (Brown et al., 2012; Bergin, 2014). While there is growing recognition of the importance of promoting prosocial behavior within schools, interventions directly targeting prosocial behavior are rare, and can be challenging to implement within a demanding academic setting (Bergin, 2014; Wentzel, 2015). Even less is known about parent-based interventions, which largely focus on preventing problematic behavior. As an exception, a meta-analysis of 50 experimental studies using Incredible Years (a parenting program that aims to promote social and emotional competence, while also preventing and treating violence and behavior problems) showed that enhancing parents' capacity to be warm and compassionate increased prosocial behavior (in conjunction with a decrease in aggression) in children under 10 (Menting et al., 2013).

Increasing prosocial behavior also has important implications for the classroom. Children who are more prosocial are not only more likely to succeed academically, but they are also more likely to be socially successful because they are more well-liked by their teachers and peers (Bergin, 2014; Wentzel, 2015). Having higher-quality friendships can help children enjoy and feel a sense of belonging at school, while teacher-student relationships predict GPA, emotional well-being, and performance within the classroom (Bergin, 2014; Wentzel, 2015). Even being around prosocial classmates is associated with higher academic achievement (Bergin, 2014).

Interventions related to prosocial behavior often target precursor skills (e.g., empathy) or mechanisms identified as fostering prosocial behavior (e.g., emotion socialization), which we previously discussed (Bergin, 2014). We will just provide a sampling of programs so that you can develop a feel for these types of interventions. For example, Ornaghi et al.'s (2015) experiment showed that a conversational intervention designed to teach preschoolers about the nature, causes, and regulation of emotions (i.e., happiness, fear, anger, and sadness) through conversations with their peers, increased children's empathy and prosocial behavior, even at four months follow-up. Similarly, Schonert-Reichl et al.'s (2015) experiment showed that a mindfulness and caring for others intervention with fourth and fifth graders effectively improved empathy, perspective-taking, and all dimensions of prosocial behavior (e.g., sharing, trustworthiness, helpfulness, being liked) except kindness. The intervention also reduced depression and aggressive behavior. Mindfulness programs (which generally increase children's self-regulatory abilities) have also been shown to be effective at increasing prosocial behavior in preschool children (Viglas & Perlman, 2018). Finally, fourth to seventh grade children who participated in Roots of Empathy, a school-based program where a caregiver and infant serve as ways to teach children about emotions, caring for others, and infant development, showed improvements on multiple prosocial dimensions and significant decreases in proactive and relational aggression (Schonert-Reichl et al., 2012). Schonert-Reichl et al.'s (2012, 2015) findings are particularly encouraging, as they advance the field by identifying strategies to promote well-being while also preventing problem behavior, such as aggression. In Chapter 9, we'll broaden our focus on school-related interventions to discuss moral and character education programs, which target a larger subset of outcomes.

Conclusion

Consistent with Dahl and Killen's (2018) suggestion, infants and toddlers may have "important precursors to morality" (p. 2), such as the moral sense and rudimentary sense of fairness described by Bloom (2013), but not the more mature morality of older children. As we argued previously, we speculate that nature or biological influences may have the most significance on morality early in development; later in development, biological pre-attuned moral dispositions can be overridden by nurture or learning. Accordingly, optimal moral development can be fostered through both early responsive parenting and ongoing moral education.

Discussion Questions

1. Which optimal parenting practices do you particularly want to remember in raising your own children?
2. If you attended preschool or a childcare center as a young child, can you remember any activities that you now see were attempting to promote prosocial behavior (e.g., sharing, kindness, helping, compassion)?
3. Do some fast research on which countries have policies most supportive of optimal child development? How do your own country's policies compare to a country that you think is doing an excellent job? Hint: Where would you go? A good place to start might be this United Nations family friendly policies report: https://www.unicef-irc.org/family-friendly

Additional Resources

Students and practitioners interested in this emerging and evolving field of early morality and prosocial development may find the following books, special editions of journals, and websites particularly useful.

- **Special issues of journals**
  - Brownell, C. [Ed.). (2013). Early development of prosocial behavior [Special edition]. *Infancy, 18*(1).
  - Smetana, J. G. (Ed.). (2018a). Early moral development [Special edition]. *Human Development*, 61(4–5).
  - Lucca, K., Kiley, J., & Sommerville, J. (Eds). (2019). Early moral cognition and behavior [Research Topic]. *Frontiers in Psychology*. doi:10.3389/fpsyg.2019.02013
  - Warneken, F. & Hepach, R. (Eds.). (2018). Early prosocial development [Special edition]. *Current Opinion in Psychology, 20.*

- If you'd like to read an accessible, but in-depth, discussion of research on infant morality, then you'll enjoy

    - Bloom, P. (2013). *Just Babies: The origins of good and evil.* Crown.

- If you'd like to watch a brief, 5-minute video of Kiley Hamlin's experiments with babies, please go here

    - https://www.youtube.com/watch?v=HBW5vdhr_PA&t=108s

7 Global Perspectives: A Sampling of Research and Issues

Although in Western countries issues of gender and ethnicity now tend to be integrated into texts and training across the professions, today's professionals will be practicing in settings, and a world, in which understanding issues of global culture will be the new necessity. For example, students in the public schools in Elly's suburban hometown in Connecticut (USA) come from homes in which more than 80 languages are spoken. No professional can hope to come to a deep understanding of dozens of cultures, but this chapter frames specific examples of moral development research and issues within an overarching frame of core moral values that can help the practitioner make sense of the multitude of cultural variations she or he will face in practice. Let's begin our exploration of global perspective with a moral dilemma from Europe.

Dilemma of the Day

In the wake of rioting by Muslim youths and growing European Islamophobia, France passed a 2004 law banning any conspicuous religious dress or apparel in public schools and universities. Although the law also covered items such as large crosses and Jewish skullcaps, it was clear that the real aim was to ban Muslim headscarves and coverings. France has long practiced a brand of secularism that removes religion from the public sphere. While endorsing freedom of worship, the state also expects immigrants to embrace common public values of liberty, equality, and fraternity.

> Many Muslims protested: The state, they insisted, should not tell young women how to dress. In the meantime, stories of girls forced to wear scarves by tradition-minded fathers abounded. When lawmakers tugged at those scarves, they found underneath... barbed questions about citizenship. Does a girl's right to

---

DOI: 10.4324/9780429295461-8

an education belong to her parents? Or to her as a future adult, a citizen whose education should enhance her ability to choose her own life?

(Cohen, 2007)

What do **you** think? Should the right of a state to promote its core values, maintain public order, and protect the rights of others, justifications offered by the French government (Boustead, 2007), override the rights of public school students to wear religious clothing?

How about the 2011 French law that bans covering your face in public (e.g., with a full-faced veil or niqab, a burqa, or a ski mask)? Again, the French government cited the need to protect the public. Might such laws be necessary for security in a world increasingly using surveillance cameras to monitor crime and possible terrorist activity? Would you feel safe if people who covered their faces with black ski masks walked around your campus? (People from far North countries and states are excused from answering this question— having lived through seven Minnesota winters, Elly can attest to the need to take extreme measures when the temperature drops to negative numbers.)

If you recall Jonathan Haidt's (2012) Moral Foundations Theory from Chapter 5, you can probably see how the French law reflects a liberal and secular reliance on the Care/harm, Liberty/oppression, and Fairness/cheating foundations, while more traditional and religious individuals are also concerned with Loyalty/betrayal, Authority/subversion, and Sanctity/degradation. Haidt (2012) maintains that morality both binds and blinds us and, in this case, we can clearly see how the two camps seem blind to the perspectives of the other. Perhaps Cohen (2007) offers us a middle way when he envisions a secularist asking the following:

Wouldn't it be more helpful to say that there is a new global assertiveness among many Muslims; it is multifaceted but also harbors some dangerous extremism. Call it 'Islamism' or whatever, but we need to distinguish extremists from the majority of Muslims, who seek common ground with non-Muslims. A Moroccan-French feminist once said to me, "I am against the head scarf and the head scarf law." Just so. (https://www.nytimes.com/2007/04/01/books/review/Cohen.t.html)

(para 7)

Might there be some common universal values as the French government and Lawrence Kohlberg argue, or do human processes such as morality and even consciousness vary across the world, as influential cultural psychologist Richard Shweder (1991, 2015, 2018) and Moral Foundations theorists (e.g., Haidt, 2012; Iyer et al., 2019) contend? Here, we encounter the core question of morality—are there universal truths and paths of development, or do culture and learning determine both moral content and development? To help you determine where you stand on this issue, we introduce you briefly to the ideas of Shweder (e.g., 1991, 2018) and Elliot Turiel (2002) as well as some exciting and influential work by Henrich et al. (2010). We then move on to briefly consider research on morality coming from diverse geographical regions (China, Africa, and Latin America) and perspectives (Islam). We end by considering current conceptions of morality in a global world (e.g., Jensen, 2015a, 2020a) and revisiting the question of universality.

Richard Shweder's "Expeditions in Cultural Psychology"

> If there is a piety in cultural anthropology it is the conviction that astonishment deserves to be a universal emotion. Astonishment and the assortment of feelings that it brings with it—surprise, curiosity, excitement, enthusiasm, sympathy—are probably the affects most distinctive of the anthropological response to the difference and strangeness of "others."
>
> (Shweder, 1991, p. 1)

As a doctoral student on my way to my first Association for Moral Education meeting in Toronto, Canada, I (Elly) was seated on the plane next to a distinguished and friendly gentleman who, it turned out, was also on his way to the conference. We had a lively conversation about my belief that justice and care/love represented universal moral values, and my seatmate's conviction that anthropological evidence supported the position of culturally relative moralities. Imagine my chagrin when I eventually discovered that I had been speaking to the keynote speaker for the conference, perhaps the premier cultural psychologist in the world today, Richard Shweder. I have since read much more deeply in his work and today take a much more nuanced view of the complex interactions between culture and morality.

In Shweder's (1991) conception of **cultural psychology**, cultural traditions and social practices not only regulate humans but also transform the human psyche. He makes the bold claim that cultural practices actually result "less in psychic unity for humankind than in ethnic diversity divergences in mind, self and emotion" (p. 73). In other words, living in different cultures literally rewires our minds in such ways that we may look at the same stimulus but perceive and feel very different things. At the heart of his vision is his **Three Ethics** (sometimes known as Big Three or Big 3 Ethics) conception of morality (Autonomy, Community, Divinity). In sum, "the moral truths or goods embraced around the world are many, not one" (Shweder, 2015, p. xiii).

> Briefly, the **Ethic of Autonomy** involves a focus on the self as an individual. Moral reasons within this ethic include the interests, well-being, and rights of individuals (self or other) and fairness between individuals. **The Ethic of Community** focuses on persons as members of social groups, with attendant reasons such as duty to others and concerns with the customs, interests, and welfare of groups. The **Ethic of Divinity** focuses on people as spiritual or religious entities, and reasons encompass divine and natural law, sacred lessons, and spiritual purity.
>
> (Jensen, 2015d, p. 3)

Shweder's work is so broad and complex (e.g., Shweder, 1991, 2015; Shweder et al., 2002; Stigler et al., 1990) that no short overview can do it justice. Instead, we will simply pull out some important insights and fascinating examples culled from reading his work. For example, his work comparing Hindu Brahman children's and American children's ratings of the seriousness of moral transgressions (Shweder et al., 1987) has deepened our understanding of the way central foundational themes for Indians (e.g., sanctity/pollution, chastity, and respect) contrast with central ones for Americans (e.g., personal liberty, privacy, equality). This work clearly laid the groundwork for Haidt's **Moral Foundations Theory.**

Shweder et al. (1987) presented the children with some culturally specific case studies/scenarios (e.g., eating with one's husband's older brother) and others representing concepts that the literature suggested might be candidates for moral universals:

- Justice
- Harm
- Reciprocity
- Protection of the vulnerable
- Altruism
- Honesty
- Loyalty
- Honoring commitments
- Prohibitions against theft, ingratitude, arbitrary assault, and so forth.

What the researchers found was that although the children all agreed that some scenarios such as breaking a promise, brother/sister incest, and discrimination against invalids were wrong, they tended to disagree about many more. For example, in contrast to American children, Brahman children saw no harm in beating a disobedient wife or giving an unequal inheritance to male versus female children. American children, in contrast to Indian ones, thought it was just fine to eat beef, have a husband cook a meal, or cut one's hair after one's father's death.

How do we make sense of such cultural variations? Can we/should we respond with astonishment and curiosity to such practices as suttee, in which Indian widows immolate themselves on the funeral pyre of their husbands? Shweder frequently raises the question of just how far we are willing to take our "Celebrate Diversity" bumper stickers. What is and should be the scope of tolerance for diverse cultural practices in a liberal democracy (Shweder et al., 2002)?

Let's return to the practice of suttee. Shweder (1991) offers a fascinating contextual analysis of the case of an 18-year-old educated widow, Roop Kanwar, who, in 1987, burned herself to death with her dead husband in her lap in front of a large and approving crowd. Indians were divided between admiration of her devotion and repulsion at an action some thought may have been due to her being crazy, hysterical, or drugged. Shweder suggests that her voluntary act can only be understood within its full cultural context. He explains that in Hindu moral doctrine, divinity is infused in the world, thus making spouses not only incarnate bodies, but also gods and goddesses. In this moral world, a husband's death transcends the material to the metaphysical sphere. In a world imbued with the doctrine of karma, or the way we reap what we sow, widowhood is perceived as a punishment for past sins. Thus, by immolating herself in a shared cremation with her husband, Roop Kanwar absolved herself of sins and guaranteed an "eternal union between husband and wife, linked to each other as god and goddess through the cycle of future rebirths" (p. 16). Within this cultural perspective, the vision of the end goal makes sense of the painful means. Shweder is willing to imaginatively conceive of the possibility that

> Roop Kanwar herself understood and experienced her immolation as an astonishing moment when her body and its senses, profane things, became fully sacred, and hence invulnerable to pain, through an act of sacrifice by a goddess seeking eternal union with her god-man.
>
> (p. 17)

What we see Shweder (e.g., 1991) arguing for is a doctrine of relativism that claims we cannot derive conclusions about what to think or feel and how to live from any universal authority. We must *also* appeal to "local authorities (scripture; communally held theories and assumptions about truth, beauty, and goodness) that are not entitled to universal respect" (p. 33). We have a glorious and astonishing diversity of thoughts, feelings, and behaviors because of the intersection between universally available experiences and both developmental and cultural differences. For Shweder (1991), humans and their sociocultural environments are interdependent. We cannot define or analyze either apart from the other. Thus, the central theme of cultural psychology proclaims that "you cannot take the stuff out of the psyche and you cannot take the psyche out of the stuff" (1991, p. 97). At the end of this chapter we give you a link to a fascinating and nuanced 2018 interview with Shweder in which he argues that although his work is often viewed as relativistic, he sees it as really "universalism without uniformity."

Elliot Turiel's Culture of Morality

Turiel (e.g., 2002) brings a very different perspective to the explanation of diverse cultural practices that arises from his belief that all humans divide their experiences into the personal, conventional, and moral domains. Hence, he gives great weight to contextual and cultural input and variations, yet holds to core universal conceptions of morality. You may recall from the discussion of **domain theory** in Chapter 4 that theorists such as Turiel believe that all people, including young children, sort issues of harm and fairness into the moral domain. According to Haidt (2012), Turiel's work suggests that issues such as loyalty, piety, and tradition belong in the social conventional domain.

Let's turn to Turiel's (2002) own words as he discusses people's reactions to former US president Bill Clinton's sexual relationship with a young intern, Monica Lewinsky, and his subsequent lies about his involvement. Turiel argues that most Americans, while troubled by the affair and the lies, "were also troubled by an investigation [impeachment hearings] of what they considered a personal and private matter" (p. 14). Turiel holds that this reaction is in line with a substantial body of research:

> Showing that Americans, as well as others, maintain distinctively different types of social judgments. Different types of judgments are made about areas of personal jurisdiction, matters of social conventions, and the morality of welfare, justice and rights... In contrast with the view of morality as entailing a fixed set of traits reflecting the incorporation of traditional values, the research demonstrates that individuals make complex moral, social, and personal judgments that often entail taking into account the context of people's activities.
>
> (pp. 14–15)

Thus, when Turiel examines the great diversity of cultural customs, he finds that theory offers him a method by which to make judgments about setting reasonable limits on tolerance. Most Western cultures, for example, have laws and norms ensuring the equality of women (and, increasingly, gay individuals). They do not allow polygamy, beating wayward wives, or female circumcision. Yet other cultures do allow such practices, and Shweder (e.g., 2015) argues that, once we understand deeply and fully the worldviews in which tradition, hierarchy, and loyalty may actually have sacred roles, we can and should hold a tolerant attitude towards diverse practices we might not choose for our own selves and cultures. Haidt (2012) echoes this stance with his anecdotes about coming to better understand the moral foundations of hierarchy after meeting educated and delightful Indian colleagues who did not accept their wives as equal in status. Turiel disagrees and offers the argument that "issues of welfare, justice, and rights" (p. 14) in which people are restricted or discriminated against on the basis of their race, class, or gender should not simply be accepted or tolerated because those in power support the practice.

Turiel (2002) argues that we must consider "whether certain cultural practices are directed at control and domination of particular groups in the society with less power and status" (p. 184). If so, then we need to be attuned to the voices of people in the subordinate positions. We must not only take the time to find out if cultural practices, such as forbidding girls to get an education or imposing strict dress codes on women, are indeed generally accepted, but also whether there is disagreement and conflict (however subversive) between people in the positions of oppressor and oppressed.

Turiel (2002) argues against Shweder's assumption (e.g., Shweder, 1991; Shweder et al., 2002) that cultural practices such as arranged marriages and gender-based inheritance rights are simply manifestations of norms accepted in some cultures and not accepted in others. Instead, Turiel contends that many practices "emerge as issues that entail complex societal arrangements and social interactions that include ambiguities and disagreements that can be the source of intense negative emotions and sometimes misery, and are sources of great conflict and argument" (p. 225). In short, if some people perceive a cultural practice as causing harm, it becomes an issue in the moral domain. And it makes a lot of sense that the people in power will often not perceive a practice as harmful if it has been benefitting them!

So here we are with two respected psychologists offering us two radically different conceptual lenses for understanding cultural differences in moral values and practices. Let's add one more perspective for consideration before turning to very situated research on moral principles, development, and education across cultures.

WEIRD (Western, Educated, Industrial, Rich, Democratic) Morality

A new generation of cultural psychologists, Joseph Henrich, Steven Heine, and Ara Norenzayan, made a major impact with their 2010 article "The Weirdest People in the World?" (e.g., Haidt, 2012; Watters, 2013). Most psychologists are all too aware that our published research relies much too heavily on the presence of the readily available subject pools on college campuses. Yet it is still striking to see journalist Watters (2013) report the stark fact that a 2008 survey of the top six psychology journals found "96% of the subjects tested in psychological studies from 2003–2007 were Westerners—with nearly 70% from the United States alone" (p. 49). Given that we may have been drawing conclusions about human functioning on the basis of a rather unrepresentative 12% of the world's population, Henrich et al.'s (2010) innovative work takes on added significance.

So, what did the researchers find? For most of our professional lives, it was pretty much a given that human brains, despite individual variations, are generally built using the same blueprint. We have basic hardwiring for universal functions such as cognition, perception, and learning. For example, all normally developing human children have the extraordinary capacity to pick up language from the language stream around them. Unless we have some special condition like color blindness, we all perceive a world of colors. However, challenges to the universality of perception began to emerge when we discovered that people who lived in differently carpentered worlds (more round-shaped environments and structures) did not perceive the classic Muller-Lyer illusion the same way as did people in Western cultures. And when Henrich et al. (2010) took an ultimatum game to people in relatively isolated cultures, their findings posed a major challenge to the doctrine of psychological universality.

Briefly, the ultimatum game involves two players who are anonymous to each other. One is given an amount of money, say $50, and told he or she must split it with the other in any way they wish. However, the catch is that if the second player refuses the split, both go away empty handed. In the past, most research using this paradigm used North American participants and found that Participant 1 generally offered a 50/50 split. If Participant 1 was less generous, Participant 2 tended to retaliate when it was his or her turn. Henrich's original research with the Machiquenga tribe of Peru (Watters, 2013) found that his participants tended to offer much lower amounts to their partners, who readily accepted the offer, no matter how low. In fact, they pretty much thought this was one crazy game. Who would ever refuse *any* amount of money?

Henrich et al. (2010) have gone on to review past research and conduct new studies of their own that have found significant cultural differences across all manner of phenomena previously understood to be universal, including spatial reasoning, categorizing, and, of most interest to our discussion, moral reasoning (Watters, 2013). In short, it appears that rather than reflecting one universal blueprint, human minds may be molded by experiences and culture in profound ways. One of the most interesting findings to emerge from Heinrich et al.'s work is that the perceptions, motivations, and behaviors of one specific group of people were particularly unusual. (You guessed it, the Westerners upon whom most previous psychological research has been conducted!) They gave this group the acronym "**WEIRD**" not only because their responses were so distinct from most other humans, but also to reflect the fact that they represented a population that was **Western, Educated, Industrialized, Rich (comparatively), and Democratic**. And, interestingly, the weirdest of the weird turn out to be Americans.

We especially like Haidt's (2012) summary of these results: "The Weirder you are, the more you see a world filled with separate objects, rather than relationships" (p. 96). In a nutshell, here are some findings that we need to consider as we attempt to answer our question about the possibility of universal moral precepts:

> Cross-cultural studies suggest that the "weird" Western mind is the most self-aggrandizing and egotistical on the planet; we're more likely to promote ourselves as individuals versus advancing as a group. WEIRD minds are also more analytic, possessing the tendency to telescope in on an object of interest rather than understand that object in the context of what is around it.
>
> (Watters, 2013, p. 51)

In summary, we're going to have to consider seriously the ways that our myriad cultural differences may have shaped not only our conceptions of fairness but also our very selves.

Journal of Moral Education *Special Issues*

Over the past decades, the flagship journal of the field of moral development, the *Journal of Moral Education (JME),* began to highlight research being done beyond the typical "weird" populations so characteristic of most of the psychological and educational research. Much credit should be given to long-time former editor Monica Taylor, whose vision, passion, and energy informed a series of special issues on moral research from China, the Muslim world, Latin America, and Africa. She and the guest editors took on the Herculean tasks of overcoming barriers of language and cultural differences in academic styles and standards inherent in such projects and produced impressive results. We can provide you only with brief samples of the important perspectives and research covered in these issues, but hope that many of you with particular interests in these countries and populations will explore further for yourself in the online databases. Although today almost any issue of *JME* will present research on diverse populations from international scholars, we want to highlight the older special issues because of their deep focus on conceptions of morality with which many people from Western countries may be unaware.

China (Maosen et al., 2004)

The challenges of Chinese language and culture have long put up barriers for Western study of the ethical ideas and practices of this 5,000-year-old civilization. Most of us have only a superficial awareness of moral perspectives in the People's Republic of China (PR China). Let's take a brief look at several layers of those perspectives—the ancient but still relevant tradition of Confucian thinking, the norms and values influenced by Leninist-Maoist ideology, and, finally, the morality emerging as China becomes more open to the world through its relatively recent capitalist global economic system.

Confucian thinking represents "a complex set of ideas of moral, social and political teaching, built up by Confucius (551–479 BD) on ancient Chinese traditions" (Fengyan, 2004, p. 429). Confucian moral education takes as its starting point the premise that human beings are born good, and that human nature is good and kind (Fengyan, 2004). We are all born with the potential virtues of benevolence, righteousness, courteousness, and wisdom. Accordingly, children were taught a system of ethical norms "based on the idea that an individual's feelings come from the inner mind, combined with external rites" (p. 429).

Other important doctrines of Confucianism hold that, despite being born good, we need to develop our nature through habit. Thus, moral behavior arises from practice in daily life. Confucius also identified filial piety (duty to one's parents) as a central virtue to be cultivated along with benevolence, righteousness, and wisdom. The ultimate goal of moral education is to develop a "noble person who is characterized by superiority of mind, character, ideals and morals" (Fengyan, 2004, p. 432). Confucianism dominated Chinese society for centuries prior to the 1949 establishment of a Communist state.

For many years, under the Communist Party of China (CPC), education was seen as synonymous with morality with the ultimate goals of forming obedient citizens and promoting current political policies (Maosen et al., 2004). However, the practice of moral education has gone through major transitions, some in response to the upheavals and suffering of the Cultural Revolution of the 1960s, and others in response to China's growing emergence on the world stage. The issue's editors report that a years-long discussion initiated by the Central Committee of the CPC in 1978 led to important ideological changes and the "liberation of people's viewpoints and beliefs" (p. 414).

> As Deng Xioping said at the time, 'It is a good cat if it could catch a mouse no matter if it is a white cat or a black cat', meaning it is right if the outcome of what a person does facilitates the country's economic development, largely irrespective of the methods used. This idea was later regarded as a standard of truth and genuinely motivated people towards economic development.
>
> (Maosen et al., 2004, p. 414)

The series editors suggest that in addition to being influenced by this new-found ideological openness, contemporary Chinese moral education is also rooted in the profound soil of thousands of years of very deep cultural traditions. These traditions include not only Confucianism but also Taoist and Buddhist ideas (Maosen et al., 2004, p. 417). In consequence, the importance of principles such as the practice of virtue continue to influence Chinese life and "gives the people a special cohesiveness and diligence in facing the challenges of contemporary life" (p. 417). Yet the editors also caution that the Chinese moral education system—with its fusion of ideological, political, legal, and moral education—while conducive to the government's political purposes, has been much less successful in cultivating the development of creative minds. They end their introduction to the issue with noting some of strengths as well as major challenges for moral education in China today:

> Mainland Chinese moral education appears successful in developing genuine patriotism. Chinese culture is shame-based and also stresses practice of virtue. Moral education has often been teacher-, textbook-, and class-centered. Positive education has often been based around slogans and explicit role models of good and bad, with criticism of students' attitudes and behavior.... However there does not appear to be any special emphasis on promoting critical thinking, reasoning skills related to moral judgement, or meeting individual needs.
>
> (Maosen et al., 2004, p. 423)

As increasing numbers of Chinese students attend Western colleges and universities, they will be exposed to systems that place a great deal of emphasis on promoting critical thinking. It will be important for Westerners to understand the worldviews and educational premises and practices that have shaped their prior educational experiences and expectations.

Islam (J. M. Halstead, 2007a)

J. Mark Halstead's (2007b) editorial comments on Islamic values can provide a thought-provoking reading for any development class's unit on moral and faith development. The United States has often struggled with tensions between its avowed separation of church and state and some constituencies' firm belief that the country should reflect Christian values. In contrast, "for Muslims faith and moral behavior are two sides of the same coin" (J. M. Halstead, 2007a, p. 283). You cannot behave morally unless you are following the tenets of your faith, and your faith is only genuine if it results in your moral behavior.

While many (not all of course) Westerners are comfortable with separating moral duties from religious ones, Muslims make no such distinction. When considering questions of what to do or how to behave, moral answers tend to be delivered using religious language because both are part of "an eternal truth revealed by God through his messengers" (J. M. Halstead, 2007b, p. 284).

> Muslims believe that God has disclosed what is *halal* (permitted and *haram* (forbidden) and it is up to individuals ultimately to choose

whether to follow the clear guidance that God has provided or to allow themselves to be led astray. Those who stick to the 'right path' (Qur'an, Sura1, v. 6) are by definition committed to a moral way of life.

(J. M. Halstead, 2007b, p. 284)

Think about the contrast of this perspective with the secular Western rational tradition underlying the theories of Kohlberg and Rest that we examined earlier. J. M. Halstead (2007b) notes that "there is no tradition of subjecting the religious base of ethics to close critical scrutiny, nor does moral education in Islam have as its goal the development of personal and moral autonomy" (p. 285). Arabic words roughly equivalent to the English term *morality* include one that focuses on people's innate dispositions or character and another that focuses on good breeding, manners, and refinement as well as concepts we would define as morality or values. We were struck by the importance of Halstead's observation that **abstract concepts "rarely carry identical meanings in different cultures"** (p. 287). They may overlap in a broad sense but differ in the details. We noted earlier that being culturally sensitive, and relatively fluent, will be a necessity for professionals in our increasingly connected global village. But we are sure you can already see the type of misunderstandings that could arise when one set of people who see autonomy as characterizing the highest form of morality interact with another set who see the perfection of morality in submission (one translation for the word Islam). Shweder encourages us to respond to the "other's" ways with astonishment, but all too often we respond with harsh judgments, frustration, and anger on both sides.

   J. M. Halstead (2007b) contends that Islamic morality's focus on carrying out the "obligations, duties and responsibilities" (p. 289) of **sharia,** or Islamic law, renders the Western value of personal and moral autonomy nonsensical. Such a perspective not only involves "usurping God's own position as the judge of good and evil" (p. 289) but also "cuts the individual off from the community of faith" (p. 289).

   The clear and prescriptive Islamic worldview of morality results in a great deal of consistency in moral education across time and place. Children are taught the differences between behavior that is obligatory, permitted, and forbidden. Permitted behavior is further divided into actions that are strongly recommended, neutral, or merely tolerated (J. M. Halstead, 2007b). Acts in accordance with sharia and done with good intentions will be rewarded in the afterlife and bad actions will be punished. This conception of religious justice echoes many Christians' conception of the paths to Heaven and Hell and the Indian conception of karma, but our evolutionary theorists would probably see all three perspectives arising from evolutionary roots in primate reciprocity.

Latin America (Frisancho et al., 2009)

As in the other special issues, the editors provide an editorial section, giving an excellent overview of the central themes addressed by the various contributors. Moreno-Gutiérrez and Frisancho (2009) note first of all that Latin America is one of the world's most diverse regions in terms of both culture and geography. For example, the number of languages spoken within individual countries ranges from 7 in Chile to 190 in Brazil. Such linguistic and cultural diversity poses difficult challenges for moral educators. One commonality, however, is the way that both individual and civic morality has been shaped by the independence struggles of the early 20th century.

Although the authors see Latin America's enormous diversity as a rich resource, the region also struggles with "a profound inequality among its people" (Moreno-Gutiérrez & Frisancho, 2009, p. 392):

> As a consequence, Latin America has a long history of social turmoil, conflicts, violent dictatorships, military *coup d'états,* and lack of democracy.... Latin America faces numerous challenges, many of which are moral in nature—such as poverty, poor access to health care, and unemployment or underemployment.
>
> (p. 392)

The recent and specific political histories of the countries in Latin America have led to distinctive efforts to implement programs such as human rights education, citizenship education, conflict resolution, and peace education (Moreno-Gutiérrez & Frisancho, 2009). Unlike the cognitive approaches to moral education favored in the United States and Europe, many countries have developed more concrete and situated **human rights education programs**. In fact, the editors found that the theme of diverse perspectives extended to the very definitions of morality and ethics. For example, some contributors conceptualized **morality** as societal customs and traditions, and **ethics** as a reflection on those traditions from a more principled and universal perspective. Recall that for Kohlberg, such a conception of morality might simply describe one stage of development; and for Turiel and Nucci it would not describe morality at all, but rather the social conventional domain!

One final observation about the climate of moral development and education in Latin America deserves note before moving to our exploration of moral perspectives from Sub-Saharan Africa. Many readers of this text may take for granted that diversity should not only be tolerated, but also celebrated. However, Moreno-Gutiérrez and Frisancho (2009) found that many Latin American nations view their cultural diversity as "dangerous and unnecessary" (p. 397) and instituted policies that promote homogenization and the invisibility of indigenous cultures. In the early decades of the 20th century, many countries instituted Hispanicization campaigns with the goal of eliminating native languages.

We regret that space considerations do not allow us to give you more detail on the many important papers in any of these special issues. Fascinating studies of such topics as the role of the Catholic Church in fostering moral and citizenship education and the Truth and Reconciliation initiatives in Peru are worthy of whole books in their own right. But move on we must, and once again you will see the powerful shaping force of culture on morality as we examine some of the unique perspectives on morality emerging from African cultures.

Africa (Swartz, 2010a)

Remember that J. M. Halstead (2007b) cautioned that abstract terms seldom have identical meanings across cultures. That is particularly true for the term **morality:**

> The term "moral" has had a chequered history in sub-Saharan Africa, mainly due to the legacy of colonialism in Africa and the history of Apartheid oppression in South Africa.... Moreover, "colonising," "civilising," "Christianising" and "moralising" were inextricably linked.
>
> (Swartz, 2010b, p. 267)

Swartz (2010b) explains that often the justification for colonization in Africa rested on the goal of "civilizing" the continent—in short, bringing Western values to a supposedly more primitive region. Today, we find this paternalistic rationalization of the colonizers' economic interests offensive and transparent, but it does help us understand the concerns with moral terms for the people of Africa. All too often under colonial rule moral education was used "as a vehicle of cultural imperialism, nationalist propaganda and social (and sexual) control" (pp. 267–278).

In all too many cases (and not only in Africa!), nations are run on the practice of **timocracy** (rule by money). Swartz (2010a) suggests that the African philosophy of *Ubuntu/Botho* offers both an antidote to timocracy and "a plausible alternative to Western approaches to morality" (p. 208). From the perspective of *Ubuntu/Botho,* "actions are right roughly insofar as they are a matter of living harmoniously with others or honoring communal relationships" (Metz & Gaie, 2010, p. 273).

Ubuntu/Botho

Metz and Gaie (2010) propose that a major strain of Sub-Saharan African thought that they call Afro-communitarianism offers a plausible alternative to the Western justice and care models of moral reasoning and action. As in Latin America, it is difficult to make general statements about morality because of the sweeping diversity. Africa is home to more than 50 countries and hundreds of ethnic groups and languages. However, Metz and Gaie believe that the international community has much to learn from underrepresented indigenous African ideas about morality.

Many of the countries of Sub-Saharan Africa have some version of the phrases: "A person is a person through other persons," and "I am because we are" (Metz & Gaie, 2010, p. 274). For Africans, the phrases are not merely descriptive but also normative. In contrast with Western approaches, African morality is *essentially* relational. The ultimate goal for humans is to become full and genuine human beings, but that is impossible without others. One's humanness is only possible through relating to others in positive ways.

Yet relating in positive ways does not mean respecting others' individual rights as it might in its Western connotation. Rather, positive relationships are conceptualized in communal terms. In short, the proper way to relate to others is to "seek out community or to live in harmony with them" (Metz & Gaie, 2010, p. 275). For Africans, developing and respecting community and harmony should serve as a guide for "what majorities want or which norms become dominant" (p. 276). The core themes in typical African discussions of community state that:

- People have **a moral obligation to be concerned for the well-being of others** in terms of both emotions (sympathy) and behavior (helping).
- People also have **a moral obligation to consider themselves as connected to others**, define themselves as members of a common group, and participate in its practices (Metz & Gaie, 2010).

Thus, a culture operating under the philosophy of *Ubuntu/Botho* will prescribe certain actions and policies as morally right. For example, property should be distributed in a way that respects communal relationships and there would not be the type of tolerance for economic inequality so typical in individualistic Western cultures such as the United States. In another example, our culture punishes adult offenders using the rationales of retribution and deterrence. *Ubuntu/Botho* instead prescribes reconciliation or the reparation of broken relationships. Even medical care would be conceptualized differently under this philosophy. We in the West expect confidentiality when we enter the health care system. In contrast, in the Afro-communitarian ethic, other members of the community have a stake in an individual's health. So not only would family or community members expect to be told about a person's health status, they would also expect to play a role in deciding how the person should be treated. Finally, in terms of moral education, Western pedagogy values activities that engage students in critical reasoning without any restrictions on which values the students eventually choose. There is a norm of respect for the students' autonomy. Although current African moral education practice has focused almost exclusively on inculcating societal norms through indoctrination, Metz and Gaie (2010) propose exchanging cultural socialization for *Ubuntu/Botho's* more worthy goal of developing personhood and facilitating students' capacity to prize community.

The Cultural Developmental Approach to Morality

Overview

Moving from the specific special issues of *JME* to a broader theoretical approach, this section relies heavily on the visionary work of psychologist Lene Arnett Jensen—both her own work and her leadership in encouraging scholars to broaden their conceptions of the moral domain. The title of her introductory chapter to the 2020 *The Oxford Handbook of Moral Development*: "Moral Development: From Paradigms to Plurality," nicely captures the shift for which she advocates. In a very broad summary, she sees the field moving from work with the kinds of theoretical paradigms we have been exploring in previous chapters to a wide range of research questions and methods. Jensen (2011, 2020b) especially wants to move the field beyond research with samples from North America and Europe to lifespan studies of diverse groups both within and across cultures (p. 4).

Interviews with Discipline Leaders: Lene Arnett Jensen, Ph.D.

Lene Arnett Jensen is a Senior Research Scientist at Clark University in Massachusetts, USA, and the originator of the cultural developmental approach to psychology. In recent years, she has also been a visiting scholar at a variety of universities, including Stanford University, Tufts University, the University of Baroda in India, and the University of Bordeaux in France.

In her own words, her research and publications "focus on moral development across cultures, and the impact of globalization on identity development—with worldviews and moral values being core components of identity." The following remarks (and the previous quotation) are taken from Dr. Arnett Jensen's February 2020 responses to our interview questions.

What Brought you to Moral Development?

I am interested in morality because it is fundamental to the human condition. Morality is not the only fundamental but, to me, it is perhaps the most interesting area of development because our moral beliefs and ideals are what provide us with aspiration, purpose, and direction in our lives and as we develop. This is true at the individual level. And it is also true at the collective level. Morality gives us hope that we can do well and that we can do better—even if that is not always how it works out.

The Committee on Comparative Human Development [at the University of Chicago] was revolutionary to my scholarship. It was like no other place in teaching one to think culturally about development, to really see human development through a cultural lens. For example, in early conversations with my graduate advisor Richard Shweder about how to analyze my master's research interviews with adults about their personal moral experiences, he introduced me to the idea of Three Ethics. At the time, the field of moral development—in my view—offered a limited set of one-size-fits-all frameworks. Together, we named them the Ethics of Autonomy, Community, and Divinity, and I developed a coding manual. To me, the idea of Three Ethics was fresh and exciting. And precisely because of its unorthodoxy, it is an idea that I have found inspiring to continue to develop and work with up to this day.

What Theorists have had the Most Influence on Your Thinking?

I've been influenced by lots of different theorists and scholars from different disciplines, psychology, anthropology, sociology, and philosophy. Instead of trying to name them, I'd like to focus on a couple of big ideas that have been crucial in my work on morality. One, as I have already mentioned, is the cultural psychology insight that we are all fundamentally shaped by the culture or cultures in which we grow up and live. For example, in some cultural communities thinking about moral issues in terms of religious or spiritual concepts—what we call and Ethic of Divinity—is common. In other cultural communities, such as Denmark where I grew up, this Ethic is uncommon.

The second big idea that has been crucial to my work is that development takes place across the life course. For example, children, even young ones, are certainly attuned to the needs of others and to their relationships with others—moral concepts that are part of an Ethic of Community. But research across many different cultures indicates that with age, from childhood into adolescence and from adolescence into adulthood, Ethic of Community concepts become more prominent in people's thinking. In my scholarship, I have found it particularly compelling to synthesize the cultural and life course perspectives, in what I term a "cultural-developmental" theoretical approach to psychology. In a nutshell, I argue that there are developmental templates that in turn are shaped by culture. From this cultural-developmental view, development is not fixed but flexible, and varies across cultures with age.

What has been Most Meaningful as Teacher, Researcher, and Writer? & What do you Hope Students Take Away from Your Classes and Textbooks?

What is most meaningful to me is to teach and research and write from a cultural perspective. In my research, I work with diverse groups within and across countries. For example, I have studied moral development among diverse religious communities in India and the United States. I have also addressed civic engagement among Indian and Salvadoran immigrant adolescents and parents in the United States. In my classes, I often invite visitors from diverse cultures—something that helps us to realize that we all have culture. In my textbooks, which I coauthor with Jeffrey Arnett, we have many cultural features including vivid videos with individuals from across the world.

What I hope that students take away from my classes, writings, and textbooks is an understanding of the diversity across today's global world. The world's population is more than 7.5 billion, and the population of the United States is about 330 million—less than 5% of the total. By 2100, the world's population is expected to reach 11 billion, with almost all growth taking place in economically developing countries. Worldwide, child development is remarkably diverse.... For college students, it is more important than ever to have knowledge of the wider world because of the increasingly globalized economy, and because so many issues—such as climate change, disease, and terrorism—cross borders.

Apart from knowing about diversity, my ultimate learning goal is for students to think culturally about development. I hope that students will learn to apply development to the work they do as well as to their own lives, and to understand that there is always a cultural basis to development. To be clear, this does not mean that biology is not important. In fact, humans have evolved to be an incomparably cultural and global species.

What is the Focus of Your Most Recent Research and What are Your Plans for the Future?

One key part of my recent and current scholarship has been to author a series of developmental psychology textbooks. Together with Jeffrey Arnett, we have four textbooks: two on child development (one with a topical and one with a chronological organization), one on adolescence and emerging adulthood, and one on the full life span. All four texts take a cultural approach. Again, to me, this is part of educating today's generation of college students for today's and tomorrow's world. In their professional and personal lives, they will be interacting with people from all over the world. My hope is that our textbooks will better prepare them for those interactions.

Another key part of my recent scholarship has been to bring the work of scholars together in edited books and handbooks in order collectively to move the field forward in new ways. I already mentioned the *Oxford Handbook of Moral Development*, but other examples of recent edited volumes include *The Oxford Handbook of Human Development and Culture* [OHHDC] published by Oxford University Press, and *Moral Development in a Global World* [MDGW] published by Cambridge University Press. The handbook brings a cultural perspective to human development with chapters by more than 100 authors. *Moral Development in a Global World* brings together scholars who are working with the three Ethics of Autonomy, Community, and Divinity in diverse parts of the world.

As to the future, I anticipate further developing my cultural-developmental approach to morality and to address globalization in relation to psychology (L. Jensen, personal communication, February 20, 2020).

New Research

We can only give you a few examples of the exciting scholarship in this new pluralistic paradigm and so we highly recommend turning to the resources Jensen notes in her interview as well as her newest edited volume, *The Oxford Handbook of Moral Development [OHMD]* (Jensen, 2020a). (Resources available in many college libraries). The goal of the latest handbook is to provide "a comprehensive, international, and up to date review of research on moral development, including moral motives and behaviors, ontogeny and developmental pathways, and contexts that children, adolescents and adults experience with respect to morality" (2020a, p. 3).

Although Jensen sometimes claims that cultural considerations have been ignored, as we noted earlier, most moral development researchers and their flagship organization, the Association for Moral Education, have also recognized the need to embrace a global perspective. For example, William Damon, long associated with classic and influential studies of human purpose recently reviewed research on the development and sustainment of purpose across the lifespan across a range of cultural contexts (Damon & Malin 2020). The growing body of international research supports his important definition of **purpose** as being meaningful to the self and having a goal of accomplishing "something of consequence to the world beyond the self" (Damon & Malin, 2020, p. 111).

MDGW (Jensen, 2015a) offers an excellent introduction to concepts and research from a cultural-developmental perspective. It proposes that the cultural developmental approach **bridges** universal and cultural perspectives on morality. In our increasingly globalized world, cultural identities are becoming too complex to be captured by broad and sometimes biased one-size-fits-all theories. Jensen uses a definition of culture as "symbolic, behavioral, and institutional inheritances that are shared and co-constructed by members of a community" (p. 4) but cautions that we need to be attuned for all the variety within a culture, especially due to differences in power that are often related to age, class, ethnicity, gender and religion. One of her most important contributions to prospective researchers is her conception of template models that propose life course trajectories for many concepts, especially patterns of moral development through the lens of the Three Ethics. In short, we need to pay attention to how culture influences ideas about the self, others and the divine at different points in the lifespan. To facilitate such research, Jensen provides four clear and helpful appendices: Coding Manual: Ethics of Autonomy, Community and Divinity; The Community, Autonomy and Divinity Scale; the Ethical Values Assessment (long form); and the Three Ethics Reasoning Assessment. These are terrific tools for researchers and a wonderful example of literally "giving psychology away." Another particularly useful essay in the book examines how religious emerging adults negotiate between their development and culture. Besides offering another crisp overview of the Three Ethics, Padilla-Walker and Nelson (2015) show how complicated it gets for young people when they must negotiate divergent or conflicting messages and norms of cultural and developmental worldviews.

Although *OHHDC* (Jensen, 2015c) repeats many of the same themes as *MDGW*, this Oxford handbook focuses more specifically on developmental emergence and life course pathways of numerous developmental concepts as well as giving a clear and helpful exposition of the "flexible and multiplicitous theoretical frameworks" for which Jensen advocates (p. 7). Essays of particular relevance to morality include Jensen's overview of the developmental emergence and life course pathways of moral reasoning among cultures (Jensen, 2015d) and Trommsdorff's (2015) exploration of the cultural roots of values, morals and religious orientations during adolescent development. Reflecting the emerging consensus on the shared moral sensibilities present on birth as well as the way moral reasoning becomes distinctly shaped by culture, Jensen's essay considers respectfully the foundational contributions of Freud's and Piaget's research questions while highlighting the necessary reframing of these questions as we become aware of how children and adults now live in "a rapidly globalizing world of cultural change." (p. 247)

Jensen's most recent compendium, *The Oxford Handbook of Moral Development* (2020a) hopes to provide "a comprehensive, international and up to date review on moral development" that "contributes to the revitalization and flourishing of the field... (p. 3). Graduate students especially will appreciate the rich resources of cutting-edge research in the areas of moral motives, moral behaviors, contexts of moral development, and applications and policies. The reference lists at the end of each chapter will allow you to delve deeply into these research topics. Given the importance of the concept of globalization for the cultural developmental approach, we will highlight McKenzie's (2020) exploration of the ways in which globalization alters moral development "by transforming the socializers to which youth are exposed" (p. 663). Urban youth often have dramatically more exposure to technology and social media and thus to narratives, images, ideas and values that may be in direct conflict with the more traditional moral teachings of their culture. Thus, both moral values and reasoning become "increasingly autonomy-driven" (p. 663).

We have been talking a lot about globalization in this section so let us take a step back to define the term. It has been defined in many ways but we liked McKenzie's use of Lewellen's 2002 conception:

> **Contemporary globalization** is the increasing flow of trade, finance, culture, ideas and people brought about by the sophisticated technology of communications and travel and by the worldwide spread of neoliberal capitalism, and the local and regional adaptations to and resistances against those flows.
>
> (pp. 7–8, as cited in McKenzie, 2020, p. 665).

As with most of the contributors to this handbook, McKenzie references the concept of the Three Ethics and agrees with Jensen's core idea that moral development is culturally situated. We find the Three Ethics in all cultures but prioritization of each varies. This essay also incorporates Jensen's approach of using cultural developmental trajectory templates to better understand how moral development unfolds—and often changes—across time and place.

At this point, we have offered you a sampling of the rich theoretical and research from global perspectives on morality. Do you see any consensus emerging from these findings and ideas?

Can We Come to Consensus on Core Moral Values?

The diverse students in one of Elly's graduate moral development classes at Columbia Teachers College in New York City were particularly fascinated with issues of universalism versus cultural relativism. Bob McNulty, a widely traveled businessman (now professor) who had spent time in a Buddhist monastery, came up with the important insight that "all cultures have universal values of justice and care. But they differ in terms of *who* deserves to be treated fairly and with care and under which conditions." Accordingly, as Jensen (2015a) argues persuasively, theories and research about morality in a global world will require psychologists to attend not only to the development of diverse reasoning across the life span, but also across cultures. The new field of cultural developmental morality holds tremendous promise for an exploration of on-going questions of universal and culturally specific values.

We lean towards the possibility of identifying core universal moral values because we do not see any contradiction inherent in accepting that common human prewiring plays out in the diverse human thoughts, emotions, and behaviors underlying cultural practices. We agree with Shweder's insight (2018) that there are deep universal principles that, in his view (and Amie's) come from a higher spiritual plane, but which more secular thinkers like Elly would attribute to evolution. Like Shweder we believe that these deep principles are always there in cultures but play out differently. In short, universal abstract principles can lead to lack of uniformity and different judgments in application because they are understood through the lens of a native or local point of view

(Shweder, 2018). Shweder (1991) has criticized general psychology's quest for a common central processing unit. However, the way we see it, our brains and related neuronal and hormonal systems probably do represent a certain basic central processing unit characteristic of the human species and designed to make meaning of the world in an evolving dance. Our minds change the world around us and the world around us changes us in perpetual cycles that we then hand down to the next generation through learning and culture. The minds we have today evolved to survive in a physical world but also adapted to surviving in the sociocultural world of human societies. Universal moral values of justice and care/love evolved out of biological and cognitive adaptations core to the survival of humans across time and place.

Discussion Questions

1. Think again about the "Dilemma of the Day" question with which we began the chapter. Then watch the TED talk mentioned in Additional Resources on the Muslim faith. If we acknowledge that the western democracies are "WEIRD," does that suggest that their laws must do a better job of understanding and accommodating the more traditional views of some of their religious and cultural minorities (as Shweder suggests)? Or *are* some moral perspectives more advanced and adequate, as Kohlberg argued?

2. We encourage our students to consider that **the way things are is not the only way they *could* or *should* be**. Think about your hometown or city. What specific changes would occur if the town/city government decided to make decisions and policies using the principles of *Ubuntu/Botho* rather than the political system now in place? How do you think the citizens (including yourself) would react?

Additional Resources

- Here's a perspective on the Muslim faith from within with messages for both believers and non-Muslim Westerners. Akyol offers an excellent analysis that distinguishes specific cultural practices from Islamic law.

    - https://www.ted.com/talks/mustafa_akyol_faith_versus_tradition_in_islam.%20html

- Shweder's work on cultural pluralism has been especially influential in calling us to notice the "weirdness" of the Western rational tradition. Thus, we believe this 54-minute 2018 clip from *The Dissenter* is worthy of an auxiliary or extra credit assignment with this chapter. Here Shweder provides a very nuanced assessment of his agreements and disagreements with Kohlberg and Moral Foundations Theory. (You can easily skip over all the ads.) *Richard Shweder Part 1: Morality, and Jonathan Haidt's Moral Foundations* https://www.youtube.com/watch?v=DiR8xRUWzSw

8 Conclusion: In a Different Mind

So what does all this information about theory and research actually mean? How can we make sense of so many complex and often contradictory ideas? Earlier, we noted that critical thinkers should always be asking the questions "Who's the audience?," "What's put in?," "What's left out?," and "Who's speaking?" It thus seems only fair to address them here before sharing our current perspective on moral theory.

Who's the audience? From the format of the book, you can see that the primary audience is all of you graduate and upper-division undergraduate students taking some kind of developmental, theory or practice class or, if you are especially lucky, a stand-alone course in moral development. We also wrote the book to be of use to practitioners in the fields of education, counseling, psychology, allied health, and social work. But no matter if you are a newcomer to your field or a veteran professional, we hope that this exposure to multiple perspectives on morality has nudged you to begin thinking about where *you* stand in the light of the text's evidence and ideas. How do *you* make sense of human moral reasoning, emotions, and actions? How do you think people come to understand what is right and wrong, good and bad?

What's put in and what's left out? From the very beginning of this book, we have tried to be upfront with you about the fact that this is a very personal selection of material from a vast and complex field. In making choices about how best to limit each chapter to a manageable domain of information, we attempted to focus on approaches with particularly well-researched and direct links to applications. We also tried to put in ideas and examples that had, quite simply, struck us and/or our students as particularly interesting, surprising, or challenging through the years. Elly reads widely across disciplines with literature being her favorite area and history, political science, and psychology coming in at a close tie for the second place. Amie's interest areas include moral and empathic development in individuals on the autism spectrum, faith development and all things Norwegian. We hope that our eclectic palates have given our worldviews a breath that reflects openness to new ideas as well as a profound respect for classic ones.

DOI: 10.4324/9780429295461-9

Who's speaking? You may already have noticed from Elly's anecdotes that her coming of age in the late 60s certainly shaped her perspective on big picture issues of morality. We were a generation that saw a flawed world and actually believed that people could organize and work to change it. Another major influence on both of our ideas comes from watching our colleagues in the field present their work across the years, reading their work and talking with them about it. This first-hand immersion with the people, theory and research in moral development has made the field very much a living presence in our lives. We've loved watching the evolution of ideas (although we have to admit to some nostalgia for the simplicity of the earlier era of the grand stage theories).

Let us now trace for you the path that has led us to our own "Here we stand" position on moral development theories and concepts. To give you an example of how people's ideas evolve over time, the next sections, edited down from the first edition, trace Elly's trajectory before ending with a "pulling things together" written and updated by the two of us.

Classic Theories of Morality

In reflecting upon how I fell in love with the area of moral development, I realized that the first step was probably an upper-division perception class I took at the University of Connecticut in which I was introduced to a high-powered blend of ecological psychology, complexity theory, philosophy of science, and developmental psychology. Although the daunting reading list eliminated two-thirds of the class by the end of the first week, those of us who persevered benefitted from the challenges of an interdisciplinary perspective on the intricate connections between perceiving, thinking, and acting. I was drawn to the idea of systems progressing towards organization and away from chaos underlying work in both cosmology and developmental psychology. I also read a primary work by Piaget for the first time (Inhelder & Piaget, 1964) and became intrigued with his ideas about developmental progression through cognitive stages.

But it wasn't until I began working on my master's in community counseling under award-winning counselor educator Tim Hatfield at Winona State University that the love affair really blossomed. In my moral development class with Tim, I read about Kohlberg's stage theory in the first textbook from a cognitive-developmental perspective (Lickona, 1976) and was completely hooked. I went on to read the hot new book of the day, Carol Gilligan's (1982) *In a Different Voice,* and integrated the two theoretical positions—justice and care—into my master's thesis: *Talking to Children about War and Peace: A Developmental Perspective.* Like many counselors, my primary interest in theory at that point was in how it could be applied to the real world.

Fast forward a few years and a thousand miles to a little bookstore in New York City where a book entitled *Freud, Women, and Morality* (Sagan,

1988) caught my eye. I'd read several biographies of Freud and found him a fascinating personality study but had very little respect for his theoretical ideas. Sagan's feminist twist on Freud's core ideas gave me my first dose of a Neo-Freudian perspective and planted the seed that taking valuable insights from multiple perspectives might be a productive way to go.

From Stages to Schemas: Kohlberg and Rest

As I moved into doctoral work at Fordham University, I had the great luck to connect with Ann Higgins (now Higgins-D'Alessandro) as a mentor and began to deepen my understanding of Lawrence Kohlberg's theory, life, and work. Ann had worked closely with Kohlberg as he refined his theory and applied it to school settings. She arranged for me to complete my doctoral internship at one of the just community schools Kohlberg founded that we write about in Chapter 9. She also introduced me to James Rest, who helped me hone the DIT-like measure I used in the research Ann and I conducted on university faculty members' moral reasoning about the real-world dilemmas inherent in affirmative action policies. Under Ann's direction, I read widely and deeply in moral development theory and research and came to evaluate Gilligan's work as an overreaching of her evidence and Rest's as a logical extension of Kohlberg's. It seemed to me that meta-analyses showing no real differences between male and female moral reasoning had pretty much decided the justice-care debate in favor of Kohlberg, and that Rest's Four Component Model of morality explained why people had found anomalies like the judgment-action gap. Kohlberg's theory of moral stages wasn't necessarily wrong—it was simply incomplete. He was focusing on moral reasoning, but moral reasoning was simply one component influencing moral behavior.

Theoretical Challenges and Vozzola's La Bamba Epiphany

So there I was, newly minted Ph.D., having figured out the answers to the field's big questions, and ready to begin my college teaching career. I was a confirmed, card-carrying Kohlbergian with a mission to spread the word. And then I had one of those "Saul on the road to Damascus epiphanies" while driving along New York City's West Side Highway in my little Toyota Tercel with Ritchie Valens's "La Bamba" blasting out of my AM/FM radio (pre-iTunes and pre-being able to afford car air conditioning). The "great Justice/Care debate" between the theories of Gilligan and Kohlberg had dominated class discussions in the summer 1994 moral development course I was teaching at Teachers College, and I had prepared some integrative remarks and questions for our final night's class discussion. Earlier that day, I had taken a break from class prep to read an *American Psychologist* article by Seymour Epstein (1994) that introduced me to the concept of dual-processing systems. Somehow the heady combination of a summer night drive along New York's Upper West Side, a great classic rock tune, my class lecture notes, and Epstein's insights came together in one of those deeply satisfying "Aha!" moments. Aha! Kohlberg and Gilligan are actually talking about two **different minds** (or parts of the brain) that speak different languages—the quick, emotional voice of care that Epstein (1994) would see as a part of his **experiential system** and the slower, more deliberative voice of justice identified as the **rational system** in Epstein's theory. It struck me that we literally hear the processing from these two systems as "different voices" (Gilligan, 1982).

Epstein's cognitive-experiential self-theory (CEST). I would like to briefly examine Epstein's cognitive-experiential self-theory (Epstein, 1990, 1994, 2003) so that you can get the sense of how evidence about the inadequacies of a focus on rationality began to converge from multiple perspectives. CEST presents an integrative theory of **personality** rather than of morality, but I think you will readily see how it gave me an epiphany about how it could be applied to the moral domain. The theory's core assumptions include:

1. Humans process information about their physical and social worlds through two interactive yet independent conceptual systems. The first is a preconscious **experiential system** and the second is a conscious **rational system.**
2. The experiential system is driven by emotions (Epstein, 2003).

In 1994, I was captivated by the idea that Epstein's theory provided a physiological explanation for the observations of researchers in the justice and care camps. Today, I see his analysis of the properties and underlying neurological structures of the two systems providing convergent evidence for the sorts of dual processing models we examined in Chapter 5 as well as linking back to Freud's classic theory. Let's examine the similarities between CEST and some of those theories.

The Rise of Theories from Neuroscience and Evolutionary Perspectives

Briefly, Epstein believes significant evidence supports the existence of an analytical **cognitive system** that moves slowly and deliberately to explore multiple facets of objects and events. Think about the sensation of studying a dense and difficult text or of grappling with understanding a very abstract and complex mathematical problem. It takes effort and concentration to use the processes of logic and reason and the tools of symbols and words. The cognitive system appears to be primarily under the control of the prefrontal cortex of the brain (Epstein, 2003).

In contrast, the **experiential system** is holistic and faster. There is less concern with future possibilities as the focus is on present action. Think about the last time you were in a situation where you had to swerve or brake to avoid a car that unexpectedly pulled out in front of you. Your emotional system went into automatic and effortless high gear to help you react quickly. You didn't run through a careful analysis of logical alternatives—you hit those brakes! Your "decision" to do so was guided by intuitions derived from prior associations. The emotional experiential system, rooted in your limbic system, played an important role in human survival in the early and dangerous human environment, and continues to provide us with intuitive quick responses that are, however, not necessarily as good a fit for the complex modern world.

One of Epstein's (1994) important insights was to point out how often the experiential system, of which we are largely unconscious, influences the rational system that we perceive to be in control of behaviors such as moral reasoning and actions. In short, he believes it is much more scientifically defensible and makes much greater evolutionary sense to see our unconscious thinking system as adaptive rather than pathological. Epstein's (1994, 2003) concept of a powerful emotional experiential system influencing our thinking would probably have been identified by Freud as **rationalization,** by Haidt as the powerful elephant of **intuition** steering the course for the rider **reason,** and by Kahneman as the interactions between **Systems 1** (fast) and **Systems 2** (slow) **thinking.** Epstein's more clinical perspective on how to integrate the latest psychological research into a coherent theory parallels the broad sweep of some of the theories we reviewed in Chapter 5, especially Haidt's Moral Foundations Theory and Narvaez's Triune Ethics Meta-Theory.

Global Perspectives on Morality

In 2012, Jonathan Haidt gave the keynote address for the Association for Moral Education annual meeting. As I worked on the first edition's chapter on global perspectives, I recalled that I had first read about the important (and humbling) concept of how "WEIRD" the Western perspective is in Haidt's book. While I ultimately saw Haidt as over-reaching his evidence and disregarding the significant research base on the ability of our rational system to develop the habit of overriding and monitoring our intuitive one, his theory stimulated me to grapple with ways in which I could best integrate my ideas about how universal moral foundations play out in specific cultural contexts. Clearly, culture not only *influences* our behaviors—it literally *re-wires* our brains.

Pulling Things Together—Who's Speaking? Elly and Amie

So how do we make coherent sense of all the disparate theories of moral reasoning, emotions, and behavior we have examined in Part I of this text? We should add two final tidbits of "Who's the speaker" before taking our

"Here we stand" position on moral theories. Neither of us are relativists. Unlike many of our esteemed colleagues, we have come to believe that there are indeed universal roots to human morality, and that the Enlightenment preference for reason over authority continues to hold great promise for humanity. We are also believers in free will and that, despite our biological pre-wirings, Harry Potter's headmaster Dumbledore had it right: "It is our choices, Harry, that show what we truly are, far more than our abilities" (Rowling, 1998, p. 333).

And so, our "Here we stand" on the ideas in Part I reflects the understanding of these particular psychologists at this particular point in time (2021), with a particular set of life and educational experiences. Although most of the key ideas continue to stand the test of time, we were very lucky to have access to many excellent recent resources that we have used to update our perspectives. In particular, not only did we review and integrate insights from Jensen's (2020a) *Oxford Handbook of Moral Development*, but we also benefitted from cutting edge research and ideas in the many excellent essays in the 2021 *Journal of Moral Education*'s 50th Anniversary issue, edited by Jim Conroy (see Resources at the end of the chapter for specific citations). After many years of deep immersion in the field, we believe that the following key ideas have, at least for now, withstood the test of time and research:

- During normal development, children's thinking tends to become more complex and more decentered as their experiential and relational worlds expand.
- Moral growth is better understood as developing more adequate and complex schemas than as "stage" growth per se.
- Which specific schema, at which level of complexity, is accessed to process an event is often heavily dependent on situational cues and social/cultural norms. In short, we are more like layer cakes than like staircases.
- Education rather than gender plays the key role in fostering moral reasoning complexity.
- Yet in terms of actual **prosocial behavior,** Eagly (2009) notes "a persistent pattern of female emotionally supportive and sensitive behavior, especially in close relationships, and male agentic behaviors, often related to strangers and to the support of social collectives" (p. 653).
- We know we need to account for the influence of a broad range of moral education experiences—both formal and informal (e.g., family, friends, religion, school, reading, media) that can either foster positive moral values or encourage antisocial ones.
- We are increasingly aware of the fact that we are biological beings whose thinking, feeling, and behaving have been shaped not only by parenting and education but also by evolutionary prewiring and

biological differences in myriad systems including our neurological and hormonal ones. Recent evidence on the importance of the microbiome suggests that the bacteria in our guts may play as important a role in the regulation of our emotions as our neurotransmitters (Pollan, 2013).

- An aspect of human prewiring of particular relevance to morality is temperament (inherited variations in patterns of behavior and mood). "Although all children are capable of feeling uncertainty, anxiety, fear, shame, empathy and guilt, they vary in the frequency and intensity of those emotions. Some of this variation, but not all, is the result of a child's temperament" (Kagan, 1998, p. 309).

- Variations of Kahneman's (2003) "thinking fast and slow" concept underlie many contemporary theories. As Epstein (1994) argued almost 30 years ago, our growing understanding of the biological underpinnings of concepts formerly labeled id, ego, and super-ego by psychoanalysts, or voices of care and justice by developmental psychologists, probably reflects whether an event is being primarily processed in the older, more emotional, quick and intuitive parts of the brain (e.g., limbic system) or the newer, slower, and more deliberative neocortex.

- If Haidt (2012) is correct, and we are biologically prewired to use a set of moral foundations whose salience is set by specific cultures, then there is both support and challenge for promoting the type of respectful dialogue and understanding central to moral education at the micro level and international cooperation at the more macro level. In short, understanding is possible but it will be difficult, especially when concrete thinkers meet complex ones. Their "righteous minds" may be initially repelled by the others' ideas, but perhaps there is a path to initial connection through the intuitive System 1.

- Finally, Jensen and colleagues' work in cultural developmental psychology offers the field, which she notes has often been too prone to build walls, a model that promotes bridges between the best of older classic theories and new perspectives arising from respectful consideration of moral perspectives developing across time and culture.

It has become very clear, as Tobias Krettenauer (2021) points out in his important review essay, that the moral sciences, as he calls them, "are markedly more pluralistic and diverse than moral psychology in the past" (p. 79). We agree with his argument that rather than clinging to Haidt's emphasis on intuition or Kohlberg's on reasoning, we need to "engage both sides of the argument in order to find out **in what way, when and how morality is emotional and rational** [emphasis added]" (p. 81). Jensen's concept of taking "individuals across the life course who are developing in tandem with one or more changing cultures" (2015, p. 7) as our unit of analysis and using broadened and deepened culturally specific concepts to understand that development would be one model for addressing this complex question. We do not know yet if her suggestion to develop such template models for life course conceptual trajectories (e.g. of the self, morality or a higher power) will become a widely accepted model for the field but it is certainly showing great heuristic value for many researchers.

Another central question for moral psychology is the extent to which human thoughts, emotions, and behaviors are due to dispositional or situational factors. The early stage theories tend to favor dispositional explanations, behavioral and cultural theories favor situational ones, and the newest theories attempt to weave a more complicated and integrative picture of the way in which our biological prewiring interacts with specific—and often changing—situations, environments and cultures. Increasingly, we expect that research in morality will attempt to understand which interactions between which brain structures, hormones, and bacteria at which stage of development in which environments influence the phenomena we describe as moral decisions, emotions, and actions. We will also look at the ways in which individuals' brains are literally shaped by early childhood experiences, learning, and culture. We may have a fairly common universal blueprint for our brains, but it now appears that not only are we sometimes reacting "in a different mind" depending on whether our experiential/fast or rational/slow system is dominant, but also that we alter that common prewiring of our brains through unique learning and cultural experiences.

Discussion Questions

1. What factors do you believe have been most important in shaping your moral identity: Temperament? Family? Education? Culture? Religion? Give specific examples.
2. Have these aspects ever been in conflict? If so, how do you decide what to do—what is right and wrong, good, and bad?
3. Which of the theories in Part I have the most value for your future or current professional life?

Additional Resources

* Conroy, J. C. (Ed.). (2021). Future directions for moral education, on the 50th anniversary of the *Journal of Moral Education* [Special issue]. *Journal of Moral Education, 50*(1).
* Gray, K., & Graham, J. (Eds.). (2018). *Atlas of moral psychology*. Guilford Press.
* Jensen, L. A. (Ed.). (2020a). *The Oxford handbook of moral development: An interdisciplinary perspective*. Oxford University Press.
* A few years ago, Oxford University Press began an ambitious project to develop an online resource made up of selective lists of annotated bibliographic citations. Then Association of Moral Education president

Sharon Lamb and Elly worked together to select and describe core books, articles, journals, and websites for the field of moral development. Our goal was to steer people new to the field to the key resources experts would turn to for categories such as a general overview of the field, moral philosophy, moral education, civic education, the ethic of care, and measurement issues. In 2015, Amie updated and expanded the entry. The *Oxford Bibliographies Online* is generally available through college library databases.

- Vozzola, E., Lamb, S., & Senland, A. (2015). Moral development. Annotated bibliography entry for *Oxford Bibliographies Online (OBO)*. http://www.oxfordbibliographies.com/

Part II

Applications of Theory to Practice

9 Applied Moral Education: Accomplishments, New Directions, and Morality (and Lack Thereof) in the Media

1. Though "No" is a very little word, it is not always easy to say it; and the not doing so often causes trouble.
2. When we are asked to stay away from school and spend in idleness or mischief the time that ought to be spent in study, we should at once say "No."
3. When we are urged to loiter on our way to school, and thus be late, and interrupt our teacher and the school, we should say "No."...
4. When we are tempted to use angry or wicked words, we should remember that the eye of God is always upon us, and should say "No." (From 1879 *McGuffey's Reader* quoted in Gorn, 1998, p. 65)

For most of the 19th century in the United States, no one questioned the fact that schools would reinforce the "central assumptions of evangelical faith and middle class morality" (Gorn, 1998, p. 9). Today, any teacher or administrator interested in moral education faces not only a bewildering array of programs but also substantial questions about how and what to teach in an increasingly pluralistic society. American practitioners are not alone. Conversations with moral researchers and educators from around the world (Association of Moral Education Roundtable, Krakow, Poland, personal communication, July 2004) grapple with how to implement moral education with children who come from cultures uncomfortable with, or sometimes hostile to, the Western values so blithely assumed to be universal in the McGuffey's readers.

In Chapter 7, we examined a sample of cross-cultural studies and highlighted the ongoing tension between conceptions of universal and culturally specific moral development that play out in different societies' specific moral education interventions. Although there is a large and lively literature on global moral education (interested readers are encouraged to search the *Journal of Moral Education*), for the purposes of this chapter, we review the best-known paradigms, as these are the approaches you are most likely to encounter in your professional lives. We then move on to look at how these approaches might play out across development. Finally, we

DOI: 10.4324/9780429295461-11

consider some current research on young people's perceptions of media's moral messages as well as how developmental research might inform the use of media in moral education.

Contemporary Moral Education Paradigms

Moral education has emerged as the central focus of moral development theory, research, and practice. However, as prominent researcher Marvin Berkowitz (2011) notes in a synopsis of what works in values education, the study of values/moral/character education has suffered for years from a "semantic morass" (p. 153) that can make assessment and comparisons difficult for researchers and practitioners alike. Berkowitz argues persuasively (personal communication, June 10, 2003) that **character education** can and should be viewed as a broad umbrella term for a broad range of approaches from violence and drug prevention programs with a character component to more comprehensive programs, such as Caring School Communities (https://www.collaborativeclassroom.org/programs/caring-school-community/). However, character education sometimes tends to have a conservative connotation in the United States (especially among researchers); thus, we prefer to use **moral education** as the broad umbrella term and discuss character education as a specific approach.

The bottom line about teaching morality in the schools is that we do (Damon, 1988; Nucci & Narvaez, 2008; Power et al., 1989; Sizer & Sizer, 1999). The more central concern should be the extent to which educators are aware of the moral messages that they are teaching and students are learning. Kohlberg often talked about the hidden curriculum of schools; those lessons students take away about what is valued and respected and what is not. Schools not only pass along the values of the culture (e.g., honesty, responsibility) but also specific values such as to work hard, be quiet, be on time, be polite to teachers, be neat, and don't cheat (Damon, 1988). Sometimes, however, schools also teach students that elite athletes who break rules will get away with doing so but that "stoners" or "outlaws" who do the same thing will not. Tragedies such as the school massacre at Columbine High School in 1999 brought many Americans to a realization of how perceptions of injustice can trigger rage and even violence in some troubled youth.

Schools in almost all cultures have two central goals: They want to help kids be smart and they want them to be good (Damon, 1988; Davidson et al., 2014; Lickona & Davidson, 2005). In earlier times, teaching children to be good meant explicit exhortations to virtuous living and habits, often from a religious perspective (Gorn, 1998). More recently, four major paradigms have emerged: **values clarification,** the **cognitive-developmental approach, character education,** and **domain-based practices.** Following a brief overview of each paradigm and an evaluation of its strengths and weaknesses, we look at a hybrid model, **integrative ethical education,** that represents the current climate of bringing together the best ideas across paradigms (see Table 9.1).

Table 9.1 Moral Education Models

Values Clarification
- **Assumptions:**
  - Children should be free to choose their own values
  - Direct moral instruction is not only wrong but harmful
- **Theoretical Roots:**
  - No explicit theoretical roots
- **Goals:**
  - Foster children's self-esteem
  - Encourage children to prize and affirm the values they chose
- **Methods:**
  - Teachers provide lots of nonjudgmental clarifying responses to children's values statements
  - Activities such as values sorts exercises and values discussions

Cognitive Developmental
- **Assumptions:**
  - Higher stage thinking is better thinking because it solves a wider range of problems, is less self-oriented, and reflects more universal values, such as fairness and human rights (Damon, 1988)
  - Higher stage thinking and civic engagement can be promoted through participatory democracy and the creation of a just school climate
- **Theoretical Roots:**
  - Piaget's phase theory of moral development
  - Kohlberg's stage theory of moral development
  - John Dewey's (1916) theory of educating for democracy
  - Durkheim's (1961) concept of group norms arising from shared group expectations and a sense of community and solidarity
- **Goals:**
  - Promote moral growth in students' moral reasoning so that they can understand complex ethical issues
  - Help students develop a sense of agency
  - Promote social and emotional development
  - Foster civic competence and engagement through the school structures, climate, and discipline practices
- **Methods:**
  - Teacher use of plus-one-matching responses
  - Peer classroom discussions of moral dilemmas
  - Democratic participation (e.g., community meetings)

Character Education
- **Assumptions:**
  - Schools should focus on moral behavior rather than thinking (This is changing as cognitive developmentalists work with character education programs to promote both moral reasoning and prosocial behavior)
  - Adults can and should identify desired moral character traits such as fairness, hard work, and integrity and teach them directly to students
- **Theoretical Roots:**
  - Early character education interventions relied heavily on Aristotle's theory of virtues
  - Currently, cognitive-developmental researchers have developed character education interventions with theoretical roots in Rest's Four Component Model, Kohlberg's theory of moral development, and Noddings's ethic of care (among others)

(*Continued*)

Table 9.1 (Continued)

- **Goals:**
    - Promoting right conduct (e.g., following rules, working hard)
    - Promoting prosocial behavior (e.g., helping, caring)
    - Promoting the development of positive character virtues (e.g., integrity, honesty)
- **Methods:**
    - Integrating character lessons throughout the curriculum
    - Discussing moral stories and moral issues related to the academic subject matter
    - Encouraging participation in character-building extra-curricular activities such as sports, community service, and clubs
    - Publicly acknowledging student accomplishments and improvements in community meetings pep rallies, posters, announcements, and so forth.

(Hybrid) Ethical Expertise Model
- **Assumptions:**
    - Character development "is a matter of building proficiency in a set of interpersonal and intrapersonal ethical skills" (D. Narvaez, personal communication, September 25, 2001)
    - Expertise building should focus on values identified as important by the local community
- **Theoretical/Research Roots:**
    - Rest's Four Component Model
    - Expertise literature in psychology
- **Goals:**
    - Help students move from developmentally appropriate novice to expert levels of ethical sensitivity, judgment, motivation, and action
- **Methods:**
    - Teachers select activities from a series of workbooks that identify and define the ethical skills
    - Teachers use the workbooks' sample lesson plans organized around activities ranging from novice to expert levels: immersion in examples and opportunities, the practice of procedures, and integration of knowledge and procedures (Narvaez et al., 2001).

Values Clarification

This approach, popular in the 1960s and 1970s (Damon, 1988; Leming, 2008), assumed that children should be free to choose their own values and that the indoctrination common to materials like the McGuffey's readers was actually hazardous to children's intellectual health. One central assumption held that schools should avoid teaching specific virtues and instead promote self-esteem and freedom. (It was the 1960s!) Goals included helping children to choose values, prize and affirm their choices, and consistently act on those values in their daily lives. Teachers used activities such as values sorts and values discussions but were cautioned not to judge any of the children's choices. Instead, they were to respond with a brief clarifying response—"I hear Johnny saying that making a fortune is his most important value"—and quickly move on. We're not going to go into the details of this approach because it is not one you will (or should) be seeing in 21st-century schools.

Strengths and challenges (mostly challenges). Although one might argue that taking no stands may be the best way to avoid controversy in a pluralistic culture, unfortunately, it also seems to weaken the role of the teacher as a moral role model. Most damning of all, evaluations showed none of the increases in self-esteem or personal adjustment the approach had promised. Children did behave better during the values discussions themselves but failed to generalize that good behavior to other settings (Damon, 1988; Leming, 2008). In short, values clarification did not deliver on its promise.

The Cognitive Developmental Approach

During the same time period, Lawrence Kohlberg and colleagues (Power et al., 1989; Power & Higgins-D'Alessandro, 2008; Snarey & Samuelson, 2014) developed a much more direct school intervention. Kohlberg proposed that some moral positions are actually better than others; thus, schools should be designed to promote their development. These higher moral positions solve a wider range of problems, are less self-oriented, and more strongly reflect universal values (Damon, 1988). While Damon sees the goal of Kohlberg's approach as helping students acquire more advanced forms (stages) of moral judgment, Ann Higgins-D'Alessandro, a close collaborator with Kohlberg on many of his school interventions, argues that it is important for people to know that Kohlberg's theory of moral education was separate from his theory of moral judgment.

Interviews with Discipline Leaders: Ann Higgins-D'Alessandro, Ph.D., Professor of Psychology, Fordham University

Ann Higgins-D'Alessandro, a Professor of Psychology, teaches in, and for many years directed, Fordham University's doctoral program in Applied Developmental Psychology. Her research interests are focused in two areas, the development of sense of self and morality across the lifespan and basing evaluation strategies for school change intervention programs in developmental and program theories. [Her] research and writing in the development of sense of self and morality focus on understanding the role of self-evaluation and the influence of institutions and groups in their development and expression in action, particularly moral actions, altruism, and self-evaluated "wrong" actions (Faculty web page, Fordham University, 2021). Ann is recognized internationally as an expert on just community schools, prosocial education, and evaluation research, publishing extensively in those fields. Relevant publications are *The Handbook of Prosocial Education* (2012) coedited with Philip Brown and Michael Corrigan. In it, she argues for the necessity of prosocial education (from whole-school improvement efforts to classroom climate, Social Emotional Learning (SEL), character, moral, civic, and contemplative interventions and service activities) to create schools as positive teaching, learning, and living places worthy of and able to uphold the respect and dignity of all within them, to foster long-term development of teachers as well as students, and to undergird and promote academic learning. As a consultant to the US Department of Education, Office of Safe and Drug-Free Schools (2005–2009), she cowrote *Mobilizing for Evidence-Based Character Education* (2007), a USDOE publication on effective partnering between educators and evaluators for character and school climate improvement interventions. In 2010, she contributed two chapters on civic engagement to Sherrod et al.'s *Handbook of Research on Civic Engagement in Youth.*

"I think it is important to know that Kohlberg's theory of moral education was separate from his theory of moral judgment. In principle, moral education should indeed promote moral judgment, but Kohlberg believed that the truly important outcomes were developing a sense of agency, developing socially and emotionally, and being able to understand complex ethical issues. The moral education research was an experiment he thought would be evaluated, maybe fade away, but be taken out someday when the world was a better place."

> What's the big thing you have learned about moral education interventions after all these years of working with them and evaluating them? "One thing I learned for sure is that you [the researcher] as someone going into a school must get and give respect to the staff. Whatever your own ideas—you have to be open to hear their input and ideas. Your job is to give them expertise in a way they can use. They need to be able to critique your ideas and take what they need/want. You become a better theorist when you learn from the practitioners. The role of the outsider is to be humble and deeply respectful of the teachers with whom you work."
>
> (A. Higgins-D'Alessandro, personal communication, June 17, 2003)

In contrast with the nonjudgmental and nondirective methods of values clarification, the cognitive-developmental approach uses directive techniques such as classroom discussions of moral dilemmas, reflection journals, and role-taking exercises. Teachers engage in **"plus-one-matching"** in which they roughly assess students' developmental level and then challenge them with statements a stage above their current level of functioning. For example, a teacher might challenge a student who claimed that he would hit anyone who hit him (Kohlberg's Stage 2) to consider another's perspective. "If you were the kid who started the fight, what would be the best way for the other kid to handle it?"

Numerous studies and meta-analyses have established the effectiveness of using **dilemma discussions** to promote students' moral development (Snarey & Samuelson, 2014). To summarize all too briefly the key findings:

- Dilemma discussions tend to produce larger (albeit moderate) effects than many other interventions; and
- The most significant effects tend to occur when all students in a naturally occurring group such as a family or classroom are empowered to discuss real rather than hypothetical dilemmas.

"Ripped from the Headlines" Dilemma of the Day: Bong Hits 4 Jesus

Elly's upper-division moral development class generally began with a dilemma of the day exercise that asked students to take a position on an issue "ripped from the headlines" or featured in the *New York Times* Ethicist column. Here's one of our favorites: "Bong Hits for Jesus."

In 2002, 18-year-old Joseph Frederick unveiled a 14-foot banner reading "Bong Hits 4 Jesus" as he and other students stood on the sidewalk outside their high school. Although it was a school day, students had been allowed outside to watch the Olympic torch runner pass by. His principal, Deborah Morse, confiscated the sign and suspended him. He, literally, took his case to the United States Supreme Court. Here's the specific dilemma we discuss: Should the principal have suspended Frederick for his actions? After a yes/no vote tally, we discuss the reasons for people's votes.

What do you think? Was Frederick simply exercising his right to free speech, as briefs in support of his position argued? Should his banner, silly and sophomoric though it might have been, be protected as free speech? Or was the principal justified in concluding that the banner promoted drug use (against which the school had a policy) and that, had she failed to act, she would be sending a message that the school condoned such a message? Do young people give up their First Amendment (freedom of speech) rights when they walk into a school?

Reflecting on Kohlberg's life, Power (2015) explained how Kohlberg's true passion was his "vocation to be a moral educator... [his] sense of his life as a calling" (p. 187) to serve and educate children. The most powerful technique developed by Kohlberg and his colleagues (Power et al., 1989) involved the transformation of an entire school into a **just community.**

Lawrence Kohlberg created the Just Community Model in the belief that certain conditions could promote more complex moral reasoning and behavior, and, hence, more engaged and effective democratic citizens. According to Higgins (1995) these conditions include the following:

- Open discussion focusing on fairness, community, and morality.
- Cognitive conflict stimulated by exposure to different points of view and higher stage reasoning.
- Participation in rule making and rule enforcement and the public exercise of power and responsibility.
- The development of community or group solidarity at a high stage (Kurtines & Gewirtz, 1995, pp. 63–64).

Evaluation evidence

Although numerous studies of cognitive-developmental interventions (e.g., Power et al., 1989) have consistently found stage growth at a small and moderate level (1/4 stage), classroom teachers were frequently frustrated at the gap between their tacit sense of the genuine benefits of the model and the explicit findings of extremely modest moral reasoning gains. With the benefit of current advances in theory and research, especially Rest's Four Component Model (Rest & Narvaez, 1994), it now seems clear that the problem with past evaluations may have been a narrow focus on growth in moral judgment. During Elly's doctoral internship at the Scarsdale A-School, one of the best-known just community high schools, she observed that in addition to fostering a strong sense of community (a goal that Power and Higgins-D'Alessandro (2008) studied intensively using their Moral Climate Inventory), the program seemed to nudge adolescents towards growth in moral sensitivity, motivation, and character (aspects for which we had no valid measures at the time). There was a norm of tolerance and sensitivity in the A-School rarely seen in traditional high schools.

In the summer of 2008, the Scarsdale A-School held a 40th reunion for which alumni had collected an e-mail list of hundreds of graduates. Back in 1993, long-time school director Tony Arenella had suggested that Elly consider doing a longitudinal study of A-School graduates that examined the long-term effects of their experiences, and she realized the reunion provided a golden opportunity to collect students' and teachers' retrospective perceptions of the A-School's influence on their lives. A-School social studies teacher Judy Rosen graciously agreed to work on the project and take the lead on interviewing the teachers and we were delighted that

Ann Higgins-D'Alessandro, a key member of Kohlberg's original research group, and her very talented doctoral graduate assistant Jacqueline Horan were also willing to work on this study.

Our first research questions centered on the broad question of student and teacher perceptions of the overall influence of the just community experience on their lives. Our second, more focused question, asked about the specific structures that were most important in promoting moral, academic, and personal development. Did the young adult and middle-aged alumni of the school believe the A-school was, to paraphrase Ann's remarks, "a valued community" that promoted development as they grappled with creating rules and norms? Did they grow up to be self-reflective, active, and engaged citizens?

We constructed a student-alumni survey that relied heavily on open-ended questions and a related set of interview questions for teachers that asked specific questions about the following:

- The immediate and long-term impact of just community structures and experiences;
- Powerful learning experiences in and out of the A-School;
- Current participation in community service and politics; and,
- Perceptions of how the A-School experience changed their thinking about self, the democratic process, and the world and the lasting influence of school climate on how they make decisions or act today.

Many survey respondents spoke eloquently of the A-School's influence on their individual development. Our preliminary data analysis suggested that the implementation of the just community educational philosophy at the Scarsdale A-School resulted not only in meeting the core goals of promoting students' moral development and transforming "the moral atmosphere of the school into a moral community" (Power & Higgins-D'Alessandro, 2008, p. 231), but also continued to influence graduates' conceptions of self, democracy, and the world long after they left the school. We did not assume that the results of one in-depth study of one school could be generalized to all schools, but we did believe that our findings highlighted the possibility of significant moral and character growth when school interventions, rooted in theory, are long enough and strong enough to truly make a difference in students' lives (Horan et al., 2010; Vozzola et al., 2009).

Strengths

Strengths of the cognitive-developmental approach include its respectful attitude towards students and the fact that cognitive advances of any sort often have positive ripple effects on children such as better judgment across a variety of settings. Power and colleagues' (1989) analysis of differences between the moral cultures of democratic high schools and their parent, comparison schools indicated that only students in the just community settings developed norms of caring, trust, collective restitution, and student responsibility to report violators of their drug rules. Higgins (1995) argued persuasively:

> The idea of responsibility for others and a shared sense of being tied together in a common group seem to promote not only individual moral reasoning development but also a strong and high-stage moral culture…results indicate that students expect themselves and others to behave in ways consistent with their best ideas about what is moral when they are in groups they value which have publicly shared prosocial norms. We see a positive moral culture as being a boost to moral behavior and as being a context in which students are challenged to think about their own identity in moral terms. (p. 76)

In his review of Kohlberg's Just Community approach, Althof (2015) noted that while the Just Community approach has continued to some extent in Europe, Taiwan, and several other places, it was never widely adopted or sustained in the United States, with the exception of the Scarsdale A-School. Despite this, the "approach generated a research base that… can be used for future programs" (Althof, 2015, p. 51). Power and Higgin-D'Alessandro (as cited in Althof, p. 51) believe that the research base also "confirms the importance of critical features of the approach such as moral discussion, student participation in decision-making, student connectedness, and community building." While Kohlberg's Just Communities have not been widely adopted, their ideals of democratic schooling are witnessed at the elementary school level through the Child Development Project, now Caring School Communities, a program that originally developed independently from Kohlberg's Just Communities. Althof described how the Just Community approach was translated to European schools and adapted from high school to elementary school settings, called "just and *caring* communities" (p. 81). Similarly, Higgins-D'Alessandro (2015) argued that prosocial interventions and interventions that focus on creating positive school climates incorporate aspects of Kohlberg's moral education ideas and conditions for moral growth, but neglect his "most radical and important educational claims and contributions" (p. 27) including his emphasis on the purposeful focus of education on development and morality.

Challenges

Contrary to the claims of Kohlberg and his colleagues, Damon (1988) saw a significant weakness in the lack of good evidence of links between cognitive developmental interventions and behavior change. Berkowitz et al. (2001) noted that criticisms of the approach also include moral elitism, "gender bias, cultural bias, and having a narrow view of moral psychology (lack of focus on affect, behavior, values, personality, etc.)" (p. 52). Space constraints do not allow for a full analysis of the lively scholarly and research literature behind these criticisms, but we concur with Berkowitz et al.'s appraisal that "each of these accusations has only partial empirical support" (p. 52).

Character Education

Character education was initially perceived in the United States as associated with conservative political and social attitudes (e.g., Wynne & Ryan, 1993) and lacking a strong research and evaluation grounding. The situation has changed radically since the 1990s, as more and more researchers and practitioners with strong cognitive-developmental backgrounds lent their expertise to teacher training and program development and evaluation. Marvin Berkowitz, William Damon, Larry Nucci, Ann Higgins-D'Alessandro, and Clark Power are among the many researchers who have helped schools and organizations to integrate developmental theory into character education programs.

Interviews with Discipline Leaders: Marvin W. Berkowitz, Ph.D., Thomas Jefferson Professor, College of Education, University of Missouri-Saint Louis

Marvin W. Berkowitz, a developmental psychologist, is the inaugural Sanford N. McDonnell Endowed Professor of Character Education and Co-Director of the Center for Character and Citizenship at the University of Missouri-St. Louis. In 2015, Berkowitz presented an invited paper to The Jubilee Centre for Character & Virtues, where he described his scholarly life journey integrating the disciplines of psychology (specifically the moral development of children and adolescents), philosophy, education, and sociology to apply science to real-world schools to facilitate character education-based comprehensive school reform.

(M. Berkowitz, personal communication, March 29, 2013)

As you look back over a very full career as a teacher, scholar, and researcher, what aspect of your work stands out as most personally meaningful? Two things stand out for me as most meaningful for my career, and they serve in a sense as bookends. Early in my career (1977–1979) I was afforded the wonderful opportunity to work on Lawrence Kohlberg's Just Community Schools project in the Harvard Graduate School of Education. Just working with Kohlberg and learning from him alone was sufficient to change the trajectory of my career. But being part of an amazing team, including Ann Higgins and Clark Power, added to the power of this experience. And the on-the-ground experience of radical school democracy allowed me set the bar high for student and staff empowerment for the rest of my career. And it also set the frame for how complex, philosophical, and sociological this work is beyond the educational and psychological dimensions. The second high point has been the opportunity for the past decade and a half to take all I know about child and adolescent development and use it to help schools and educators radically transform what they do to optimally promote both learning and moral (character) development. Seeing these school leaders experience pedagogical epiphanies and then lead their schools to wonderful journeys of success is the capstone of my career.

What distinguishes **character education** from other approaches? As with moral education, we are talking about a broad tent under which you will see numerous philosophies and approaches. The meaning of the term varies by time, place, and ideology. Berkowitz (2002) argues persuasively that we need to move beyond theory disagreements and begin using our research to help students become good people. He chooses to use character education as the umbrella term for all efforts to promote moral and character development, including youth development programs that facilitate children and adolescents' deliberate ethical engagement through program culture, relationships, and activities (Larsen et al., 2020). Although we prefer to use **moral education** as the broad umbrella term, we whole-heartedly concur with his call for sharing knowledge and best practice in the service of children's development, no matter the theoretical orientation. In this section, we use the definitions Berkowitz and Bier (2006) use in their influential evaluation of character education practices: "**Character education** targets a particular subset of child development, which we call character. **Character** is the composite of those psychological traits that impact the child's capacity and tendency to be socially and personally responsible, ethical, and self managed" (p. 4). Controversy over the definition of character education continues to this day and more recently Berkowitz and colleagues (2017) extended the definition to read: "the intentional attempt in schools to foster the development of students' psychological characteristics that motivate and enable them to act in ethical, democratic, and socially effective and productive ways" and the definition of character as "the set of psychological characteristics that motivate and enable one to function as a moral agent, to perform optimally, to effectively pursue knowledge and intellectual flourishing, and to be an effective member of society" (p. 34). Traditional character educators, with roots in Aristotelian virtue theory, tend to focus efforts on the cultivation of virtues and early habit formation. Educators coming from the rationalist tradition put more emphasis on individual moral reasoning and justifying moral actions on the basis of the principles of justice. A third approach puts more weight on the role emotions play in moral decisions and actions (Nucci & Narvaez, 2008). While acknowledging the breadth of approaches that make up character education, we can pull out some underlying principles that characterize the most effective practices (Berkowitz & Bier, 2014; Berkowitz et al., 2017, 2020). Not surprisingly, character education works best when it is well designed and implemented. Given the broad range of practices, it is also not surprising that the outcomes vary across programs. Yet Berkowitz et al. (2017) identified six common principles, the PRIMED Model, that can be used to guide program development (p. 38). These include

- **Prioritization**—School-wide embracement and commitment to character and social emotional development.
- **Relationships**—Intentional focus on fostering nurturing relationships among members of the school community, as well as a commitment to involving families and communities.
- **Intrinsic Motivation**—Promotion of prosocial identity and ownership of values.
- **Empowerment**—Promotion of opportunities for autonomy and decision-making for members of the school.
- **Modeling**—Provision of role models and mentors.
- **Developmental Pedagogy**—Schools intentionally foster growth in character, using developmentally appropriate methods (Berkowitz et al., 2017; see also Berkowitz & Bier, 2014).

Students particularly interested in character education will appreciate Berkowitz's (2021) latest book *PRIMED for Character Education: Six Design Principles for School Improvement,* where he provides an in-depth discussion of and implementation strategies for each PRIMED principle, as well as other resources (books, videos, web-sites) to pursue to learn more about specific design principles.

Strengths and Challenges

Many of the character education resources education students find most valuable provide concrete examples of goals and objectives, lesson plans, and classroom activities. Such materials abound and range from the free exchange of ideas on the Internet among teachers, to online materials provided by character education organizations, to research-based programs developed by seasoned professionals and researchers, to workbooks and materials offered by for-profit companies. In short, one strength of the movement has been the profusion of resources available to school systems and teachers interested in developing student character. However, quality varies widely and not all the materials or lessons have either sound theoretical and research grounding or any proven effectiveness. A related problem can occur when well-intentioned systems or individuals attempt to implement character education programs without proper professional development for school staff. Students notice gaps between the words and actions of adults and if the hidden curriculum of actual school policies and interactions conflicts with the noble words of a character education program, the outcome is more likely to be the development of cynicism than the development of character. The proliferation of programs has also outpaced the need to adapt programs to various cultural contexts (e.g., inner cities, indigenous populations) or unique populations (e.g., students with developmental disabilities), and to determine which programs work best for which students, under which circumstances.

Domain Approach

Larry Nucci (2001, 2009; Nucci & Powers, 2014) has led efforts to translate the social cognitive domain theory of moral development you read about in Chapter 4 into research-based educational applications. Recall that social cognitive domain theory posits that from a very young age, people make distinctions between issues of morality (involving harm or unfair treatment) and social conventions (based on social norms). Researchers also found that people used a third distinction for issues of privacy or personal choice. Interestingly, they have also found that reasoning about moral situations involving harm or helping often follows a U-shaped rather than linear pattern, with a low point occurring during the middle school years. Clearly, such findings have important implications for school settings. Nucci and Powers (2014) see domain theory educational applications as situated within the tradition of developmental and constructivist approaches. What they add to these approaches, however, is "a set of analytical tools for identifying moral and non-moral aspects of educational experiences along with domain appropriate teacher strategies for fostering moral and social development" (p. 127). Those of you going on for teacher certification will want to explore the many examples of lesson plans with specific goals and procedures laid out by Nucci (2009) in the text listed in the Additional Resources section at the end of this chapter. For our purposes in this section, we focus on the general assumptions guiding the domain approach.

First, this approach assumes that **social climates** of classrooms and teachers' and administrators' **behavior management policies** provide core sources for children and adolescents' social development (Nucci, 2009; Nucci & Powers, 2014). The domain approach would thus begin by establishing a caring school classroom environment (Noddings, 2002) in which students know they can take the risk to be emotionally vulnerable and engage in caring acts towards others.

Second, domain approaches stress the importance of making **domain-appropriate responses to student transgressions** (Nucci, 2009; Nucci & Powers, 2014; Turiel, 1983). Students evaluate most highly those teacher responses that are appropriate to the domain of the misbehavior (Nucci, 2001). Research suggests that most school misconduct comes through violations of conventions rather than morality. For example, we all understand that it is a moral issue (preventing harm) to forbid weapons in schools. Yet many current zero-tolerance policies impose the same strict penalties (expulsion or suspension) on a student who inadvertently leaves a penknife in a knapsack that they would on a student bringing an Uzi! Such a domain-inappropriate response does not lead adolescents to respect either rules or the adults who enforce them.

Third, educators need to understand developmental shifts in conceptions of social conventions (Nucci & Powers, 2014). The highest rates of violations of school norms/conventions occur at approximately ages 8–10 and 11–13. These are ages in which children and young teens redraw their boundaries between social conventions and issues they see as private and personal. Things get even messier when children are negotiating not only developmental but also cultural differences between how they see things and how the adults around them see things.

Nucci and Powers (2014) note that in the **just community** approaches we examined earlier in this chapter, even moral transgressions such as stealing can be used as teachable moments in which adults engage students in honest moral discussions about the consequences of moral misdeeds. Having watched students in community meetings engage in frank discussions of the harm done to teachers and classmates when students arrive late to class, Elly can testify to the effectiveness of nudging students to consider the moral implications of actions they may have previously seen as merely conventional. When students in traditional school settings get a perfunctory detention for lateness, they often see rules as petty conventions imposed on them by authorities. In contrast, when a young person is called out by a peer for being disrespectful to a dedicated teacher, light bulbs sometimes go on.

Finally, domain approaches stress the importance of using the academic curriculum in domain-appropriate ways. All too often, adults assume that young people are taking away an intended moral message from a text or video. In reality, students' understanding is filtered through their intellectual, moral, and social developmental levels (see e.g., Narvaez, 2001). Yet when the focus of classroom readings and discussions matches with the domain of the issue under consideration, the curriculum can make a significant impact on social and emotional learning. One of the strengths of using a domain approach is that teachers can help students see how domains so often overlap in the real world. For example, think about the headscarf discussion in the global chapter. At one level, students could examine and discuss two competing moral visions—the religious duty to obey an interpretation of a sacred text versus a citizen's obligation to respect France's endorsed value of equality. At another level, students can consider whether the wearing of headscarves is indeed a social convention that can and should be changed by legislation if it proves disruptive, a moral obligation that should be respected, or even a matter of personal choice that should be up to students themselves.

Let's consider another dilemma of the day in light of a domain approach.

Dilemma of the Day: Athletes, Alcohol, and the Big Game

Any of you who played high school sports are probably familiar with the pledge high school athletes and their parents sign, in which they agree not only to forgo using alcohol and drugs themselves, but also not to be in the presence of alcoholic beverages or illegal drugs. Several years ago, five starters from a religious high school's boys' basketball team were benched for a semifinal tournament game and had to sit and watch as a squad made up primarily of junior varsity players struggled valiantly but eventually lost that important game. The five starters had attended a weekend party where alcohol was served and when the principal found out, he suspended all of them from the team for violating the school's athletic code. Here's your dilemma:

1. Identify how the five players, the coach, the parents, and the principal probably conceptualized the domains of (a) signing the pledge and (b) drinking.
2. What might be a domain-appropriate response to these specific student transgressions?
3. Using a pair/share and/or an open-class discussion: How well did athletic pledge policies work at your high school? Do you think school policies should be revised to better reflect developmental research or is it important to send a strong message (domain appropriate or not) about using drugs and alcohol?

Strengths and Challenges

We find the domain approach to be especially valuable for giving teachers and administrators a better perspective on student resistance to many school rules. Understanding the three domains and developmental changes in their use opens up the possibility of providing "nudges" to growth rather than simply becoming frustrated at dealing with the steady stream of student transgressions that can drain the souls of dedicated educators. The major challenge we see is that given the frequent overlaps in domains and cultural, individual, and age-related changes in domain use, it is not such an easy thing to assess and respond in domain-appropriate ways. However, we believe that anyone willing to take the time to explore this approach in more detail will find a real value in integrating knowledge about social domains into their teaching practice.

Integrative Ethical Education

Darcia Narvaez is another leading scholar-practitioner who has brought her cognitive developmental expertise to the development, implementation, and evaluation of moral and character education programs. Let's take a look at her innovative hybrid program in some detail to give you a flavor of a promising theoretically based and research-evaluated moral education model. Several years ago, the Community Voices and Character Education Partnership Project paired a team of researchers from the University of Minnesota with the Minnesota Department of Children, Families and Learning to develop a character education program for middle school students. Narvaez and her colleagues used an ethical expertise model to design and pilot a series of four activity booklets now available commercially to interested educators (Narvaez et al., 2009). After a brief overview of the model's assumptions and research base, we'll give you a description of the four booklets and a sampling of the activities they provide.

Integrative ethical education proposes to "reconcile the insights of traditional character education and rational moral education with current research" (Narvaez, 2006, p. 716). Rest's Four Component Model of morality provided the theoretical foundation for the program and the foundational concept of moral expertise guided the development of specific content. The term **expertise** "refers to a refined, deep understanding that is evident in practice and action" (p. 716). Psychological research has found that experts differ from novices in having more and better organized knowledge about an area, noticing more details about the area, and being able to solve problems in automatic and effortless ways (Narvaez, 2006). Think, for example, about how much effort it took you to start up and drive a car when you were a new driver compared with the way you sometimes arrive at your destination today, with little consciousness at all of the many driving maneuvers and decisions that got you there. Once the research team had identified moral expertise in the four components of morality as the goal of character education, operational definitions of the components guided the development of curricular materials.

Ethical Sensitivity

The first activity booklet (Endicott, 2001) defined ethical sensitivity as "the empathic interpretation of a situation in determining who is involved, what actions to take, and what possible reasons and outcomes might ensure" (p. 5). The academic and social skills identified as contributing to such sensitivity included reading and expressing emotion, taking the perspective of others, caring by connecting to others, and identifying the consequences of actions and options. Although, of course, the researchers had realistic expectations for developmentally appropriate levels of expertise in this component, they could use the endpoint of development as an anchor for their thinking. Mature experts in moral sensitivity are able to quickly and accurately "read a moral situation" and determine "what role they might play" (Narvaez, 2006, p. 716). They are able to put themselves into the shoes of others and control their personal biases so that they can be morally responsive to the needs of others.

Here is an example of a sample activity for middle school students aimed at helping to create a climate that promotes the reading and expressing of emotional skills. The activity asks students to "discuss discussing" (Endicott, 2001, p. 18). They are first asked to write down two things that their peers do during class discussions that make them feel good and two things that make them feel bad. After sharing their ideas in small groups, the class comes together for two "circle whips" in which each student first contributes one positive discussion behavior and then, in the second round, one negative behavior. The students take notes and end by choosing something they want to improve.

Ethical Judgment

The second activity booklet in the series (Bock, 2001) begins with a definition of ethical judgment as involving "reasoning about the possible actions in the situation and judging which action is most ethical" (p. 5). The skills targeted in the booklet include developing both general and ethical reasoning skills, identifying judgment criteria, reflecting on the reasoning process and outcome, and planning implementation. Mature experts in this component have multiple tools for solving even the most complex of moral problems and can reason about abstract concepts such as duty, responsibility, and ethical codes (Narvaez, 2006).

To help students develop skills in implementing ethical decisions, the booklet provides a series of activities from the level of immersing in examples to integrating knowledge and procedures. In intermediate-level activities, students are guided to attend to facts and skills so that they become familiar with prototypical situations and build their knowledge base. Bock (2001) suggests that students might be encouraged to interview an adult who works in a setting such as social services, where he or she must make ethical decisions. Students would be asked to take notes on the kinds of moral decisions the professional makes, what planning is done, and which decisions are the most difficult and report back to the class.

Ethical Motivation

In the series' third volume, Lies and Narvaez (2001) define ethical motivation as "prioritizing ethical action over other goals and needs" (p. 5). Accordingly, in their booklet, they developed activities to foster the ethical skills of respecting and helping others, cooperating, acting responsibly, and developing a conscience. Experts in ethical motivation, later renamed **ethical focus** (Narvaez, 2006), "cultivate ethical self regulation that leads them to prioritize ethical goals" (p. 716).

In each workbook, teachers are reminded that the components build upon each other. For example, in order to help others, students must have developed skills at caring for others (ethical motivation) as well as taking the perspective of others and identifying needs (ethical focus skills). As an advanced activity for developing helping skills, Lies and Narvaez suggest that a class might decide to adopt a child in need from another country. Students would have to figure out the cost and agree that they are willing to bring in or raise the money. Once the decision is made, they can write letters to their child.

Ethical Action

The final activity booklet focuses on the central component for most character education programs—actual moral behavior. Narvaez et al. (2001) define ethical action as having the knowledge to implement action and "following through despite obstacles and difficulties" (p. 5). Skills needed for this component include perseverance, courage, communication, and working hard. At the mature expert level, individuals know how to "stay on task and take the necessary steps to get the ethical job done" (Narvaez, 2006, p. 716).

Developing ethical skills in this final component can be particularly challenging for middle school students, many of whom are transitioning into adolescence and are much too insecure to step up with the kind of moral courage required to face obstacles and challenges, especially in peer interactions. Yet it is important to introduce them to skills for resolving the inevitable conflicts and problems of early adolescence. A simple but effective activity (much beloved by teachers and students alike) involves watching a film to generate a class discussion. In the fourth activity booklet, Narvaez et al. (2001) suggest watching a film on interpersonal conflict, discussing the perspectives of each party, and assessing whether the outcome was successful. Students are then asked to write an alternative outcome.

Using Films for Moral Discussions—For Which Child? Under Which Circumstances?

One practical problem for teachers is that many of the finest films depicting aspects of character strengths or significant moral dilemmas may have an R rating and thus be prohibited by school policies for classroom use. Luckily, technologically savvy teachers can often use YouTube or other sites to pull up short clips with PG segments. For example, as Elly was thinking about good films for discussion she remembered *My Bodyguard* (Bill, 1980) and easily found the iconic "ass-kicking" scene where the scrawny protagonist and his bodyguard take down the bully who had been tormenting them. Watching it again reminded us of the importance of knowing "for which child, under which circumstances?" While the scene might have great potential for generating a discussion about bullying and revenge among mature students, we suspect it would only add fuel to the fire of the "eye for an eye" Stage 2 moral reasoning of many middle school students. Two other films with much potential for moral discussions are

(Re: moral courage): *Hotel Rwanda* (George, 2005)

(Re: perseverance and justice): *Just Mercy* (Cretton, 2019)

Strengths and Challenges

Integrative ethical education is grounded in clear and well-supported theoretical and research roots. The program was designed and implemented with extensive feedback from practicing teachers and carefully evaluated by a top-flight group of researchers. Teachers have a multitude of activities from which to choose as they integrate ethical skills components into the academic curriculum. This hybrid model advocates teaching both moral virtue and moral reasoning, and that is surely the common-sense consensus emerging in the field today. Effective character education should not be a forced choice between nurturing character traits or moral reasoning. "Smart and good" schools (Berkowitz & Bier, 2006; Lickona & Davidson, 2005) use multiple methods to achieve a broad range of goals; integrative ethical education provides a concrete example of effective methods and clear goals for the middle school (10–13-year-old) level.

The challenge for this model is that more simplistic, atheoretical packages and programs developed by commercial firms have the ability to market their products to teachers and school systems in ways researchers cannot.

Principals and teachers are much more likely to get a shiny brochure selling a commercial program than they are to hear about the integrated ethical education model. Here is where organizations such as the Character Education Partnership and the Collaborative for Academic, Social, & Emotional Learning (listed in the Additional Resources section) come in. By exploring these websites and attending conferences they sponsor, practitioners can educate themselves about best practices that are grounded in sound theory and research.

Morality (and Lack Thereof) in the Media

Kohlberg was fond of stressing how students are always acutely aware of the **hidden curriculum** of their school that is manifested in how the adults and students treat each other. Those interactions send powerful messages about morality such as whether rules apply impartially to all, whether adults respect students and each other, and which values or virtues get rewarded and which do not. If the football team gets a lot more praise and attention than the chess club does, that is noted. If students are expected to talk respectfully to teachers but some teachers yell at or embarrass students, that is noted.

Today young people are picking up moral messages not only from school settings but also from a second hidden "curriculum" of messages arising from their immersion in a complex and easily accessible world of video games, text-messaging, Twitter, Facebook, Instagram, TikTok, YouTube, streaming movie sites and, more disturbingly, pornography sites and the Dark Web. In a major study conducted prior to the 2020–2021 pandemic shutdowns pushing students to even more reliance on their screens, the Common Sense Media Census found that 8–12-year-old US children were spending 4.4 hours a day on non-school screen time and 13–18 year olds were spending 7.22 (Rideout & Robb, 2019). In an example of the rapidly changing norms of media use, 69% of U.S. 12-year-olds in 2019 had their own cell phones—up from 41% in 2015.

A year later, a nationally representative group of 804 young people from 13 to 18 surveyed about sources that influenced them found that YouTube and Instagram were becoming preferred news sources for this age group (Robb, 2020). In 2020, 77% reported obtaining news and headlines from social media sources and 28% gave their preferred news source as influencers or personalities such as PewDiePie, Trevor Noah, Beyoncé and Donald Trump. Although they may have gotten their news from these sources, participants did not necessarily see them as trustworthy; with 55% claiming to be able to evaluate fake news. (We can only hope!)

As with the knowledge we get from fMRI scans, we know more about the gross "whats" of young people's media use than the "hows" of that usage—or the "whys.' And of course, the whats, hows and whys become even more complex and convoluted when we consider the kind of multi-tasking so common today—texting on a phone while watching a TikTok video on a tablet with TV or music playing in the background. Since a comprehensive analysis of morality in the media would be a book-length project, our brief remarks simply introduce you to several useful theories and give you some examples of how we applied those theories to our own research. We'll also discuss a recent survey of research into gaming and morality before offering our reflections about the impact of media's moral messages.

As described in more detail in Garmon et al. (2018), numerous theories attempt to explain interactions between media content and people's attitudes, behaviors, and perceptions. One of the best known is social learning theory (Bandura et al., 1961) which describes how observers imitate the behaviors that real life or media characters model. Most theories assume that the media drives the effect on people using it (e.g., Coyne et al., 2013). Accordingly, a good deal of research in the area tends to focus on correlations between exposure to content (such as violent or misogynistic music or video games) and consumers' attitudes, behavior and/or thoughts (e.g., Krcmar & Cingel, 2020). While certainly social learning theory explains some instances of the influence of media, we find the **Uses and Gratification Approach** (Rubin, 1994) even more helpful for understanding how media sends moral messages to young people. This theory asserts that individuals should be viewed as **active participants in the consumption of media.** In this approach, individual differences are presumed to influence individuals as they make different choices about the type and amount of media they will consume. The approach "emphasizes the role of social and psychological factors in mediating (and mitigating) individuals' media consumption" (Arnett, 1995, pp. 520) because they "have specific needs and they gravitate toward the media to fulfill and satiate these needs" (Coyne et al., 2013, p. 127).

In a similar vein, Jane Brown and colleagues (Brown et al., 2002) developed another active model of media consumption, the **Media Practice Model,** which proposes that adolescents' identities influence the media sources to which they attend (e.g., MSNBC or Fox News, Twitter or *The New York Times*, Rachel Maddow or PewDiePie). Brown sees individuals very actively evaluating and interpreting specific media offerings. Sometimes they incorporate media messages into their identities and sometimes they resist them. It may be useful to think of the Uses and Gratification Approach as explaining an initial choice involving exposure to some media content and the Media Practice Model as explaining not only how identities shape those choices, but also how the choices may further hone identities.

Building on the Uses and Gratification approach, Arnett (1995) offered five self-socialization uses which might motivate adolescent media consumption. Coyne et al. (2013) believe the uses are also relevant to emerging adults (18–29 years of age).

- *Entertainment* is use of media as "simply… an enjoyable part of their leisure lives" (p. 521).
- *Identity Formation* involves using media to cultivate "a conception of one's values, abilities, and hopes for the future" (p. 522).
- *Sensation Seeking* is often highest during adolescence and involves using media for "intense and novel stimulation" (p. 523).
- *Coping* involves using media "to relieve and dispel negative emotions" (p. 523).
- *Cultural Identification* involves using media to provide "a sense of being connected to a larger peer network, which is united by certain youth-specific values and interests and provides common ground" (p. 524).

Our own research began with a "How" question about the wildly popular *Harry Potter* series of books and films. While young people were simply enjoying them, teachers and librarians tended to see the books and films as promoting positive virtues and offering opportunities for moral reflection and discussion. In stark contrast, some religious groups were deeply worried about possible messages of sorcery that are explicitly forbidden by a literal reading of the Christian *Bible*. The books were banned and challenged in many locations with the stated fear that they were leading children to the occult and rule-breaking. Our core research question in a series of studies was simply—What moral messages are children and adolescents **actually** taking away from the books and films (Whitney et al., 2005)? Using a measure based on Rest's Four Component Model (FCM) we queried participants from elementary schools to doctoral students at an Ivy League college about their perceptions of the moral messages in the series and the moral sensitivity, judgment, motivation and character of Harry Potter, his friend Hermione and the morally ambiguous Potions Master Snape. Our findings showed that children were definitely not being led to Satan and the occult but rather seeing themes of friendship and courage. They did see that Harry broke rules but understood that he did so to save lives. All ages perceived Hermione as the most moral character along FCM components but, as expected, younger readers were captured by the mean teacher archetype of Snape while older, more educated readers perceived his complexity.

Building on this work, we (Senland & Vozzola, 2007) recruited families with children ages 9–18 from three liberal Protestant churches and a biblical church for a study in which the adults took a scriptural literalism scale, noted whether or not they allowed their children to read the Potter books or see the films, and provided open-ended responses to a key biblical passage. Children who had read one or more of the books completed the same FCM-based scale as in the original studies. Both parents and children were presented with passages from the *Harry Potter* books in which the headmaster Dumbledore allowed rule breaking and were asked why they thought he did so, if it was fair to others, and whether they either admired or looked down on him for doing so. We were intrigued to see that when interpreting Deuteronomy 18:10–11 ("Let no one be found among you... who practices divination or sorcery, interprets omens, engages in witchcraft, or casts spells, or who is a medium or spirits or who consults the dead.") many Biblical parents took the prohibition literally and did not allow their children to read the books. Liberal parents and biblical parents with higher scores on the scriptural literalism scale tended to see the prohibition as against actual sorcery—not sorcery in fantasy works. Both biblical and liberal children identified courage and friendship as major themes and understood that Dumbledore allowed rule breaking for a higher good. However, although biblical children valued the result of saving a life, they were more likely to question the rule breaking as a means to that end. In short, not only did age (generally associated with the complexity of moral reasoning) filter perceptions of the Potter narrative, so also did the lens of religious beliefs—especially the weight given to taking a literal interpretation of holy texts.

The *Harry Potter* studies and subsequent studies exploring the *Potter, Twilight* and *Hunger Games* franchises (Garmon et al., 2018) and media's moral messages in television programming (Glover et al., 2011) took place in an era where we focused on print and film media and presupposed much common consumption among children, teens and emerging adults. Today, research is moving on to look at screen time in general with special concerns about social media bullying, sexting and a continuation of long-term research into violent video game use. For example, Graver and Blumberg (2020) examined the moral choices inherent in digital game play. As they note, research is still relatively new on the real-world ramifications of online game decisions to cheat or commit violent acts in order to win. Although gaming is popular across the lifespan, research has most commonly been conducted using only undergraduate participants. Graver and Blumberg's survey of this developing area of study concludes that the focus has remained largely on decisions to commit violent transgressions. Some studies use Haidt's Moral Foundations Theory (MFT) as a theoretical base, but rarely explore beyond the care/harm dimension. The authors would like to see research exploring developmental differences in moral choices during play as well as ways to identify "gaming behaviors that demonstrate congruence between decisions and moral actions" (p. 720).

What we take away from research on media's influence on morality (and lack thereof) is that once again we are led to our developmental credo of always asking; For which child? Under which circumstances? Most teens will play first-person shooter games without becoming violent in the real world. Many listen to music with decidedly non-prosocial messages. But for some young people, the perfect storm of immersion in misogynistic music, violent video games and racist web sites can, and tragically sometimes has, led to real world atrocities including school shootings, gay bashing and rape. Identifying and intervening with these youth will require school settings in which caring adults have relationships not only with the "bright pennies" in their classrooms (as Marv Berkowitz often notes) but also with the "tarnished ones"—those youths harder to like—and to reach.

We expect that many studies are going to emerge that look at the impact of both high screen time usage during the global pandemic and a world of frightening and often inaccurate news dissemination that shows little sign of abating. For example, both Facebook and Google have algorithms that know your previous history of "likes" and site visits and select links for you that reinforce your preferences. Thus, a student who has been following the conspiracy theories of Q-Anon and types "climate change is" into a Google search may get a list of sites purporting to show it is a hoax. Another student, one who has been researching credible sites, may get information that suggests it is the most pressing issue of our time. Many schools have explicit guidelines discouraging or even prohibiting the discussion of politics, especially political discussions that seem to favor one political party or candidate and disparage another. But how can we develop moral citizens who have not engaged with and thought deeply about the justice of political policies and the characters of the leaders of their countries? Real and hypothetical dilemma discussions in both classrooms and homes offer a powerful tool for exposing young people to multiple perspectives and levels of moral reasoning. For example, asking students to do some fast online research about Q-Anon's almost laughably unrealistic theories of Democrat child slavery and sacrifice rings or Facebook's and Google's algorithms keeping them in their own bubbles can put the responsibility for using this knowledge on the young people themselves. "Now that you know this, what *should* you *do*? What do you think you *will do*? In an ideal world, what would you hope most people *would do*?" One-minute writes followed by pair/shares or go-arounds at minimum give the knowledge away. At best, they nudge youth to an awareness of the moral choices they make in their consumption of media.

We believe one of the most important jobs for moral educators and parents will be to help children of all ages understand how curated their media sources are and the importance of seeking out multiple perspectives and credible sources. As we attempt to study media's influence on morality, the Four Component Model helps us understand that moral messages are filtered through levels of moral and empathic development. The Uses and Gratification and Media Practice Model remind us that youth are not passive consumers of media but come to it with particular identities, personalities and cultural/religious value systems that determine whether they accept or reject underlying messages. But adults have to give young people effective tools to make those decisions and become better aware of media attempts to influence them with false and or hateful content. Learning the habit of regularly asking the four critical thinking questions about news and opinions could go a long way towards shaping better citizens. (Who's speaking? Who's the audience? What's put in? What's left out?)

Equally important, we need to help young people understand a second key developmental credo: **We become what we do**. Yet policing media choices has become near impossible, especially as teens' technology skills and work arounds far outpace those of parents and teachers. We will be most effective in addressing the second "hidden curriculum" when we guide students to an understanding of the messages they are getting from media and their power to use media experiences for uses "ranging from" sheer entertainment and sensation seeking to "shaping a mature moral identity". Assignments and conversations that allow students to reflect on what media they are consuming **and why** open the door to making wiser, more informed choices.

New Directions

Theory and research provide us with powerful tools for practice. Yet the field of educational practice can sometimes seem to drift from one "flavor of the month" to another as the political and cultural winds shift. In the United States (and many other Western countries), the social change movements of the 1960s encouraged innovation and freethinking (for both good and ill) in classrooms as well as the wider culture. The more conservative 1980s and 1990s brought us a back to basics "adults know best" focus on rules and good behavior. More recently, the turn of the century corporate focus on "value added" results brought in an era of high-stakes testing that often pushed out time for the arts, humanities, and social-emotional learning programs.

One of our central goals in writing this text was to introduce not only education students, but also all of you who are or who will be parents to see that few initiatives are more important for any society than to raise good children. We know that in our media-saturated culture schools and parents are not the only source of students' moral messages. However, good moral education programs can help students evaluate these multiple messages and develop the critical thinking and ethical skills necessary to rise above the often-shallow and material perspectives dominating popular culture. You may have noticed that we gave a great deal more space to the section on just community schools than to other perspectives. There is a reason for that. Many of us who work in the fields of moral development and moral education have come to see the just community model as perhaps the best and strongest intervention for promoting social-emotional and moral development. It is not an easy model—it takes enormous amounts of time, energy, passion, and commitment to get it right—but when we do get it right, we transform young people's lives.

What we learned from the reflections of students who had attended the Scarsdale A-School (Horan et al., 2010; Vozzola et al., 2009), some of them four decades ago, was that long enough and strong enough moral education programs play a powerful role in shaping caring, just, and effective democratic citizens. "We become what we do," states the developmental credo, and the graduates who responded to our survey reported that they became better and more engaged citizens through participating in direct democracy, better listeners though listening to multiple perspectives, better people through participating in service, and better thinkers through the constant challenges of the values-infused curriculum. Currently, the United States is spending enormous amounts of time, money, and effort on high-stakes testing. If we really want to help our children be both smart *and* good, perhaps the time has come to move in a new direction that uses best practice social-emotional and moral education programs like just communities to develop the kind of character traits and reasoning skills that we know are essential for both academic and life success.

Discussion Questions

1. In 2012, a 17-year-old student at Wolcott High School in Connecticut (USA), to protest his opposition to gay marriage, showed up at the school's Day of Silence (an event designed to acknowledge the silencing, abuse, and bullying faced by gay, lesbian, and transgender youth) wearing a homemade t-shirt of a rainbow with a slash through it (the classic "No" icon). Interestingly, in this case, courts upheld his right to do so on the rationale that he had a right to free speech on the issue. If you were the principal of this high school, how would you plan for and structure the upcoming Day of Silence in which this student and 19 of his friends announced that they intended to attend wearing their "no gay marriage" shirts?
2. You can easily find the Supreme Court ruling and rationale in the Bong Hits 4 Jesus case through a simple Google search. How do you think teachers and administrators at a just community school would have handled the situation?

Additional Resources

Following are texts and websites that students going into the field of education have found particularly useful, as well as an outstanding handbook with contributions from many of the major figures in moral education.

- Practice-Oriented Resources:
  - Character Education Partnership (CEP). www.character.org/ The Partnership's mission states that it provides vision, leadership, and resources for schools, families, and communities to develop ethical citizens. This extensive and easily navigated website should be the first stop for teachers and school systems to consider when implementing a character education program.

- Center for Character and Citizenship. https://characterand citizenship.org/ This newly updated and growing website gives numerous links and resources for educational practitioners.
- Collaborative for Academic, Social, & Emotional Learning (CASEL). www.casel.org. You will find a treasure trove of information and resources at the site of this respected organization. Early childhood education students and practitioners will find a rich source of classroom ideas in

  - DeVries, R., & Zan, B. (1994). *Moral classrooms, moral children: Creating a constructivist atmosphere in early education.* Teachers College Press.

- Another excellent resource that offers concrete examples of best practice activities for both elementary and high school classrooms is

  - Lickona, T. (2004). *Character matters: How to help our children develop good judgment, integrity, and other essential virtues.* Touchstone Books.

- If you'd like to see how to promote moral development using the domain approach, you'll enjoy

  - Nucci, L. (2009). *Nice is not enough: Facilitating moral development.* Pearson.

- Education students and practitioners will appreciate Berkowitz's latest book (2021), which offers a rich source of classroom ideas for implementing the PRIMED Model of character education

  - Berkowitz, M. W. (2021). *PRIMED for character education: Six design principles for school improvement.* Routledge.

Research-Oriented Resource

- Nucci, Narvaez, D., & Krettenauer, T. (2014). *The handbook of moral and character education* (2nd ed.). Routledge. Readers interested in a more comprehensive survey of the chapters' topics will find *The Handbook of Moral and Character Education* to be an invaluable compilation of articles reviewing classic and contemporary approaches to moral education both in and out of the classroom. The editors invited many of the major figures in the field to contribute overviews of research and practice in their particular areas of expertise. Not only will you find excellent and current summaries of moral education theories, practice, and evaluations, but also you will be able to use the reference lists at the end of each chapter to conduct literature searches of your own if you should choose to explore specific topics for a paper or presentation. For example, in addition to extensive coverage of the moral education topics discussed in this chapter, the book has chapters on service learning, developing character through sports, and fostering moral and civic development in college students.

10 Developmental Therapy: Helping Clients Grapple with Core Moral Issues

Clearly in such a complex area as how to promote human growth and development, there is an urgent need for more applied research... and for training programs designed to produce a host of professional helpers. Role-taking programs require modification and expansion as a means of achieving the general goals of psychological maturity. The conventional... curriculum for schools, colleges, or professional training programs rarely, if ever, addresses the issues of human relationships and moral judgment.

(Sprinthall, 1994, p. 97)

Given the rise of character education programs in school systems and the centrality of some of the (im)moral behaviors that often bring people into counseling (e.g., abusing drugs or alcohol, infidelity, anger, aggression, acting out, breaking rules/laws), you might expect that helping professionals receive a strong grounding in moral development theory and research. Sadly, the reverse is true. Current accrediting guidelines leave little to no room in most graduate counseling or clinical psychology curricula for much more than a brief summary chapter on moral development in a Human Development course. However, some individual professors and programs have, in the words of legendary counselor educator Norm Sprinthall, "kept a place at the table" by encouraging new generations of counselors and researchers to explore applications of the moral development perspective to emerging practice issues.

As the space constraints of this text preclude a comprehensive survey of moral development and counseling, we limit our focus to several particularly useful applications. This chapter first examines a classic approach to promoting moral growth, Norm Sprinthall's Deliberate Psychological Education (DPE) model (Sprinthall et al., 2001). Next, we survey key ideas of several influential developmental counselors that we assess as still valuable and important to introduce to today's helping professionals. We then present an attempt to pull together the way moral development influences the core issues clients bring to counseling. The chapter ends with some of the newest research on promoting well-being and treating moral injury and

DOI: 10.4324/9780429295461-12

a call to better integrate knowledge about moral development into counseling training and practice.

A Problem is a Finding

In a 1984 article on the implications of moral development research for counseling psychologists, James Rest noted the profusion of relevant research. However, as we looked back over the past 5–10 years of published research and reached out to practicing counselors for input, it became evident that there was a scarcity of recent publications. Counselor educator Rick Halstead's memory of the line from a research methods class that "a problem is a finding" helped guide our own thinking about this chapter's revisions. He offered us the useful observation that the framing of client issues "has evolved (maybe devolved) onto other and various avenues of inquiry as the need for understanding clients' lived experiences as intersectionality has emerged from social influence theory. In other words, it just may be that the connection between moral development and counseling may no longer be linear but just one vector within the counseling relationship. Of course, that is the way it has always been in the real world but the thinking in the 1960s–1980s was necessarily reductionistic as theory was being built" (personal communication, September 28, 2020). Thus, we came to see that "keeping a place at the table" for moral development should involve revisiting some of the folks highlighted in the first edition, updating their work when possible, and then introducing some of the latest counseling/psychotherapy best practice ideas from research on promoting well-being and purpose and on conceptualizing and treating moral injury.

Developmental Counseling

> The heart of the cognitive developmental framework… does not lie so much in its account of stages or sequences of meaning organizations, but in its capacity to illuminate a universal, on-going process (call it "meaning making," "adaptation," equilibration," or "evolution") which may very well be the fundamental context of personality development.
>
> (Kegan, 1982, p. 264)

Robert Kegan's influential concept of an evolving self integrates perspectives from human development with the core meaning-making process so often explored in therapy. His counseling orientation, like that of most of the practitioners described below, rests on two central assumptions: (1) **constructivism** (that humans construct their realities) and (2) **developmentalism** (that we can observe patterns in organisms' evolution or growth across time). Among numerous counseling frameworks centering on meaning making, those with the most influence on counseling practice tended to be the neo-psychoanalytic (e.g., Anna Freud, Erik Erikson) and the existential-phenomenological traditions (e.g., Carl Rogers, Abraham Maslow). Kegan (1982) notes that while psychoanalytic theory now has very little influence in the academy, it continues to guide practice in many hospitals and clinics. In contrast, cognitive developmentalism, with a strong academic research tradition, has had only limited influence on the field of counseling. However, among counselors and counselor educators who have managed to "keep a place at the table" for moral development, research guides practice. Despite differences in emphasis, the sample of practitioners we discuss in the following sections all note the importance of adapting counseling strategies and techniques to provide an optimal level of challenge and support for clients' developmental levels.

Although Kegan (1982) downplays the importance of stages and stresses the larger issue of development in meaning making, others situate their frameworks squarely in major cognitive-developmental stage theories such as Piaget's, Erikson's, Kohlberg's, and Loevinger's (e.g., Hayes, 1991, 1994; Sprinthall et al., 2001). As you read through some of the following specific counseling and prevention strategies, begin thinking about how Piaget's concept of schemas, or generalized knowledge structures, might tie together some of the diverse perspectives. If humans are indeed hardwired to make meaning of their worlds, physical and social, then how can counselors and therapists best help clients whose schemas or meaning-making structures are developmentally inappropriate, maladaptive, or damaged?

Norman Sprinthall

Sprinthall et al. (2001) believe that an extensive body of research supports resting a cognitive-developmental model on three assumptions:

1. Humans construct meaning from their life experience using cognitive processes that develop through structural stages.
2. These cognitive structures develop in a hierarchical, invariant, and sequential way from less to more complex thinking.
3. Stage growth occurs across the life span as individuals interact with their environments and thus is influenced by factors such as culture and ethnicity (p. 112).

For Sprinthall and his colleagues Ralph Moser and Lawrence Kohlberg, these assumptions suggested the possibility of developing primary prevention interventions to promote cognitive-developmental growth (Sprinthall, 1994). After many a false start, Sprinthall and Moser took the then-innovative step of "giving psychology away" to high school students by teaching them basic counseling skills, providing opportunities for significant role-taking experiences, and asking students to reflect on those experiences. Decades of carefully evaluated research with populations including high school students, student teachers, counselors in training, and experienced helping professionals have validated the effectiveness of using role-taking activities as well as traditional individual and group-counseling strategies. The **Deliberate Psychological Education (DPE)** model holds that optimal client growth occurs when counselors design role-taking activities with the following conditions:

Significant role-taking experiences—Clients or students must be put in complex situations that will "nudge" them to think in more complex ways. For example, high school students might interview veterans about their experiences or counselor trainees might be asked to design an optimal developmental discipline program for the school in which they are interning. A depressed client might be encouraged to choose meaningful volunteer work that pushes him or her to attend to the needs of others.

Guided reflection—Journals and or discussion allow the counselor/supervisor to provide developmentally appropriate feedback. Reiman and Thies-Sprinthall's (1998) work on dialogue-based and developmentally-based guided reflection provides specific tips for optimizing this component of DPE. Their research has documented the necessity for journal writing when people are put into complex new roles and thus into a period of disequilibrium. They stress the importance of a warm and trusting relationship between supervisor/counselor and intern/client as well as the need to balance support (an understanding of the person's current developmental stages) and challenge (responses that promote deeper and more complex reflection).

Balance between reflection and experience—A regular (weekly is often ideal) sequence of experience followed by reflection and self-analysis provides for an ongoing examination of the student's or client's adjustment to the new role.

Support and challenge—This developmental credo highlights the insight that new roles throw people into states of disequilibrium as they struggle to meet new demands that may tax their skill levels and coping abilities. Thus, the counselor or supervisor needs to assess individual needs and provide appropriate levels of both support and challenge.

Continuity—In a therapeutic environment often driven by the constraints of managed care and in school systems reeling under many an unfunded mandate, counselors are often pressured to conduct brief therapies or organize one-size-fits-all school assemblies to address serious issues. Yet the common-sense truth, based on more than 50 years of research, is that **development is a process, not an event**. It takes time. Sprinthall and his colleagues have found that cognitive/moral structural changes require continuous, ideally weekly, experiences over a period of 6–12 months (Sprinthall et al., 2001).

Interviews with Discipline Leaders: Norman Sprinthall, Professor Emeritus, Counselor Education, North Carolina State University

In reviewing my 50 plus years of professing, there are three connected themes of significance that stand out: the Kohlberg, Mosher, and Thies-Sprinthall colleagueships. At the outset, as I had become dissatisfied with many of the then-current theories for counseling, I met Larry as he arrived in Cambridge. Somewhat ironically, I was also doing the statistical analysis on Bill Perry's research. This was followed by "discovering" the same themes in Jane Loevinger, David Hunt, Piaget, and a very long et al. Talk about a rich post-doc. I realized that these multifaceted theories overlapped and could liberate applied psychology from behaviorism, the empirical dust bowl, and even humanistic theory. I said at the time I had one foot on the dock of Carl Rogers and one foot in the canoe of cognitive development. Larry shoved the canoe. This colleagueship was long lived and clearly instrumental in my work.

Another fortuitous connection started earlier, in my second year at Harvard meeting the brilliant Ralph Mosher. I soon realized the meaning of a complementary relationship as Ralph drilled into me the meaning of Dewey's conception of learning. I can still hear him in my head and heart saying, "Education cannot remain only from the neck up," and, "we must work in schools and classrooms not in counseling offices" (e.g., in the Little Red School not the Little White Clinic). As a result, we started a long series of try-outs of our best ideas. We attempted to extract a pedagogical theory from practice. We failed many times, "Once more snatching defeat from victory," Ralph would say. Then gradually the success of our role-taking program emerged, the adolescent as a psychologist with peer counseling, cross-age teaching, activities; the five conditions to promote human growth. This also included a long series of research studies documenting [success] through a meta-analysis of outcomes. The dependent variables were from multiple indices of development to make sure our studies were Campbell and Stanley "proof." Deliberate Psychological Education (DPE) was alive and well, as 20 years of publication attested.

The third important event was the expansion of social role-taking to include professional adults. My closest professional (and personal) colleague Lois Thies-Sprinthall took the lead in a teacher mentor program. The pedagogy was parallel with action-reflection vis-à-vis a match and (gentle) mismatch of the developmental levels of experienced teachers; one more application both research and theoretically based with subsequent publications and recognition.

Of course, there are significant barriers today for all such developmental programs such as role taking, dilemma discussions, or broad curriculum changes (school within a school). The obsession with the SAT, the cut back on counselor positions, the reduction in R&D money, the prevalence of pro-forma service learning (experiential education on the cheap), the virtue of the week character education, back to pre–Hartshorne-May. Yet I'd have to say, with apologies to Freida Fromm-Reichman, we didn't exactly live in a Rose Garden either. Our era was filled with racism and sexism, and the relativistic message of values clarification was everywhere. The professional associations APA, ACA (née APGA) were not thrilled with our view of giving psychological counseling away to teenagers. Nor were those in the association who saw us as a threat to their interest in promoting private practice. The education of the whole person, however, is at least as important today as before. So as Harriet Tubman said in a different and ever more difficult context, it is critical not to give up; instead, she said, "Keep going." So, to my present and future colleagues I also say, "Keep going, the torch is now in your hands." Remember my final words: Prevention, Prevention, Prevention.

(N. Sprinthall, personal communication, May 13, 2013)

Richard Hayes

Hayes (1994) argued that Kohlberg's ideas about promoting moral development can and should be applied to counseling interventions. Kohlberg held a deep belief that democracy provided the most effective context for the stimulation of development and thus urged any counselors working with groups to

> consistently demonstrate your belief in the democratic process, a belief which you are trying to instill in the group members. Your authority… will come from your ability to be an objective mediator, from our insistence on fairness and responsibility, from our willingness to stand up for unpopular causes and individuals for the sake of fairness, and from the appropriate recognition you give to moral development in individual community members.
>
> (Kohlberg et al., 1974, p. 111, as cited in Hayes, 1991)

Hayes (1991) believed that the conditions Kohlberg and colleagues outlined for moral change and development offered promising guidelines for counselors. To promote moral development, counselors should attend to

- **Considerations of fairness and morality**—Specifically, clients should be encouraged to consider moral aspects of their presenting concerns by examining the relationship between their reasoning and their actions, and by reflecting on the consequences of acting on prior moral decisions. For example, a counselor might point out the following: "You know, for the past two weeks, you've been talking with me about how much you hate spending so much time in detention and we've talked a bit about what you are thinking when you make decisions to do things like skip class or shoot spitballs. I was wondering why you think places have rules anyways. What do you think?"

- **Exposure to cognitive conflict**—Cognitive developmentalists believe that growth occurs when new information can no longer fit into older ways of thinking. So a goal of counseling is to expose a client to alternative viewpoints that challenge immature or maladaptive thinking patterns. "From what you're telling me, this new buddy of yours Carl is a really cool guy—into the same kind of music you like, has a great sense of humor, and is willing to be there for his friends 24/7. Yet it sounds like he somehow manages to be cool and still follow rules—you said he's never had a detention or suspension. How do you think he thinks about rules? What must he be saying to himself about going to class?"

- **Role-taking opportunities**—"What is maturity but the ability increasingly to take the perspective of others in deciding what is right or fair or good?" (Hayes, 1994, p. 264). Hayes notes that from a Kohlbergian perspective, group counseling may prove to be the best venue for clients whose problems are distinctly social in nature. A well-run group encourages participants to put themselves in other people's shoes as they discuss core issues and begin to see how their own and others' behaviors are perceived by group members.

- **Active participation in decision making**—The very act of participating in the counseling session itself requires the client to provide direction to the treatment. Skilled counselors, even those using activist tactics, always have the goal of helping clients make good decisions for themselves. The classic opening query—"So how have things been going since we last talked?"—allows the client to choose the issues and events that seem most salient at that moment.

- **Exposure to higher levels of thinking**—Taking the strategy of "plus one" statements developed in educational interventions, Hayes suggests that counselors not only clarify a client's arguments (active listening) but also call her or his attention to arguments at a slightly more cognitively complex level. "So I'm hearing you say that in your school, if someone gets up in your face, you pretty much better get up in his face back. I guess I'm wondering what might happen if a guy was to try a different strategy that showed he was a bigger man—that he didn't have time for kid's stuff like playground fighting?"

- **Intellectual stimulation**—If cognitive development and role-taking ability are the necessary but not sufficient conditions for moral development, then counseling techniques such as bibliotherapy, giving information, and counselor self-disclosure can help clients take more complex perspectives as they grapple with life problems.

Hayes was always deeply involved in the training of school counselors and thus much of his later work (e.g., Hayes & Paisley, 2002; Paisley et al., 2010) addressed initiatives to transform school counseling preparation and practice. Just as his suggestions for individual counseling stressed the need to focus on considerations of fairness and morality, his work on counselor training stressed models of preparation that enhance students' commitment to social justice.

Gil Noam

Noam (1988a) has been quite critical of clinicians who apply the hard stage concepts of cognitive or moral development (structural wholeness, sequentiality, and hierarchical integration) to the development of the self. Instead, he offers a developmental perspective that suggests that the most developed or mature aspect of the self may not represent the actual overall self (Hayes, 1994).

Noam finds that psychopathology and other normal, but difficult, struggles of life develop when the most recent developmental stages/advances come in conflict with schemas from an earlier developmental level. The most important implication for counselors "is that clients may be assessed at functioning at a most mature perspective while simultaneously being influenced by processes that reflect more primitive perspectives" (Hayes, 1994, p. 196). Noam calls the more primitive processes **encapsulations,** which are basically less developed schemas that have resisted becoming incorporated into more developed schemas as the person matured. For example, a child whose parents divorced when she was 5 years old was likely to have processed the experience as a concrete thinker at a level of moral development at which children believe that you do the right thing so you don't get punished. When a mom or dad leaves, small children often believe their own bad behavior ("Daddy was angry I didn't listen") caused the parent's departure. Even though the 16-year-old may now know her occasional naughtiness did not cause Dad to run off with his secretary, she may, however, react in current romantic relationships "as if" any imperfections on her part will chase away the current partner. In short, she has constructed a schema, or story, with "themes and attributions about the self and important relationships" (Noam, 1988b, p. 289) that remains an important and influential part of her internal self.

In short, encapsulations remain encoded with the logic (and emotions) of the developmental level of the child at the time they occurred. The role of the therapist, then, is to help clients explore the disparities between the more primitive encapsulations and the clients' current level of meaning making. Counseling helps clients to transform and integrate their encapsulations with their current, more mature developmental structures (Hayes, 1994). "I've come to understand that when my boyfriend acts at all displeased or distant, that triggers old feelings and thoughts about my dad's leaving. I get terrified that he will leave me too and I start acting like a needy 5-year-old—I cry and pout, which makes him even more distant, and me even more scared. I think I need to come up with a way to remind myself that this is now and that was then and he's definitely NOT my dad."

Noam's work with the Clover Model of Development (formally the RALLY program—Responsive Advocacy for Life and Learning in Youth) brings together years of his work on developmental therapy and interventions (Malti & Noam, 2016; Noam & Malti, 2008). This school-based inclusive intervention and prevention model to promote resiliency sees children as neither "at risk" nor invulnerable but rather falling along a tiered continuum. All children need to develop resilience as well as strong academic and interpersonal skills, and these strengths are best developed through positive relationships with adults in classroom settings rather than through pull-out services. Noam's concept of developmental worlds provides an especially useful conceptual framework for educators and counselors. Although you will note vestiges of Kohlberg's theory of moral development underlying Noam's work, Noam and colleagues (Malti & Noam, 2016) acknowledge that the four worlds often coexist within a youth:

1. The **world of actively engaged youth** has strengths of spontaneity and curiosity but egocentric thinking holds the risk of impulsivity and attention problems.
2. As development progresses, in the **world of assertive youth,** adolescents can regulate feelings, act assertively, concentrate on tasks, and resolve conflicting interests between self and others through instrumental exchange. However, a risk at this stage is that some young people use their assertive ability to manipulate or exploit others.
3. As teens move into **the world of belonging,** they develop a Golden Rule based ability to see the world through the perspectives of others. This more mature perspective-taking ability can lead, on the positive side, to altruism, and on the negative side, to social conformity. The deep need to be liked common to this world also leaves young people vulnerable to depression or anxiety should peers ignore or reject them.
4. Finally, in the developmental **world of reflection,** strengths include growing responsibility and thoughtfulness, while risks include feelings of aloneness or perfectionism.

Noam and colleagues (e.g., Malti & Noam, 2016) note that effective enhancement and prevention interventions need to be tailored in developmentally differentiated ways based on observing students' developmental capacities in multiple settings, as well as adapted to specific contexts and cultural settings: "In summary, the developmental perspective suggests that understanding students' development and resiliency is essential for the prevention process because it helps to situate mental health problems in the broader context of resiliency, risk and development" (Noam & Malti, 2008, p. 37).

Dilemma of the Day

Almost every year, our local newspaper reports on a particularly newsworthy senior class prank. Mice and crickets have been let loose in cafeterias, small cars and other large objects have been carried into buildings, and, in Simsbury, Connecticut, firefighters had to rescue four goats from the roof of the local high school. In another Connecticut high school (which shall go nameless to protect the innocent—and the guilty), two enterprising seniors filled 15,000 polystyrene cups with water and placed them in a hallway. That prank did little but slow down entry to part of the school building, but later in the day, students began tossing beach balls around the cafeteria at lunch, which led to tossing food, which led to major food fights and a major mess. Classes were canceled, dozens of students were suspended, some were fined, and the staff spent a day or more cleaning up. Imagine that you had been a counselor at that high school and the principal had turned to you for advice on how to handle the situation. What might a developmental counselor suggest? Why? How about the case of the seniors and the goats? Would your recommendations be different? Why?

Robert Selman

Kohlberg's Harvard colleague Robert Selman focused his early research on children's developing ability to take the perspective of others (**social role taking**) and its relationship to their moral development. He found that

> the child's cognitive stage indicates his level of understanding of physical and logical problems, while his role-taking stage indicates his level of understanding of the nature of social relations, and his moral judgment stage indicates the manner in which he decides how to resolve social conflicts between people with different points of view.
> (Selman, 1976, p. 307)

Selman describes five developmental levels of social perspective taking that children use as they attempt to analyze and understand interpersonal issues:

1. Level 0 (approximately ages 3–5): An egocentric and physicalistic level focused on understanding the child's own perspective. *What do I think/ want/need?*
2. Level 1 (early elementary): The child attempts to understand another's perspective, understands it is different from his or her own. *What might* **you** *think/want/need?*
3. Level 2 (late elementary): Child begins to understand another's view of her or his subjective perspective. *What do* **you** *think/feel about what I think/feel/want/need?*
4. Level 3 (middle school): Young teens begin to figure out what a person might think of the child's group. *What might he or she think about us?*
5. Level 4 (high school): Older teens come to understand their own perspective as being situated in the context of multiple perspectives. The child now comes back to *What do I think/feel/want/need?* at a much more complex and contextual interpersonal level (Adapted from Selman, 2003, p. 21).

Selman's applications of theory to practice range from promoting social awareness in classroom settings (Selman, 2003) to facilitating growth in children's interpersonal relationships through **pair therapy** (Selman & Hickey Schultz, 1990). Specifically, pair therapy uses the insights of developmental theory to help socially inept children learn mutual collaboration.

Therapists interested in exploring pair therapy will find Selman and Hickey Schultz's (1990) book to be an invaluable resource that integrates theoretical foundations, case histories, and concrete practice suggestions. This innovative treatment for children suffering isolation from peers because of either severely aggressive or withdrawn behaviors helps them learn what it means to have and be a friend. The key to developmental growth is a structured set of sessions in which children are paired with each other and have to work out interpersonal issues in the here and now, not some artificial retrospective session of talk therapy. The therapist has the challenging role of creating a safe setting where the children can not only experience positive social interactions but can also work through those situations when unpleasant or negative emotions emerge. The children learn specific strategies for controlling feelings while coming to understand the mutual perspective taking necessary to form and sustain friendships (or any relationships).

Selman harbors no illusions that it is an easy process to put two struggling, sometimes severely troubled children in a session together and expect miracles. However, he believes that however buried or distorted it may be, children have a basic motivation to make connections with others. Thus, the therapist must be prepared to

> set the scene, keep their patience and consistency constant, maintain their confidence in the face of no visible results, and if and when the time arrives that the work and waiting can pay off, their alertness,

sensitivity, and skill should be at the ready to facilitate the children's growth at key moments.

(Selman & Hickey Schultz, 1990, p. 160)

In addition to his clinical practice work, Selman has long been associated with the Facing History and Ourselves project that uses education about events that led to the Holocaust and other genocides to combat bigotry and nurture democracy. Facing History trains middle and high school educators to use their curriculum to "learn to combat prejudice with compassion, indifference with participation, and myth and misinformation with knowledge" (https://www. facinghistory.org/about-us). Selman and Kwok (2010; see also Kwok & Selman, 2017) have reported some very promising work on a measure to evaluate student gains in informed social reflection after participating in such programs. Informed social reflection ideally develops when students are taught to think "critically and reflectively about history, civic issues and ethics— through the pedagogical tools of course work and the teacher's capacity to foster a safe and vibrant classroom climate" (p. 657). The goal, of course, is that after developing the capacity for informed social reflection, students then apply it in school and societal situations and actually make the moral choice to stand up for victims of prejudice, racism, or other forms of social injustice. Any helping professionals interested in valid, developmentally grounded student outcomes measures should find this work of particular interest.

When asked to reflect on which aspect of his career had been most personally meaningful to him Bob's initial response was that it was the decision to work with Lawrence Kohlberg on an NSF grant, as "That's how it all began." He later sent the more extensive reflection below.

Interviews with Discipline Leaders: Robert Selman, Roy Edward Larsen Professor of Education and Human Development, Professor of Psychology, Harvard University

Robert Selman is the founder of the Prevention Science and Practice Program and served as its first director through 1999. At the Harvard Medical School, he is professor of psychology in the Department of Psychiatry, where he serves as senior associate at the Judge Baker Children's Center and at the Department of Psychiatry at Children's Hospital Boston. The following spotlight has been excerpted from Selman's reflection on the impact of his work.

For the past 20 years, I have studied and implemented educational programs that integrate social and academic competencies in kindergarten through high school. Currently, my research and practice partners and I connect practice and research in three active projects, one each at the elementary, the middle, and the high school level. In partnership with the for-profit educational publisher, Highlights for Children, we have developed a literature and writing curriculum at the elementary grade level, "Voices Literature and Writing," that focuses on the integrative development of literacy skills and the awareness of social and psychological themes, e.g., social identity, conflict resolution, social awareness, and civic understanding. At the middle school level, I have partnered with Catherine Snow and the Strategic Education Research Partnership (SERP) to apply our developmental and cultural theory of social perspective coordination—and its measurement—into a social studies and science curriculum for students in schools whose students tend on average to struggle to read comprehensively and deeply in these subject matter areas. At the high school level, I have partnered for 30 years with Facing History and Ourselves, a non-profit organization that works with educators throughout their careers to improve their effectiveness in the classroom, as well as their students' academic performance and civic learning. We have developed and validated measures of the way students understand historical evidence, causality, and agency. We also have studied how the approach promotes the development of the students' "informed social reflection" on their civic and moral choices.

All three of these applied developmental approaches to education serve as contexts for fundamental research that looks at how students understand their social world, make their social, ethical, and civic choices. At the elementary grade level we have studied, and are studying, questions such as how students make sense of social issues such as the history of racism and psychological issues such as self-awareness through their interpretation of grade-appropriate children's literature, for example, *Freedom Summer*, by Deborah Wiles. At the middle school level, we have studied and are studying how students understand their choices when they are put in the position of a witness to the all-too-common events such as bullying, harassment, teasing, and violence in schools, through interviews, surveys, focus groups, and observations. At the high school level, using similar research methods, we are studying how students deal with incidents of racism, sexism, and homophobia in their schools, neighborhoods, and societies.

(R. Selman, personal communication, November 15, 2012)

Robert Enright

After years of careful research, Enright and the Human Development Study Group have operationally defined the concept of forgiveness and mapped out a developmental framework for understanding it (Enright & North, 1998; Enright & Song, 2020). Of particular interest to clinicians, a meta-analysis of counseling and clinical research (Baskin & Enright, 2004) has found that forgiveness is associated with psychological well-being: "Forgiveness is a willingness to abandon one's right to resentment, negative judgment, and indifferent behavior toward one who unjustly injured us, while fostering the undeserved qualities of compassion, generosity, and even love toward him or her" (Enright et al., 1998, p. 47).

People who have been wronged or deeply hurt by another person respond with a variety of strategies ranging from vengeance to repression, but Enright and colleagues have discovered they do not consider forgiveness. In response to findings that people who did forgive evidenced positive outcomes such as decreases in depression and anger and increases in well-being, the Human Development Study Group devised a model to teach people how to forgive (Enright & North, 1998):

1. In the **Uncovering Phase,** counselors can help clients examine their defenses, confront their anger or shame, understand the possible permanent and adverse changes to self caused by the offense, and become aware of how they may have been ruminating on the event.
2. In the **Decision Phase,** the clients are helped to see that strategies they have been trying are not working and begin to consider the option of forgiveness. This phase ends with a commitment to forgive the offender.
3. Now begins the difficult task of the **Work Phase.** Here clients use role-taking strategies to begin to reframe their conception of the offender. Viewing the offender in context ideally triggers some measure of empathy and compassion that eventually allows the client to accept and absorb the pain she or he has been feeling.
4. Finally, in the **Deepening Phase,** clients become aware of decreased negative affect and feel an emotional release. They find meaning in their own suffering and in the forgiveness process.

Enright's colleague North (1998) notes that the process of **reframing** is central to the forgiveness process. She cites the Study Group's definition of reframing as "a process whereby the wrongdoer is viewed in context in an attempt to build up a complete picture of the wrongdoer and his actions." Most commonly, the counselor guides the client to consider the personality and developmental history of the offender in order to understand the particular pressures he or she may have been under at the time of the wrong. Clearly, both counselor and client must keep a delicate balance in acknowledging both the offender's humanity **and** her or his hurtful actions.

Enright and colleagues (Klatt & Enright, 2011) have also studied the process of forgiveness outside the counseling setting, and findings suggest that the aforementioned Forgiveness Process Model accurately describes the sequence of steps people take in natural settings without a counseling intervention.

While study findings supported earlier work on the importance of reframing and empathy, they also suggested the need to teach clients strong communication skills so that they could, if they wish, engage in productive dialogue with their offenders. Such skills include learning how to control emotions such as anxiety and fear, as well as training in assertiveness to assure that clients keep the session focused on their needs rather than the offender's possible desire to blame the victim. Obviously, counselors will need to be sensitive to the fact that "personal contact with offenders may require the presence of a third-party mediator and may not be appropriate in all situations" (p. 39).

Although Enright and colleagues stress the therapeutic value of forgiveness, McNulty and Fincham (2012) offer an important caution about promoting concepts of positive psychology such as forgiveness in a noncontextual way. They challenge the assumption that particular psychological traits are "inherently beneficial for well-being" (p. 101). Their review of several longitudinal studies of marriages found that forgiveness does indeed predict better relationship well-being *in healthy marriages*. However, spousal forgiveness in *troubled marriages* predicts many negative outcomes such as a partner staying in a violent relationship and abuse escalating.

Pamela Paisley

Counselors practice in many settings in which they are responsible not only for individual and group therapy, but also for implementing primary prevention programs, such as character or moral education. Unfortunately, amid the profusion of how-to lists, worksheets, and videos generated by the Character Education movement, there is a scarcity of materials for school counselors coming specifically from the developmental perspective. Paisley and Hubbard's (1994) text on developmental school counseling stands out as a model for blending theory and practice. Elly used her work for many years in a moral development class for prospective school counselors, who highly rated Paisley's clear presentation of developmentally appropriate goals, objectives, and lesson plans. Although we would love to see an updated version of this book for the 21st century classrooms and issues, we briefly discuss the 1994 edition because of its still relevant and valuable perspective.

For example, the chapter on effective problem-solving notes how educators try perennially, with varying degrees of success, to teach children how to make appropriate decisions. Paisley and Hubbard note that all too often, however, adults fail to match the technique to the child's developmental stage. This is particularly ineffective when adults do not notice adolescents' growing higher-level thinking skills and continue to treat them as children who must "Do as I say." Further adding to the challenge, when adults do allow older children and teens to make their own decisions, it can be discouraging to see those decisions swayed (and often not in a positive way!) by peer pressure. Paisley and Hubbard suggest that an understanding of developmental stages holds the key for counseling interventions and programs that consider the developmental needs of young people growing in their ability to make complex decisions. For developmentalists, such progress is always a process, rather than an event.

Their text offers exercises such as dilemma discussions that "go with development." In contrast to younger students, adolescents and emerging adults have skills in using formal operational thinking as well as an emerging understanding of the tensions between individual rights and relationships and societal goals and constraints. They enjoy exercising these abilities in group or classroom settings and enjoy not only contributing their own opinions but also hearing the perspectives of others. Elly has used a "dilemma of the day" opening class activity for years in an undergraduate moral development class and has consistently observed gains in moral sensitivity and complexity in responses throughout the course of the semester.

Paisley writes frequently on topics related to school counselor training (e.g., Johnson et al., 2016; Paisley & Milsom, 2006; Paisley et al., 2010) and brings the same developmental perspective to counseling preparation that she does to actual counseling practice. As Paisley and Milsom (2006) note, the Transforming School Counseling Initiative (TSCI) calls for school counselors to extend beyond traditional responsibilities, such as counseling and guidance, and take on new roles of "educational leadership and advocacy" (p. 9). These new roles require that school counselors develop complex understandings of social justice and their responsibilities as citizen advocates for the youth they serve. In short, training programs need to nurture the moral development of the counselors—a fact which may account for the fact that in our literature search for recent counseling research on moral development, we found numerous studies assessing the moral development of counseling students and trainees but very few assessing the moral growth of counseling clients or groups.

Putting It All Together—Moral Development and Client Core Issues

> An individual's living story consists of the repetitive reenactment of his or her personal truth expressed through relational interactions over time…According to Kegan (1982), we are constantly in a process of making observations about the world and then cognitively constructing an organized meaningful whole from those observations…. Because personally constructed truths, by their nature, reflect an encapsulated reality, there is often very little awareness of alternative pathways.
>
> (R. Halstead, 2007, pp. 54–55)

In the United States especially, the professions exist in a climate of accountability and assessment. Fields such as counseling and psychology now provide extensive coursework and training in assessment, and many clinicians find themselves in positions where doing assessments rather than providing therapy occupies most of their time. Of particular relevance to moral development, R. Halstead (2007) published a well-received book on assessing client core issues that is deeply grounded in the broad developmental tradition and provides a useful frame for pulling together some of the key ideas presented in previous sections.

Similarly to Noam's (1998a) stress on the concept of encapsulation, R. Halstead (2007) believes that when counselors help clients understand what he calls their "childhood survival story" (p. 67) and how it developed as a response to their specific childhood environment, they can then begin to link that story to core problem issues with which they may have been struggling with across their development.

Morality in the Media

Movies are made to entertain people, not to accurately portray the therapy process, making it difficult to find good examples of good therapy. However, two fine older films will give you a good glimpse of positive therapeutic encounters in which clients grapple with core issues and, in the case of *Ordinary People,* quite literally must face up to the influence of a "childhood survival" story. If you haven't already seen them, we think you will see many of the concepts in this chapter come alive in *Ordinary People* (Redford, 1980) and *Good Will Hunting* (Van Sant, 1997).

R. Halstead (2007) conceptualizes client core issues as artifacts of clients' "acceptance of early maladaptive schema" (p. 17). Readers will see echoes of Noam's work on developmental encapsulation and Piaget's concept of schemas in Halstead's analysis of how problematic inter- and intrapersonal meaning-making systems can generate habitual, problematic behaviors and responses. Halstead draws heavily on Young and colleagues' (e.g., Young et al., 2003) work on how core unmet emotional needs (for secure attachment; autonomy and competence; expression of needs and emotions; spontaneity and play; and realistic limits) can lead to associated maladaptive schemas. For instance, when the need for secure attachment goes unmet, individuals may develop a "Disconnection and Rejection" schema. Similarly, the unmet need for spontaneity and play can result in clients developing "Over-vigilance and Inhibition" schemas.

R. Halstead (2007) notes the consistency between Young et al.'s (2003) four core emotional needs and other developmental models (e.g., Erikson's (1963) theory of psychosocial stages and basic human needs). Such similarities suggest "there must be a favorable psychosocial environment associated with being a well-adjusted individual" (p. 13). Thus, early childhood relational interactions establish children's schemas about relationships—schemas that will influence future relationships.

After explaining the concepts and literature on core issues, R. Halstead (2007) lays out a clear and comprehensive step-by-step model for assessing core issues and the nature of the client's living story:

1. Exploring the client's presenting problem;
2. Generating an initial core issues hypothesis;
3. Tracing the client's psychosocial history to test the validity of that hypothesis;
4. Assessing how the client expresses and responds to her or his core issues (a chart on typical examples of maladaptive coping responses is especially useful, p. 43); and, finally,
5. Establishing a full core issues conceptualization that can serve as a basis for establishing treatment goals and deciding on appropriate therapeutic intervention (Adapted from pp. 31–44).

Recently, R. Halstead (personal communication, September 28, 2020) noted that moral development assessment could provide important information to therapists to guide their treatment plans. This seems to us a particularly useful suggestion. Using valid and reliable measures like the Defining Issues Test or the Sociomoral Reflection Measure (SRM; Gibbs & Widaman, 1982) would greatly enrich therapists' ability to assess how the client is both expressing and responding to core issues.

This brief overview of Halstead's work in no way does justice to the importance of his short text for practicing clinicians. We believe that it should be on any therapist's shelf right next to their copy of the *Diagnostic and Statistical Manual of Mental Disorders (DSM)*. Helping professionals need to use the *DSM* to provide a common diagnostic language, but they also need to do a developmental assessment of clients' core issues and moral reasoning complexity if the therapeutic outcome is to be successful.

Nudging Clients' Better Angels

To give you a better idea of newer approaches that integrate moral psychology into therapy, we will highlight two themes: (1) the growing use of interventions focused on promoting well-being through gratitude, prosocial behavior, and purpose, and (2) the consideration of advancements in the field of moral psychology when conceptualizing and treating moral injury.

While therapy has historically focused on improving symptoms, interest has recently grown in how it can also enhance well-being. In their review of positive psychology interventions, Jankowski et al. (2020) argued that virtue-based treatments (e.g., forgiveness, compassion, gratitude interventions) and psychotherapies promoting flourishing, are effective at promoting well-being (although perhaps not at reducing clients' symptoms) and may be useful for counselors to consider in conjunction with more traditional approaches for alleviating clients' symptoms. For example, Bronk and Mangan (2016) encouraged therapists to help adolescents develop a sense of **purpose,** "a stable and enduring intention to accomplish something that is at once personally meaningful and at the same time leads to productive engagement of the world beyond the self" (Damon et al., 2003, as cited in Bronk & Mangan, 2016, p. 408), through gratitude, goal setting, and a clear identification of how their values and skills can be applied toward meaningful change in the world. Experiments have shown that Bronk and colleagues' purpose-based and gratitude interventions for adolescents and young adults are effective and can be applied in therapeutic settings to decrease stress and enhance well-being (Baumsteiger et al., 2019; Bronk et al., 2019).

In addition to purpose-based and gratitude interventions, a large body of research also shows a small positive relationship between prosocial behavior and well-being (Hui et al., 2020). Over a six-week longitudinal experiment, Nelson et al. (2016) found that prosocial behavior, including acts of kindness toward others, promoted psychological flourishing more than simply being kind to oneself. Experiencing positive emotions after helping others likely partially explained the relationship between prosocial behavior and well-being. While less effective at reducing clients' symptoms of mental illness, positive psychology and virtue-based treatments have been shown to enhance clients' well-being (Hui et al., 2020; Jankowski et al., 2020). In addition to becoming practitioners of interventions that promote flourishing, counselors trained in moral psychology can also design research-based interventions targeting constructs well-known in the field such as prosocial behavior, purpose, gratitude, and forgiveness.

Counselors trained in moral psychology may also want to be engaged in treating and designing interventions for **moral injury**, the "lasting psychological, biological, spiritual, behavioral, and social impact of perpetuating, failing to prevent, or bearing witness to acts that transgress deeply held moral beliefs and expectations" that often befall soldiers and those engaged in military combat (Litz et al., 2009, as cited in Lancaster & Miller, 2020, p. 156). More recently, this term has also been applied to healthcare workers responding to the COVID-19 pandemic, who often worked without appropriate PPE and made ethically challenging decisions about how to prioritize potentially life-saving equipment such as ventilators (Shortland et al., 2020).

Highlighting the important impact counselors trained in moral psychology could make in working with those with moral injury, Farnsworth et al. (2014) argued that conceptualizing moral injury and linking it to mental illnesses such as PTSD could be enhanced by considering recent advances in the field of moral psychology and moral emotions (e.g., shame, anger, and disgust). For example, Lancaster and Miller (2020) found that when military veterans were more altruistic, they were more likely to appraise war-time acts in a way that led to moral injury, suggesting a need to consider the role of moral decision-making in the appraisal process when conceptualizing and treating moral injury. In addition, Forkus and Weiss (2021) found that for veterans, the binding (but not individualizing) moral foundations were positively associated with moral injury and PTSD, suggesting that the same moral emotions that foster loyalty and cohesion within the military also make one vulnerable to moral injury. Accordingly, in addition to current PTSD treatments for veterans, Farnsworth et al. (2020) argued for the use of interventions drawing on positive moral emotions, as well as newly designed interventions that targeted the negative moral emotions typically experienced by those with moral injury (e.g., an intervention promoting self-forgiveness to ameliorate shame over time).

Applications and Implications for Helping Professionals

We hope this chapter has helped you to see how the theories of Part I can and should continue to inform counseling practice. Ideas rooted in the cognitive developmental tradition can help practitioners get a fix on their clients' developmental strengths and challenges, as well as their healthy and not-so-healthy schemas. Counselors' next task involves offering appropriate levels of challenge and support so that their clients can come to understand their own past developmental trajectories and the future path back to wholeness and effective functioning.

Let's end with an example of how we might conceptualize developmental counseling today if we moved beyond the focus on moral reasoning in many of the aforementioned approaches and broadened our scope to a more inclusive developmental model. In Chapter 3, we introduced James Rest's Four Component Model of morality. How might that model look as applied to counseling? (see Table 10.1).

Table 10.1 Applications of Rest's Four Component Model to Counseling

Component	Application
Moral Sensitivity	For some clients, help to effectively address empathic distress through nudging to take appropriate action. For others, help to develop a stronger moral compass. Consider role-taking exercises, bibliotherapy, and YouTube clips.
Moral Judgment	Work on identifying and reframing unhealthy or encapsulated schemas.Identify client core issues and choose appropriate therapeutic techniques for the assessed developmental level.
Moral Motivation	Promote positive moral emotions such as pride, empathy, care. Assign homework such as acts of kindness and gratitude journals.Identify and move beyond crippling emotions such as shame and anger.Where appropriate, teach forgiveness.
Moral Character	Primary prevention—interventions such as moral education and character education that promote positive youth development.For those with significant deficits in empathy or moral reasoning, develop long enough and strong enough programs such as EQUIP (see Chapter 11) to address these deficits and "equip them with new skills."

As you read this chapter, you probably noticed that the focus was on working with clients with problems in living rather than with serious biological pathologies and disorders. In the next chapter, we explore how some of the theories we have been examining may play out when development goes very seriously awry.

Discussion Questions

1. Which of the theorists/practitioners in the chapter seem to rely particularly heavily on Piaget's ideas of cognitive schemas? Kohlberg's stage theory?
2. Can you see ways to integrate ideas from Haidt's more intuitive model into rationalist "meaning making" perspectives of the cognitive developmentalists? If not, why not?
3. What concerns might a counselor have about encouraging a client to move through Enright's Forgiveness Process? Are there any developmental or situational factors you see that might influence which clients would benefit most from this approach?

Additional Resources

- Noam's Clover Model of Development (https://www.thepearinstitute. org/) is part of a larger after-school initiative, PEAR, a program dedicated to education, after school, and resiliency. Dedicated to the "whole child—the whole day," PEAR continuously integrates research, theory, and practice for lasting connections between youth development, school reform, and mental health. PEAR creates and fosters evidence-based innovations so that increasingly "young people can learn, dream, and thrive." PEAR is located at McLean Hospital and Harvard Medical School. Its programs and projects are a part of a number of Boston schools replicated in other parts of the country.
- To learn more about the **Facing History, Facing Ourselves Curriculum** and programs visit: https://www.facinghistory.org/

11 When Development Goes Awry: Deficits in Moral and Empathic Development

In Chapter 5, we took a broad look at the biological underpinnings of morality. Our focus was on genetic mutations that had been selected for their adaptive value. Yet sometimes rather than genetic variations or mutations solving an evolutionary challenge, they lead to problematic developmental paths for individuals. Recall also how in Chapter 6 we explored the connection between empathy and prosocial behavior, and in Chapter 5 noted a consensus among theorists that human attachment systems play a key role not only in ensuring the success of vulnerable human infants, but also as the foundation for key moral virtues such as empathy and care. In this chapter, we examine two important theories that can help us understand what happens when development goes awry, leaving individuals with deficits in empathy and morality. We examine two specific diagnoses, autism spectrum disorder (ASD), and psychopathy, where deficits in empathy have been identified as central criteria. Interestingly, these deficits play out in very different ways in terms of moral development. We will also consider briefly a more widespread and disturbing way that development goes awry—the mechanisms by which ordinary people morally disengage in order to commit reprehensible acts. We think you'll find this chapter's application of theory to practice particularly fascinating as we consider the limits of free will.

Martin Hoffman's Theory of Empathy

> [The] combination of empathic distress and the mental representation of the plight of an unfortunate group would seem to be the most advanced form of empathic distress.
>
> (Hoffman, 2000, p. 85)

Although most of us have an ordinary language understanding of the term *empathy*, this is probably a good place to note the specific definitions used by major theorists and researchers in the area. Martin Hoffman, whose influential stage theory of empathy has been widely accepted in developmental psychology, defines empathy as "a vicarious response to others; that

DOI: 10.4324/9780429295461-13

is, an affective response to someone else's situation rather than one's own" (Hoffman, 1981, p. 128). Autism researcher Baron-Cohen (2011) adds a cognitive piece to his definition, "our ability to identify what someone else is thinking or feeling and to respond to his or her thoughts and feelings with an appropriate emotion" (p. 16). Many researchers and theorists consider empathy to be a multi-component process that includes both **cognitive empathy** (the extent to which we are able to take another's perspective) and **affective empathy** (our capacity for empathic concern—warmth and compassion—for another's experiences) (e.g., Davis, 1983; Decety & Cowell, 2014). It is beyond the scope of this text to provide an extensive background on empathy as a moral motivator, but interested practitioners can turn to the *Handbook of Moral Development* (Killen & Smetana, 2014) for a comprehensive overview of research on the influence of empathy, emotions, and aggression on moral development.

In a very brief overview, Hoffman has posited that the biologically pre-attuned human propensity to feel empathic distress at another's distress leads to helping behavior and to observers feeling better after the helping. Empathy develops over the lifespan from its most primitive form, the newborn's reactive cry at the crying of others, through to its most mature form, empathic distress at another's life condition (Hoffman, 2000). Hoffman currently identifies three immature developmental stages during the early preverbal years and three mature ones during later development:

1. **Global empathy,** such as a newborn's reactive cry to the cry of another infant.
2. **Egocentric empathy,** where the toddler has not yet developed a sense of self and other and often reacts to another's distress by comforting herself.
3. **Quasi-egocentric empathy,** where the toddler now has achieved a sense of self but is still likely to try to comfort another with something that actually comforts himself or herself rather than the other.
4. **Veridical empathy,** where the child feels what another would normally feel given the circumstances.
5. **Empathy beyond the immediate situation,** when young people can truly put themselves in another's role and feel for his or her distressing life situation.
6. **Empathy for distressed groups,** the final mature stage in which people who have achieved advanced cognitive and social perspective-taking stages can feel empathy for the abstract issues concerning the suffering of groups of people (Adapted from Gibbs, 2019; Hoffman, 2000).

Challenges to Hoffman's Theory

Offering a thought-provoking perspective on empathy in *Against Empathy: The Case for Rational Compassion,* Paul Bloom (2016) argued that empathy, "the act of coming to experience the world as you think someone else does" (p. 16), makes the world worse as empathy is just a "spotlight focusing on certain people in the here and now" (p. 9). He believes that empathy's tendency to lead us to personal or tribal biases can cloud our judgment and lead to poor decisions. Instead, he proposes that we rely on **rational compassion** in which we make decisions with our heads rather than our hearts. This concept mirrors the mature stages of Hoffman's theory (stages 5–6) so perhaps Bloom's work would be better entitled 'The case against immature stages of empathy and the importance of nurturing its mature forms.' (Not so catchy but more accurate in our opinion).

We agree with Gibbs (2019) that Bloom (2016) points out many of the limitations of immature (stages 1–4) empathy already addressed by Hoffman (2000) including:

- **Empathic bias**—our tendency to empathize more deeply and readily with family members, friends, and people who are similar to us (our in-group) (**familiarity bias**), as well as our tendency to empathize more deeply and readily with those who are present in the immediate situation (**here-and-now bias**).
- **Empathic overarousal**—our tendency to experience personal distress, which can reduce our likelihood to act prosocially, when we are exposed to highly salient distress cues.

Bloom's (2016) argument may help to explain research that shows that for some children under certain circumstances, such as family environments characterized by chronic depression, marital conflict, alcoholism/substance abuse, or poverty, highly empathic children may experience anxiety or depression (Tully & Donohue, 2017; Zahn-Waxler & Schoen, 2016). However, not all children in such environments experience "costly altruism," and for most children, empathy is associated with emotional well-being (Zahn-Waxler & Van Hulle, 2011, p. 324). While Bloom maintains that our moral decisions and actions need to be shaped by "reason and cost-basis analysis… a more distanced compassion and kindness" (p. 39) instead of empathy, Zaki (2017) argued that people deserve more credit for choosing to direct and control their empathy appropriately. Similarly, while acknowledging that empathy can interfere with morality, Decety and Cowell (2014) highlighted how people have constructed social structures for "upholding moral principles to all humanity, such as human rights and the International Criminal Court" (p. 533) and emphasized how research supports that we can expand our empathy beyond our in-group by engaging in perspective-taking opportunities through fiction, the media, and acting.

Like Gibbs (2019), we find Hoffman's postulation of empathy as **the** root of moral motivation an overreaching of the evidence. We are also in agreement with Gibbs that cognitive motivations, such as justice and reciprocity, play central roles. (Although we are unaware of any specific studies in this area, we suspect that faith provides a third powerful source of moral motivation for many people.) However, like Zaki (2017) and Decety and Cowell (2014), we also believe that people have the capacity to reflect on and grow beyond empathy's immature states and limitations, with Hoffman's (2000) theory emphasizing how broadening one's view of who deserves care is a typical part of development.

"Friends don't let friends lose their capacity for humanity," concludes Barbara Frederickson (2013) in a *New York Times* (p. SR 14) synopsis of research published in *Psychological Science* (Kok et al., 2013). Although this chapter's primary focus is on psychopathology, Frederickson's work on the neurological effects of digital versus face-to-face human connections suggests that future research on empathy and its deficits will need to look closely at the way our reliance on our cell phones may be rewiring our empathic capacities. It is a cliché in neuroscience that neurons that "fire together, wire together," or, more simply, our habits shape our brains. Frederickson and colleagues found that a randomly selected treatment group who participated in six weeks of a "lovingkindness" meditation technique actually altered the tone of the vagus nerve that connects the heart and the brain. The higher the vagal tone, the better able people are to regulate a variety of internal systems, including "facial expressivity and the ability to tune in to the frequency of the human voice." The researchers claim that increased vagal tone underlies increased capacity for "connection, friendship and empathy." If they are right, perhaps we all need to be concerned about the hours we are spending texting with our thumbs instead of exchanging the face-to-face micro-expressions that, in essence, build our empathic capacities.

Dilemma of the Day

Parents of the small children murdered at Sandy Hook School in Newtown, Connecticut, USA, in 2012 successfully lobbied the state legislature to block public and press access to photos of the crime scene and victims. One parent noted that the only kind of person who would want to see these photos would be someone like the children's alleged killer, Adam Lanza, who is reported to have collected photos of massacres such as an earlier one at Columbine High School. Do you agree that, in deference to the feelings of family and friends, media should not publish graphic photos of crime scenes? What would your vote have been and why?

Now consider the case of one of the iconic images of the Vietnam War (aka the American War in Vietnam), a photo of a little girl horribly burned in a napalm attack. The photo (you can easily Google it or see the link in Additional Resources) won a Pulitzer Prize and sensitized many Americans to the Vietnamese people's suffering in a way that news reports never had before. Does its power to activate global empathy give you pause when you think about legislation banning photos of wounded or murdered children? What should take priority, our empathy for the suffering of the Newtown parents or the possible power of such photos to motivate people to work for a less violent society? **In free and open societies, who gets to decide?**

Albert Bandura's Theory of Moral Disengagement

Almost everyone is virtuous at the abstract level. It is in the ease of moral disengagement under the conditions of life where the differences lie. Some [moral disengagement practices]… are built into the organizational and authority structures of societal systems. The ideological orientations of societies shape the form of moral justifications, sanction detrimental practices and influence who gets cast into devalued groups. [But] people are the producers as well as products of their social systems. They have the agentic capacities to change the nature of their social systems.

(Bandura, 2002, pp. 115–116)

Less than two months after the terrorist attacks on the World Trade Center in New York City on September 11, 2001, Albert Bandura delivered the 14th annual Lawrence Kohlberg Memorial Lecture to a sober group of attendees at the 27th annual conference of the Association for Moral Education. His message that moral agency involves both the "power to refrain from behaving inhumanely and the proactive power to behave humanely" (Bandura, 2002, p. 101) struck a responsive chord with us all. Editing this chapter only days after the horrors of the 2021 siege on the US Capital Building, we were struck again by the power and importance of his explanatory ideas about the human capacity for inhumanity.

Bandura (2002) believes that moral behaviors are governed more by "self-reactive selfhood rather than by dispassionate abstract reasoning" (p. 101). A simple example of self-regulation occurs when someone cuts you off in traffic and you are tempted to blow your horn or flash an obscene hand gesture but catch yourself and decide it's not worth potentially triggering a retaliatory response from this jerk. There cannot be a police officer on every corner to control aggressive behavior, but luckily most people develop self-regulatory mechanisms that act as our inner cops. However, these mechanisms work for us only if they are activated. Unfortunately, there are numerous psychosocial mechanisms by which our moral self-sanctions can be **selectively disengaged** from inhumane conduct, potentially creating a catalyst for aggression, antisocial behaviors, bullying, and cyberbullying (Bandura, 2016; Bussey, 2020; Hymel & Perren, 2015).

To morally disengage from **reprehensible conduct,** people use the following mechanisms:

- **Moral justification** (We link our actions to some socially worthy purpose or moral cause. "We had to destroy the village to save it." "We are saving humanity from evil-doers.")
- **Advantageous or palliative comparison** ("Yes, we may have used waterboarding to gain confessions but those prisoners lived through it—unlike our citizens who died in the burning Twin Towers on 9/11.")
- **Euphemistic labeling** (Sanitizing language allows us to reduce personal responsibility for killing or maiming as "wasting," "servicing the target," or "surgical strikes.")

To morally disengage from **detrimental effects** of our actions, we use the following mechanisms:

- **Minimizing** ("The My Lai massacre was an isolated incident.")
- **Ignoring** (Some authorities send subordinates a clear message that they should be kept uninformed about questionable practices. For example, some police departments have routinely ignored evidence that a colleague might be planting evidence or beating prisoners.)
- **Disregarding, distorting, or misconstruing the consequences of one's actions** (Hierarchical chains of command protected the generals in World War I from the horrific conditions in the trenches or the senseless slaughter of their commands to attack across No Man's Land. In contrast, few Americans could ignore the harm caused by our bombing campaign when they viewed the photo of the little Vietnamese girl fleeing in agony, her clothes burned off by napalm.)

To morally disengage from our **victims** as fellow humans, we rely upon the following mechanisms:

- **Dehumanization** (We label the other or the enemies as "savages," "gooks," "infidels," and "cockroaches" in an attempt to distance ourselves from our common humanity.)
- **Attributions of blame** ("I am a faultless victim driven to violence by provocation." From Adolf Hitler to Osama bin Laden bringing the world to war, to soldiers' justifications for battlefield atrocities, to our own US presidents' authorizing drone strikes—the blame for violent actions is placed squarely on the shoulders of the victims of our attacks.) (Adapted from Bandura, 1999, 2002, 2016).

Bandura (2002) argues that these mechanisms have allowed displacement or diffusion of responsibility for inhumane or reprehensible behavior in ordinary people across time and cultures. However, he notes that although we are often captured by sensational accounts of how easy it is to bring out the worst in people (e.g., the Milgram study), we also know that (a) acknowledging our contribution to harm or (b) attending to the humanity of another fosters **moral engagement** and **moral self-control**: "What is rarely noted is the equally striking evidence that most people refuse to behave cruelly, even with strong authoritarian commands towards *humanized* [emphasis added] others..." (p. 109). He cites an inspiring example of moral heroism: the young helicopter pilot who flew over the My Lai massacre, saw a wounded little Vietnamese girl mowed down by a soldier, landed his helicopter in the line of fire, and ordered his gunner to fire on anyone who attempted to harm a terrified woman and baby before he could airlift them and other survivors to safety: "These people were looking at me for help and there is no way I could turn my back on them" (Bandura, 2002, p. 112).

Let's now move from Hoffman's theory of normative empathic development and Bandura's explanation of how people disengage from normal feelings of empathy to some specific examples of psychiatric diagnoses in which deficits of empathy play a central role.

Psychopaths and Individuals with Autism Spectrum Disorder—Deficits in Empathy but Widely Different Outcomes

So what do we actually know about empathy (and lack thereof) in individuals on the autism spectrum versus empathy (and lack thereof) among people diagnosed as psychopaths? As you might imagine, what at first appears to be a simple underlying deficit manifests in widely different patterns of behavior. Why might this be so, and what are the implications for counselors? Work in neuroscience (Sinnott-Armstrong, 2008) has explored the fascinating fork in developmental pathways of individuals diagnosed with ASD or as psychopaths. Variations in underlying brain abnormalities related to empathy in ASD and psychopathy (Klapwijk et al., 2016) may underpin results from many studies that show that ASD is more associated with deficits in cognitive empathy while psychopathology is more linked to deficits in affective empathy (e.g., Georgiou et al., 2019; Oliver et al., 2016). Both conditions list deficits in empathy as symptoms but those deficits appear to have widely varying influences on moral agency and behavior. An understanding of the emerging science into the roots of these empathic deficits can assist helping professionals working with individuals with either diagnosis tailor their approaches to the clients' unique needs and abilities.

Empathic and Moral Development in Individuals on the Autism Spectrum

News accounts of ASD diagnoses in 1/54 children (Centers for Disease Control and Prevention [CDC], 2020) have generated both intense concern and intense interest among professionals and parents. Part of the extensive diagnostic process for ASD in the *Diagnostic and Statistical Manual of Mental Disorders, 5th Edition* (*DSM-5*) includes establishing that the individual has (a) impaired social communication and interactions (e.g., difficulties with social reciprocity such as turn-taking, challenges with nonverbal communication such as difficulty initiating or maintaining eye contact, or problems with "developing, maintaining, and understanding relationships" and (b) "restricted, repetitive patterns of behavior, interests, or activities" (e.g., strong resistance to change, intense and/or focused interests) (American Psychiatric Association [APA], 2013, p. 50). Of those diagnosed with ASD, about 33% also have an intellectual disability (CDC, 2020). Such deficits present daunting challenges for counselors, educators, and parents hoping to provide children on the spectrum with the sort of peer interactions and perspective-taking opportunities that Piaget, Kohlberg, and others posited as necessary but not sufficient conditions for moral development.

McGeer (2008) argued, however, that Kennett's (2002) study of individuals with ASD who are deeply motivated to do the right thing suggests that we may need to rethink whether empathy actually is a necessary condition for moral agency. In fact, she concludes, although a lack of empathy makes it a real challenge for individuals with ASD to act in "morally appropriate ways, it does nothing to undermine their interest in so acting, it does nothing to undermine their moral concern" (McGeer, 2008, p. 235). At least among individuals with higher functioning ASD, the interactions among their primarily intact reasoning abilities, their passion for order, and a desire to "make sense of their own and other's behavior, seems to support the emergence of a sense of duty and conscience, that is, by contrast, entirely lacking in the psychopathic population" (p. 237).

While people often assume individuals with ASD lack empathy due in part to initial uncertainties about their empathic capacities (e.g., Baron-Cohen, 1995; Gillberg, 1992), recent research incorporating a multidimensional view of empathy (considering both cognitive and affective empathy) reveals a more nuanced view of the empathic strengths and weaknesses in ASD, especially at the higher end of the spectrum. The research remains controversial and fluid, complicated by variations in definitions and measurements of empathy, as well as participants' varying ASD severity, gender, and age. A general summary is that compared to typically developing individuals, studies consistently show that those with ASD have impaired cognitive empathy (Bos & Stokes, 2019; Rueda et al., 2015; Senland & Higgins-D'Alessandro, 2016; Song et al., 2019), while the research for empathic concern is more mixed, with some studies showing that empathic concern is also impaired (Bos & Stokes, 2019; Song et al., 2019), while others show preserved empathic concern (Rueda et al., 2015; Senland & Higgins-D'Alessandro, 2016). We believe that feeling empathic concern may help to motivate those with ASD to continue to develop morally, as Hoffman's (2000) theory of moral development argues that such feelings of empathy are critical for moral development. Research from the cognitive-developmental perspective suggests that those with ASD continue to develop morally. While those with ASD may have less advanced moral reasoning than their typically developing peers (Senland & Higgins-D'Alessandro, 2016; Takeda et al., 2007), the difference can be best accounted for by the hypothesis that delays occurred prior to the time-period that Amie (Senland, 2017) researched–adolescence and emerging adulthood. She found that the gap in moral reasoning ability between the TD and ASD groups was the same size for adolescents and emerging adults, which suggests that the ASD group continued to grow in moral reasoning at the same *rate* as their TD peers (neither catching up to their peers or falling further behind). Obviously a longitudinal study is needed to actually draw a conclusion about growth/change.

Cognitive empathy interventions may improve well-being and outcomes in individuals with ASD, a place where the skills and resources of moral educators and practitioners could be vitally important (Bos & Stokes, 2019; Senland & Higgins-D'Alessandro, 2016). In her dissertation research with young adults with ASD who were on the higher end of the spectrum, Amie found that those who were able to describe using perspective-taking to reason about and resolve challenging sociomoral situations had better developmental outcomes than those who could not do so (i.e., more success at friendships, independence, and education and employment) (Senland & Higgins-D'Alessandro, 2016). Similarly, Bos and Stokes (2019) found that higher empathic concern is associated with positive well-being for adolescents with ASD, but only when coupled with cognitive empathy. We argue that this, as well as consistent research showing that those with ASD have higher personal distress than their typically developing peers (e.g., Senland & Higgins-D'Alessandro, 2016; Song et al., 2019) is congruent with the empathic overarousal limitation of Hoffman's (2000) theory. If individuals with ASD experience compassion and concern for others but have difficulty identifying others' perspectives, they may experience heightened personal distress when they are unable to translate their empathy into prosocial action. The deficit in perspective-taking could be addressed through cognitive empathy interventions. Moral educators and practitioners, with their emphasis on designing moral education programs, facilitating positive social relationships, and facilitating sociomoral and empathic growth, could be key players in designing interventions that address the nuanced empathic strengths and challenges of those with ASD (Senland & Higgins-D'Alessandro, 2016).

Morality in the Media

If you are interested in a list of films featuring individuals with autism spectrum disorder (many of which are available on DVD or streaming platforms), visit: https://www.autism.org/autism-movies/ Do note the caveat that the films are often not reliable re: causes of autism.

One of Elly's personal favorites is a quirky but poignant film based on the real-life love story of two young people with ASD. *Mozart and the Whale* (Næss, 2006) provides an honest look at the challenges these individuals face in forging relationships. We have also enjoyed the creative Netflix coming-of-age TV series *Atypical* (Rashid, 2017-2021), in which the protagonist with ASD navigates love, friendships, work, family issues, and independence. A favorite of students has been the Belgian-Dutch film *Ben X* (Balthazar, 2007) about a boy with ASD who retreats into a world of video games to escape the relentless bullying of his school peers.

Empathic and Moral Development in Psychopaths

In sharp contrast to individuals on the autism spectrum who are attempting to do the right thing in a world of emotions they struggle to understand, psychopaths appear to understand others' emotions only too well. Kiehl (2008) concisely sums up the clinical portrait of psychopathy as "a personality disorder characterized by a profound lack of empathy and guilt or remorse, shallow affect, irresponsibility, and poor behavioral controls" (p. 119).

When we think of people most lacking in morality or any inner sense of conscience, we think of the psychopath. Such individuals are responsible "for a disproportionate amount of repetitive crime and violence in society" (Kiehl, 2008, p. 122). The *DSM-5* (APA, 2013) classification of antisocial personality disorder focuses on the presence of antisocial behaviors. In contrast, the most common diagnostic tool, the Hare Psychopathy Checklist-Revised (Hare, 2003), gives a fuller picture of the emotional and interpersonal characteristics that professionals consider central to the disorder; for instance, a grandiose sense of self-worth, callous lack of empathy, and cunning manipulation. The Hare checklist represents a two-factor view of psychopathy: (1) an interpersonal and affective factor and (2) a social deviance factor. Revisions to the *DSM-5* did include more interpersonal and affective criteria as associated features that could support a diagnosis.

Evidence is mounting that psychopathy arises from some sort of dysfunction in the paralimbic system (Kiehl, 2008, p. 148) but, to date, this line of research does not offer any biological remedies for the condition. Given the serious consequences to society when individuals with glib but superficial charm and a lack of remorse or guilt indulge in such checklist behaviors as "juvenile delinquency" and "criminal versatility"—to say nothing of "promiscuous sexual behavior," "many marital relationships," and "pathological lying" (Hare, 2003)—it is no wonder that so many psychopaths find themselves frequent flyers in the criminal justice system.

Unlike individuals with higher functioning ASD, whose profiles of empathic concern and desire for order offer promise for a positive, if different, path of moral development, psychopaths' intact intellect but lack of moral behavior challenges therapists attempting to find effective clinical interventions. We suggested earlier that individuals with ASD could learn to fake it until they make it. In contrast, psychopaths can fake it, but not make it (Kiehl, 2008, p. 120). Psychopaths are commonly perceived as "moral monsters" (Ellis, as cited in Marshall et al., 2017, p. 240), and some have argued that psychopaths do not have the moral understanding to be held "morally responsible for their crimes" (Malatesti, 2010, p. 337). While research remains mixed, recent research from using multiple morality-related measures suggests that in general they can tell right from wrong (e.g., Aharoni et al., 2014; Larsen et al., 2020; Marshall et al., 2018) but *choose* to do wrong.

Mental health researchers Harris and Rice (2006) believe that there is not sufficient evidence to draw meaningful conclusions about the efficacy of treatment for psychopathy. It may be that we have not yet found effective treatments because (a) the proper evaluations (perhaps with higher doses/intensities of treatment) have not been done, (b) because an effective therapy is lacking for this particular disorder, or (c) that no treatment can ever be effective—we can only limit the harm psychopaths do—not cure them. They note that research has shown that psychodynamic, insight, or emotionally evocative therapy programs have proven ineffective and also may actually increase violent recidivism of psychopaths. Given that psychopaths appear to have a different physical makeup, it may be that some future drug treatment may reduce the risk of psychopathic behaviors. For the present, in cases where psychopaths have committed crimes and have a high risk of future violent behavior, Harris and Rice believe the best evidence supports an institutional (e.g., prison setting) behavioral program with an explicit token economy and consistent consequences based on observable behavior—never on inmates' self-report.

Harris and Rice paint a grim picture of the prospects of treating psychopaths. But what if we took a more developmental perspective and tried to intervene early with antisocial youth, a group that may be at high risk of becoming adult psychopaths?

Antisocial Behavior and the EQUIP Program

Over several decades, John Gibbs and colleagues have designed, implemented, and evaluated an innovative program for teaching youth to think and act responsibly through a peer-helping approach (e.g., Gibbs, 2019; Gibbs et al., 1995; see also Potter et al., 2015 for how this program has been translated into a program for adult offenders. Note: A second edition of the print version of *EQUIP* is forthcoming). This theoretically based and research-supported intervention method aims to prevent or reduce antisocial behavior by equipping adolescents with tools to decrease their self-serving cognitive distortions, increase their moral reasoning complexity, and improve their social skills. EQUIP programs have been implemented in various correctional facilities in the United States, Canada, and the Netherlands. There is now quite a bit of evidence with regard to its effectiveness.

Interviews with Field Leaders: John C. Gibbs Ph.D. (Harvard University 1972) Professor of Developmental Psychology Ohio State University

Gibbs's work on moral judgment and cognitive distortion assessment and on interventions with antisocial youth has not only seen widespread use in the United States and Great Britain but also has been translated and adapted for use in France, Germany, Italy, Taiwan, Spain, the Netherlands, and other countries. Dr. Gibbs and coauthors' EQUIP intervention program won the 1998 Reclaiming Children and Youth Spotlight on Excellence Award. He has served as a member of the Ohio Governor's Council on Juvenile Justice as well as the Social Cognitive Training Study Group of the Centers for Disease Control and Prevention (Division of Violence Prevention). In addition to intervention programs for conduct-disordered individuals his work has also concerned developmental theory and assessment of social cognition and moral judgment development. His authored or coauthored books include *Moral Development and Reality: Beyond the Theories of Kohlberg, Hoffman, and Haidt* (2019) and *Moral Maturity: Measuring the Development of Sociomoral Reflection (1992).*

> When asked what has been particularly meaningful to him in his years of working in the field of moral development theory and applications Dr. Gibbs reflected on the way his life had intersected with theorists, researchers, and clinicians to inform the comprehensive ideas he developed from being on "both the treatment and assessment side of things." In his early work at a school for antisocial youth judged to have "severe behavioral handicaps" it quickly became clear to him that "great though Lawrence Kohlberg's stages were there was a lot more to conduct disorder" than low-level moral reasoning. As he worked cooperatively with clinicians he began to synthesize ideas from the positive peer culture literature, anger management and anger control programs, and social skills training programs. However, he found that often programs were "too Spartan—too behavioral." Gibbs sees EQUIP as offering a "synergistic character" that blends best practice ideas to enhance social skills and empathy training with a "more cognitive, more constructive, and more positive" focus.
>
> (J. Gibbs, personal communication, April 30, 2013)

Counselors working with antisocial youth, in or out of the criminal justice system, know that this is a difficult population to reach and one that tends to show high rates of recidivism. They will find Gibbs's (2019) book, *Moral Development and Reality: Beyond the Theories of Kohlberg, Hoffman, and Haidt* an invaluable guide that concisely summarizes relevant theory and then moves into a detailed overview of understanding and treating antisocial behavior. Gibbs notes that the research literature on patterns of antisocial behavior such as conduct disorder or opposition–defiance disorder consistently describes antisocial and aggressive youths as sharing three problematic tendencies: arrested moral and social-emotional development, a tendency to blame others, and a lack of knowledge about how to handle problems constructively. Gibbs (2019) calls these limitations the 3 Ds:

- Developmental *delay* in moral judgment;
- Self-serving cognitive *distortions;* and
- Social skills *deficiencies* (p. 180).

Students in Elly's moral development classes, especially those going on to careers in the helping professions or education, have particularly appreciated Gibbs's inclusion of specific exercise handouts, such as a self-assessment measure for thinking errors and "problems" (e.g., low self-image, problems with authority, being easily angered, or having problems with drugs or alcohol). This assessment measure introduces the client to a language that will be used throughout the EQUIP intervention. For example, the primary thinking error, self-centered thinking, is defined for the youth as meaning that

> You think your opinions and feelings are more important than the feelings of other people. You may not even consider how another person might feel about things. [It]… can also mean that you think only about what you want right now and do not think about how your behaviors will affect you or others in the future.
>
> (Gibbs, 2010, p. 158)

The measure also introduces classic secondary thinking errors: minimizing/mislabeling, assuming the worst, and blaming others. At the end of the exercise, the youth are asked how many thinking errors they have and which are their most common.

The EQUIP curriculum, a highly structured mutual help program, is designed in 31 sessions and thus is particularly useful for incarcerated youth or those in a structured halfway house or group home setting. The goal of the sessions is to "equip" youth with three sets of skills: mature moral judgment, managing anger and correcting thinking errors, and social skills. The antisocial youth in EQUIP groups help each other learn to identify problem behaviors and thoughts and to practice skills that will help them overcome their deficits and, eventually, deal with the world more prosocially and effectively.

Implications for Practitioners

To date, Gibbs's (2019) EQUIP program has been used primarily with juvenile delinquents, but some variation of his highly structured approach to address developmental deficits may hold promise for the treatment of psychopathy. During EQUIP meetings, facilitators and fellow group members consistently confront offenders' distorted thinking and teach them that self-serving cognitive distortions, especially about the harm done, are not simply "different but rather wrong, erroneous, faulty, inaccurate and in need of correction" (J. Gibbs, personal communication, February 28, 2012). In a section on social perspective taking for severe offenders, Gibbs (2019) writes that although positive outcome evaluation findings for the EQUIP program suggest its promise for working with antisocial youth, it may require strengthening or supplementation for more serious and chronic offenders. For example, techniques such as crime reenactment role-plays have been shown to break down offenders' defenses, help them understand the perspective of their victims, and even, ideally, to feel remorse (p. 232). Gibbs notes, however, that serious offenders who have been helped by social perspective-taking approaches were not necessarily formally diagnosed as psychopaths (Personal communication February 28, 2012), thus, by definition, that last step of "feeling remorse" may remain elusive for this population.

Although work on effective moral education interventions for individuals with higher functioning autism remains in its infancy, Amie's research suggests that counselors and teachers should look for evidence of affective empathy in their clients or students and support their genuine concern for others. What higher functioning individuals on the spectrum clearly need from helping professionals are very specific cognitive tools and strategies for more effectively translating their feelings into appropriate behaviors. Senland and Higgins-D'Alessandro (2016) found that the teens interviewed in their study of empathic and moral development often thought they did a better job of helping and "being nice" than they actually did. Many times, scripts and role-plays in the safe atmosphere of an individual or group therapy session can help ASD individuals "fake it till they make it." An obvious caution, however, when working with individuals with such high needs for structure, routine, and predictability, is that the world of social interaction is a messy, constantly fluid world. Haddon's (2003) wonderful novel about an adolescent with Asperger's syndrome, *The Curious Incident of the Dog in the Night-Time,* captures poignantly his autistic protagonist Christopher's sense of frustration at this human messiness:

> And in [my favorite] dream nearly everyone on the earth is dead because they have caught a virus. But it's not a normal virus. It's like a computer virus. And people catch it because of the meaning of something an infected person says and the meaning of what they do with their faces when they say it... And eventually there is no one left in the world

except people who don't look at other people's faces and who don't know what these pictures [inserts a string of emoticons] mean and these people are all special people like me. And they like being on their own and I hardly ever see them because they are like okapi in the jungle in the Congo, which are a kind of antelope and very shy and rare.

(pp. 198–199)

In sum then, theory and research (e.g., Baron-Cohen, 2011) suggest that strides in neuroscience may provide direction for attempts to work with clients across a range of empathetic deficits. This includes not only individuals with ASD or psychopaths but also those who are narcissists or who have borderline personality disorder. In the meantime, attempts to promote the moral and empathic development of neuroatypical individuals remain in their infancy and await the careful empirical evaluation and replication of promising interventions.

Discussion Questions

1. Do psychopaths have free will? What evidence can you cite to support your position?
2. In Haddon's novel, the teenage protagonist Christopher is not only overwhelmed easily by people and change, but also takes things very literally. In response to school lectures on "Stranger Danger," he takes a knife with him when he travels on a train so that he can defend himself from strangers. Aside from legal issues, would you see him as morally responsible if he became frightened and struck out with that knife? Why or why not?

Additional Resources

- We have always found it fascinating to hear theorists and researchers in person. With today's technology, you have many options for tracking down video talks by major thinkers. At the writing of this book, Googling "Bandura and Moral Disengagement" brings you to numerous sites, including: https://www.youtube.com/watch?v=JjuA4Xa7uiE&feature=emb_logo
- For a creative and moving glimpse into the worldview of people diagnosed on the higher end of the autism spectrum, you will probably greatly enjoy the novel referred to earlier: Haddon, M. (2003). *The curious incident of the dog in the night-time*. Doubleday.
- If you would like to read a 40-year follow-up story about the Pulitzer Prize–winning photo of the little Vietnamese girl, you can visit this weblink: http://abcnews.go.com/blogs/headlines/2012/06/the-historic-napalm-girl-pulitzer-image-marks-its-40th-anniversary/

12 The Role of Faith, Religion, and Spirituality in Morality

Amie K. Senland

Worldwide, we see religious trends including growing fundamentalism ("a global religious impulse, … that seeks to recover and publicly institutionalize aspects of the past that modern life has obscured") (Wacker, 2000, para. 2; see also Emerson & Hartman, 2006; Orva, 2015) in some places, and rising secularism in other places (Pew Research Center [PEW], 2015a, 2019). Recent PEW (2015a, 2019) surveys of religion in the United States show that the percentage of adults identifying as Christian has declined significantly while those identifying as religiously unaffiliated has grown, a trend occurring across races, regions of the country, and educational levels. Adults are also attending church less often. Trends for religious affiliation and attendance are most pronounced among young people. This rise in secularism in the United States is also consistent with other Western countries such as Canada and Europe, where religion is perceived as becoming less important over time (Poushter & Fetterolf, 2019). These countries are predicted, along with the United States, to experience a continued rise in people identifying as religiously unaffiliated (PEW, 2015b). Despite these trends for rising secularism in some places, the importance of religion varies geographically, with Poushter and Fetterolf (2019) highlighting that more countries across the world favor an *increased* role for religion over time. Looking forward to 2050, those identifying as religiously unaffiliated are predicted to continue to grow in some geographic regions of the world, but their percentage of the global population will *decrease*, given expected patterns of birth rates in geographic areas where religion remains very important (PEW, 2015b).

Across the globe, 45% of people think that a belief in God is necessary to be moral and have good values, with non-religious, highly educated people with high incomes living in developed countries less likely to answer in the affirmative (PEW, 2020). For example, in that 2020 survey, only 9% of those in Sweden thought that belief in God was necessary for morality while 96% of those in Kenya did so. Similarly, McKay and Whitehouse's (2015) thoughtful analysis of the relationship between religion and morality notes that although more than half of Americans believe morality impossible without a belief in God, "some aspects of 'religion' may promote

DOI: 10.4324/9780429295461-14

some aspects of 'morality,' just as others serve to suppress or obstruct the same, or different aspects" (p. 465). Correspondingly, a wide body of research in recent decades links religiosity to positive outcomes including less risky behaviors and depression, enhanced well-being, and higher self-esteem (e.g., King & Furrow, 2004; Smith, 2009; Yonker et al., 2014). However, religion can also be a source of distress, with spiritual struggle, associated with increased psychological distress, decreased physical health, lowered self-esteem, and less growth in religiosity and spirituality (Bryant & Astin, 2008).

Given the importance of religion worldwide, people's assumptions about the relationship between belief in God and morality, and links between religion and positive developmental outcomes, one may speculate that the field of moral psychology has fully explored the relationship between faith and morality; however, in fact, the opposite is true. As Jensen (2015d) highlighted,

> there is a 'lacuna in contemporary moral psychology' (as cited in Pandya & Bhangaokar) in research on Divinity considerations… that at a minimum goes back to Piaget, who argued that any references to religion and the supernatural mask the structure of genuine moral reasoning."
>
> (p. 12)

Importantly, and to the contrary, Lawrence Kohlberg maintained an interest in religion, conceptualizing his own theory of religious development with Clark Power (Kohlberg & Power, 1981; Kuhmerker, 1991) that ultimately contributed to James Fowler's (1981, 2003) faith development theory, which remains the most dominant theory of faith *development.*

Most universalist theories of faith development, including Kohlberg's theory of religious development and Fowler's theory of faith development, have emerged from the cognitive-developmental tradition of morality. More recently, these universalist models have been seriously challenged by the cross-cultural, more global perspective of the Ethic of Divinity (e.g., Jensen, 2015a; Shweder, 2015). We agree with Jensen (2015a) that recent researchers have become more interested in studying the importance of religion in people's moral lives, particularly regarding the Ethic of Divinity. However, this chapter will give substantial coverage of universalist theories of faith development, as these theories have historically dominated the field, and Fowler's theory remains the most influential and utilized theory of faith development. After describing theories of faith development, we'll discuss what *is* known about the relationship between faith development and moral development. Due in part to the "lacuna" (Jensen, 2015a, p. 12) of research on morality and faith development, until recently, much of the research came from a Western perspective. Jensen's (2020a) moral development handbook provides many good examples of research with more globally diverse samples. Jensen's (2015a, 2020a) cultural-developmental theory of morality, with its inclusion of the Ethic of Divinity, offers a solid framework to advance future research on more global, cultural developmental perspectives on faith. Considering both Fowler and Jensen identify adolescence and emerging adulthood as a crucial time-period of developmental change in faith development, we will end this chapter by concentrating more specifically on emerging adults' faith, religiousness, and spirituality, and applications for helping professionals.

Definitions

Both dictionary entries and common usage of the term *faith* encompass two related but distinct definitions—(1) a belief and trust in God or some transcendent power; and (2) a belief in and adherence to the traditional doctrines and practices of a specific religious orientation. In the classic *Varieties of Religious Experience*, psychologist William James (1902) made a distinction between institutional and personal religion. Aspects of what James called worship, theology and ceremony are captured by religious affiliation and religious practice, while what James called personal religion is more closely aligned with what later scholars would identify as spirituality. Current studies of faith development tend to operationalize and measure the two concepts separately (Astin & Astin, 2010; Barry et al., 2010; Dalton et al., 2006; Redden, 2007) and use the term **religiosity** to refer to organized and institutionalized aspects of religious beliefs and practices (e.g. Barry et al., 2010) and **spirituality** as a search for "connection to transcendence (e.g. God, nature, and other people)" (Hardy et al., 2014, p. 339). The current chapter's operational definition of **faith** as belief in a higher power aligns most closely with the concept of spirituality.

Theories of Faith Development

Kohlberg and Religious Development

Although not as well-known as his theory of moral reasoning, Lawrence Kohlberg remained intrigued by religion, developing a stage theory of religious development with his colleague, Clark Power, and engaging in discussions with James Fowler and Fritz Oser about the relationship between faith and moral development that ultimately strongly influenced their own faith/religious theories of development (Kuhmerker, 1991). Swiss psychologist Fritz Oser (1980; Oser et al., 2003) developed a related cognitive-developmental stage theory of religious judgment, which has had considerable influence in Europe and has been well supported in intercultural and intervention studies. As we'll discuss shortly, Fowler's theory has had the most influence in the fields of moral development and pastoral counseling and is still widely considered the most current leading faith development theory.

Kohlberg believed that moral reasoning and faith development were clearly distinct but related processes. For Kohlberg, religion is "a conscious response to, and an expression of the quest for ultimate meaning for moral judgment and action" (Kohlberg & Power, 1981, p. 336). As Kuhmerker (1991) explained, "Kohlberg focused on the *structure* of thinking about moral issues and saw religious beliefs as part of the *content* of thinking about moral issues" (p. 157). Accordingly, Kohlberg's moral education technique of dilemma discussions has been adopted by religious leaders across denominations (e.g., Catholic, Protestant, and Jewish) to facilitate growth in justice, a key goal of many religious groups, without regard to religious content or denomination (Kuhmerker, 1991). Kohlberg believed that growth in moral reasoning preceded faith development, with his research suggesting an 81 percent agreement between moral and faith development stages (when there was disagreement between stages, the moral stage was higher than the faith stage) (Kohlberg & Power, 1981).

Kohlberg and Power's (1981) cognitive-developmental stage theory of religious development parallels Kohlberg's theory of moral reasoning and focuses on people's increasingly complex understandings of God/a higher power and the meaning of life. In Stage 1 of Kohlberg and Power's (1981) model, God/a higher power is all-powerful, makes everything happen and rewards people when they obey Him/Her but punishes them when they disobey His/Her rules. In Stage, 2 when people are good to God/a higher power (e.g., by praying and engaging in religious practice), God/that higher power is good to them. By Stage 3, people believe God/a higher power wants them to have personal trusting relationship with Him/Her. Those reasoning at Stage 4 believe that God/a higher power has given people His/Her laws and it is their duty to live by those laws but no longer think that God will personally intercede in their lives. Upon reaching Stage 5, people understand that God/a higher power has given people the responsibility to make good moral choices. Finally, believers who reach Stage 6 perceive that there is a Supreme Being who is known to all the major faiths and there are many ways to relate to Him/Her (Kohlberg & Power, 1981).

Fowler's Structural Stage Theory of Faith Development

While Kohlberg and Power's (1981) theory offers a focused model for assessing growth in cognitive complexity in understanding a higher power, Fowler's faith development model can explain how life history shapes purpose and meaning. Drawing on the developmental theories of Piaget, Kohlberg, and Erikson, James Fowler's (1981, 2003) structural-developmental approach to faith development

> was pioneered... as a framework for understanding the evolution of how human beings conceptualized God, or a Higher Being, and how

the influence of that Higher Being has an impact on core values, beliefs, and meanings in their personal lives and in their relationships with others. (Fowler & Dell, 2006, p. 34)

In contrast to Kohlberg, who believed that moral development facilitated faith development, Fowler believed that faith development preceded moral development, "adding meaning and motivation to the moral quest for justice" (Hanford, 1991, p. 308).

Fowler's (1981) theory of faith development suggests that all "human beings are genetically potentiated—… gifted at birth—with readiness to develop in faith" (p. 303), which may or may not be expressed through religion. Just as Kohlberg (1984) argued that cognitive maturation facilitated an increasingly complex view of who deserves justice, Fowler believed that cognitive development led to more complex, abstract, and encompassing visions of values and meaning. While higher stages represent more complete and accurate ways of knowing, the goal of education, therapy, and nurturing should be to realize, integrate, and maximize the strengths of each stage rather than to propel an individual toward the next stage without the time or experiences necessary for growth (Fowler, 1987).

Fowler's (1981) six stages of faith development are based on his original cross-sectional research from 1972 to 1981 that involved 359 interviews with mostly White, Christian participants, aged 3.5–84; each participant engaged in a Faith Development Interview accessing life-changing experiences and relationships, existing values and commitments, and religious conviction. An overall pattern emerged with progression through the stages resembling a "stairstep pattern" (Fowler, 1987, p. 319) of change and equilibrium until approximately age 40, when the pattern became more spread out with adults reaching long-lasting equilibrium anywhere from Stage 2 onward. While faith stage transitions in childhood/adolescence are more predictable and parallel with changes in cognitive and psychosocial development, change at any age involves a reorganization and accommodation of thinking and knowing that is often lengthy, painful, and confusing (Fowler, 1981).

During infancy, prior to the six formal stages, Fowler (1981; Fowler & Dell, 2006) described a pre-stage of Undifferentiated or Primal Faith, where later development and relationships are influenced by the extent that an environment of basic trust is established and trust, hope, and love are communicated. As language emerges, children transition to Stage 1, **Intuitive-Projective Faith** (Toddlerhood and Early Childhood), creating a world based on imagination and becoming captivated by stories, symbols, and images that serve as models of living life and relating to others. Given the power of imagination to construct faith and visions of the world at this stage, the specific stories and images imparted can strongly influence development, confirming a world of love, faith, and courage, or instilling a world of fear and "the hell of fiery torments" (Fowler, 1981, p. 132).

With the emergence of concrete-operational thinking, children typically transition to Stage 2, **Mythic-Literal Faith** (Middle Childhood and Beyond), where they begin to actively separate fact from fiction and to formulate a knowledge of the world based on logic (Fowler, 1981; Fowler & Dell, 2006). An understanding of the world is constructed in terms of reciprocity, and God is viewed as a powerful judge of a world where people are rewarded/punished based on their actions. With the advent of formal-operational thinking and mutual interpersonal perspective taking, individuals have the reflective capacity necessary for the transition to Stage 3, **Synthetic-Conventional Faith** (Adolescence and Beyond; Fowler, 1981; Fowler & Dell, 2006). As individuals structure an interpersonal world based on a system of tacit/unexamined values, their choices and behavior become guided by the expectations and potential judgments of significant others. God, too, becomes a "divinely personal significant other" (Fowler, 1981, p. 154) to whom individuals look for guidance, companionship, and support as they consolidate their identity, values, and commitments.

Movement to Stage 4, **Individuative-Reflective Faith** (Early Adulthood and Beyond), generally emerges as individuals critically examine previously assumptive values, beliefs, and commitments and take personal responsibility for their system of values and commitments (Fowler, 1981; Fowler & Dell, 2006). Family religious beliefs and traditions (as well as secular worldviews) may be questioned while alternative faiths are explored. As one develops an "executive ego" (Fowler, 1981, p. 179) of personal authority for making decisions and choosing values, he or she begins to formulate an understanding of the world based on an explicit, individualized, clearly defined system of values and meanings.

By Stage 5, **Conjunctive Faith** (Adulthood), individuals formulate an understanding of a world where truth is multidimensional (Fowler, 1981; Fowler & Dell, 2006). As individuals move beyond a world of clearly defined boundaries and traditional class, racial, and religious barriers, they become free to explore a world of paradoxes and contradictory truths. Recognizing that their experience of the world/God is incomplete, limited, and distorted, individuals at this stage are ready to risk immersing themselves in interfaith and intercultural experiences to grow in understanding while retaining the capacity to remain rooted in their personal value and belief systems. While individuals at Stage 5 may be attuned to the complexity and broadened inclusion, individuals in Stage 6 (**Universalizing Faith**) live out and apply principles of absolute love, justice, and selflessness to personal visions aimed to rectify conditions crushing, exploiting, destroying, and stunting the potential for human growth (Fowler, 1981; Fowler & Dell, 2006).

Current evaluation of Fowler's theory

While Fowler's theory (1981; Fowler & Dell, 2006) "has proven influential in pastoral care and counselling, pastoral and practical theology, spiritual

Table 12.1 Strengths and Challenges of Fowler's Theory

Strengths include:
- Heuristic value: Most influential theory of faith development, with continued modern popularity and widespread use in pastoral care and educational settings.
- Simplicity, comprehensiveness, and practicality: Differences in faith described in seven stages across development, which can easily be used to assess students' and clients' current level of functioning to support and challenge their growth.
- Focus on structure rather than content of faith allows for broad application of theory across religious denominations, as well as those who identify as unaffiliated.

Criticisms include:
- Methodological: More research is needed to determine whether the theory is accurate, particularly longitudinal research studies (Parker, 2010; Piper, 2002).
- Overemphasized cognition, potentially neglecting other key aspects of faith development (Piper, 2002; Streib, 2001).
- Universalist models have been seriously challenged by the cross-cultural, more global perspective of the Ethic of Divinity (e.g., Coyle, 2011; Jensen, 2015a; Shweder, 2015).

---

direction, and Christian education, … it has also been subject to substantial critical evaluation" (Coyle, 2011, p. 1) (see Table 12.1 for an overview of the strengths and weaknesses of Fowler's theory). In a review of over three decades of research on Fowler's faith development theory, Parker (2010) pointed that Fowler's theory remains the most well-supported theory of spiritual or religious development, but empirical support for the theory "continues to present a mixed picture" (p. 246). With some caveats, research has supported a relationship between age and stage (at least through adolescence) and that the stages are characterized by the structure of one's faith, rather than the contents of one's beliefs (Parker, 2010). However, as Parker argues, a longitudinal study is needed to evaluate whether Fowler's stage sequence is truly hierarchical (each stage is more complex than the prior stage, with previous stages contributing to, and supporting, the current stage) and invariant (each stage happens in a specific sequence—people cannot skip a stage or follow a different journey through the stages).

Heinz Streib has been at the forefront of critically evaluating and advancing Fowler's theory. According to Streib (2001, 2020), faith development involves a sequence of five multi-layered religious types rather than a sequence of irreversible structurally whole stages. In recent research, Streib et al. (2020) confirmed the presence of four distinct, hierarchically ranked religious types across three samples of 667 late adolescent and adult participants (the first religious type was not assessed because it is predominately found in childhood). Streib's revision of Fowler's faith development theory is similar to how Rest and colleagues (e.g., Rest, 1986; Rest et al., 1999) revised Kohlberg's theory to include moral schemas. As discussed in Chapter 3, Kohlberg's theory of moral reasoning was expanded to highlight how context influences moral development schemas, just as Streib's revision of Fowler's theory illustrates how individuals may typically rely on an overarching religious type to shape life's meaning and guide life's interactions but earlier schemas for viewing the world reemerge under certain circumstances and within certain relationships. As individuals develop in faith, they have an increasing number of schemas to "pull on" when responding to specific environments, interactions, and religious commitments. Streib (2007) provides the example of adult fundamentalism potentially representing a regression into or a revival of earlier religious styles, as the reciprocal-instrumental style (similar to Fowler's Stage 2) becomes the dominant style used in religion while other more advanced styles are utilized in other areas of life. Consequently, an individual's religious style may influence how he or she constructs meaning and thinks about the world, but one's specific circumstances and relationships can influence the ways that he or she ultimately relates to the world, living out and communicating values and commitments.

Shweder and Jensen's Ethic of Divinity

While not a direct critique of Fowler's (1981) theory of faith development, the cross-cultural, more global perspective of the Ethic of Divinity (e.g., Jensen, 2015a; Shweder, 2015) offers a formidable challenge to universalist models such as Fowler's, as well as Kohlberg and Power's (1981). As we discussed in Chapter 7, Jensen's (2015a) cultural-developmental theory of moral development tries to account for how Shweder (2015) and Jensen's (2015a) Three Ethics (Autonomy, Community, and Divinity) develop across the lifespan and vary across cultures. As you may remember from Chapter 7, the Three Ethics are defined as follows:

> The **Ethic of Autonomy** [emphasis added] involves a focus on the self as an individual. Moral reasons within this ethic involve a focus on the self as an individual. Moral reasons within this ethic include the interests, well-being, and rights of individuals (self or other) and fairness between individuals. The **Ethic of Community** focuses on persons as members of social groups, with attendant reasons such as duty to others and concern with the customs, interests, and welfare of groups. The **Ethic of Divinity** focuses on people as spiritual or religious entities, and encompass divine and natural law, sacred lessons, and spiritual purity.
>
> (Jensen, 2015a, p. 3)

Shweder (2015) explained that one of the most important contributions of Jensen's (2015a) cultural-developmental theory of moral development is her inclusion of the Ethic of Divinity within the moral domain. We will present some of her research on the Ethic of Divinity in religious samples in the next section.

Research on the Relationship between Moral Thinking and Religious or Spiritual Beliefs

Some studies have looked specifically at relationships between moral reasoning and religious or spiritual beliefs. Historically, much of the research was conducted with the Defining Issues Test (DIT) and consistently showed that religious conservatives had lower moral reasoning than religious liberals (Getz, 1984; Rest et al., 1999). Needham-Penrose and Friedman (2012) questioned the singular reliance on the DIT to assess the moral maturity of conservative Christians. Results showed that conservative Christian graduate students scored lower on the DIT but higher on moral identity, and Needham-Penrose and Friedman argued that religious conservatives responded to the DIT using Jensen's (2015a) Ethic of Divinity.

More recently, Jensen and McKenzie (2016), using a cultural-developmental lens, found that by the age of 10, evangelicals and mainline Protestants diverged on the use of the Ethic of Divinity for public moral issues, such as capital punishment or interracial marriage, and private moral issues that have happened in their own lives. Mainline children, adolescents, and adults relied on the Ethic of Divinity for private issues but evangelical children, teens, and adults relied on it especially for public issues such as capital punishment or interracial marriage. In a study of emerging adult Latter Day Saints, Padilla-Walker and Nelson (2015) also highlighted the interaction between culture and development, with participants struggling to reconcile the moral worldviews of the Ethic of Autonomy and the Ethic of Divinity, for example, regarding sexuality.

Walker and Reimer (2006) argued that the results from research involving real-life moral dilemmas (similar to what Jensen and McKenzie (2016) called private moral issues) and **moral exemplars** help to illustrate the significant impact of religion and spirituality on people's moral thinking. A major theme in Walker and Reimer's research suggested that people relied on their faith to resolve their real-life moral dilemmas, using their religious beliefs and values to guide their moral choices. Colby and Damon (1992) interviewed a small sample of moral exemplars, individuals identified as leading lives of sustained moral commitment. While their religious affiliations differed, and religion was not part of the selection criteria, 80% of the sample discussed how faith-based values drove their moral commitments. Across various studies of moral exemplars, Walker (2020) has shown that exemplar and comparison groups are differentiated by moral reasoning and **epistemic development**, what Fowler referred to as faith development. As Walker notes,

> Mature epistemic development is predictive of exemplary moral character because it entails openness to the ambiguity and complexity of multiple aspects of reality... It entails a striving toward the transcendent, a grappling with questions of meaning and purpose, and with notions of what is good and true. And, especially pertinent, mature

epistemic development embodies an expanded inclusiveness, the humanizing of all people. This expanded and inclusive circle of concern clearly can undergird committed moral action.

(Walker, 2020, p. 8)

Emerging Adults' Faith, Spirituality and Religiosity

Both Fowler and Jensen identified emerging adulthood as a crucial time-period for faith development, and a specific focus of current research is emerging adults' faith, spirituality, and religiosity. Clearly, Erikson's (1968) theory of identity development influenced both Fowler's older work (e.g. 1981) on faith development, as well as more recent research on religious and spiritual beliefs of emerging adults (EAs) (Arnett & Jensen, 2002; Barry & Abo-Zena, 2014). Of specific relevance to the current chapter is Arnett's (2000) argument that the Eriksonian period of identity exploration in adolescence, including exploration of religious identity, now takes place during emerging adulthood (18–29) in western industrialized cultures. Fowler (1981) specifically identifies college as a context that can facilitate (or stall) the transition to Stage 4, Individuative-Reflective Faith.

The college years often immerse EAs in very specific cultures of learning and socialization. Although results of several major national studies of EAs' religious and spiritual lives suggest that contemporary US college students' participation in organized religion is declining at a steep pace (Pew Research Center [PEW], 2015a, 2019), findings from other studies argue that this does not necessarily mean that EAs are not searching for spiritual meaning (e.g., Astin & Astin, 2010; Bryant et al., 2003; Barry & Abo-Zena, 2014; Dalton et al., 2006; Smith, 2009). Smith's (2009) extensive longitudinal study of religiosity and spirituality in American adolescents and young adults found EAs less religious than older adults, but differences by age often varied based on religious affiliation, with black and evangelical Protestants showing higher levels of religiousness across age groups. Smith also identified a cluster of beliefs he labeled **Moralistic Therapeutic Deism (MTD)**, including the ideas that (a) although God wants people to be nice, good and fair, he does not need to be particularly involved in one's life; (b) good people will go to heaven when they die; and (c) the central goal of life is to be happy and feel good about oneself. Barry and Abo-Zena (2014) argued that emerging adulthood is an "untethered time" (p. 41) in which many young adults put religion in a "lockbox" (p. 163), where it is just not all that important. In findings complementing Smith's work with younger participants, Arnett and Jensen (2002) found that EAs' beliefs tend to be highly individualized. The 140 EAs in their sample of 21- to 28-year-olds took bits and pieces of various religions (and popular culture) to form their own diverse beliefs independent from parents and religious institutions.

Developmentalists understand that both individual differences and cultural contexts shape worldviews and behaviors. They ask: "For which people?

Under which circumstances?" Findings from Barry and Nelson's (2005) study of the role of religion during the transition to adulthood suggest the importance of attending to influences of specific college cultures. Students who chose to attend religious institutions may be significantly different in terms of devotion than non-students. For instance, in a study of highly religious college students, Cook et al. (2015) found that this population was less likely to accept the "watered down" MTD faith identified by Smith (2009). The prevalence of more traditional and committed conservative belief systems in their sample highlights the importance of not generalizing about the faith experiences of contemporary EAs.

Our own research has used both questionnaires and interviews to explore samples of EAs at two different universities (one faith-based and one secular) to develop a deeper understanding of developmental trends in first-year and senior college students' perceptions of religion, spirituality, faith, and God/a higher power; as well as a more nuanced understanding of the contextual factors supporting or challenging their religious and spiritual growth (Senland, 2019; Vozzola, 2019). Given that many large national studies of EAs' faith development often miss nuances of development and context, we began our research aiming to provide university communities and leaders with a more contextualized, developmental perspective about the faith of their student populations. In addition, we found no research suggesting that Kohlberg's theory of religious development (Kohlberg & Power, 1981) had been tested, so we aimed to do some initial construct validity on a measure that we designed to assess Kohlberg and Power's faith development stages.

Our results highlight the fruitfulness of exploring faith development across multiple contexts, as well as the need to examine faith participation norms at individual colleges. Qualitative results indicated that students at the faith-based university identified more aspects of the college context that fostered faith while those at secular university noted more that encouraged students to put faith into a "lock-box" (Barry & Abo-Zena, 2014, p. 163). Student characteristics likely interacted with context; students may have self-selected their institutions such that those open to spiritual growth were more likely to attend the faith-based university whereas those who may already have been moving their faith into a "lock-box" for this stage of their life chose to attend the secular university. However, Hill's (2009) results and Hall et al.'s (2016) findings that evangelical Christians attending a Christian college declined in spiritual practice, involvement, and commitment across college, highlight the crucial point that simply attending a faith-based institution does not necessarily facilitate spiritual growth, even for students who may arrive religiously and spiritually committed. Our results for the faith-based university are more aligned with Cook et al. (2015) who found stability in religious practice and beliefs for evangelical conservative Christians at another Christian college.

While we believe there is value in developing a faith development measure reflecting growth in cognitive and moral complexity (goals of many colleges), we concluded that the Kohlberg/Powers model, rooted in the universalist assumptions of its time, may not adequately capture students' development in spirituality or conceptions of their faith tradition. Developing a valid and reliable measure will require going back to the drawing board and finding ways to integrate the most relevant concepts from Jensen and colleagues' (2015) fine work on assessing the Ethic of Divinity, Fowler's Faith Development measure, and those concepts from Kohlberg and Powers' theory congruent with a global developmental perspective. Future studies should especially consider the inappropriateness of assessing items such as "I see God/a higher power as all powerful; makes everything happen," as a low stage of development, as that ranking biases against those of strong religious faith. Researchers should also consider whether a pantheistic highest stage accurately captures mature moral development across diverse religious orientations or simply reflects tolerance for multicultural perspectives.

Although there have been widespread assumptions that the well-documented decline of religiosity in emerging adulthood arises from the secularizing influence of higher education, in fact, the opposite is true (Hartley, 2004). A consistent finding across many studies has been that while religious practices may decline during the college years, college does not seem to play a role in changing students' core religious beliefs (e.g. Barry et al., 2010; Stoppa & Lefkowitz, 2010). Furthermore, it is actually EAs who do not attend college who exhibit the largest decline in religious practice. Both college attendance and marriage curb religious decline, while non-marital sex and drug and alcohol use promote it (Uecker et al., 2007). Another study of the effect of higher education on religious practices and beliefs (Schwadel, 2011) found that for mainline Protestants and other religions, but not for evangelical Christians, education does weaken the viewpoint that there is truth in only one religion. It also weakens a belief in the Bible as the literal word of God for both mainline and evangelical Protestants. Interestingly, education positively affects belief in a higher power rather than a definite belief in God—a finding that may correlate with the rise of spiritual but not religious young people.

In a particularly extensive study of the religious and spiritual dimensions of first-year college students' faith experiences, Bryant et al. (2003) noted a discrepancy between students reporting a commitment to becoming more spiritual yet admitting they were becoming *less* spiritual. Perhaps one explanation for this can be found in the Higher Educational Research Institute (HERI) data from 2010 (HERI, 2010) that suggested that while first year students care about spiritual matters, they do not find adequate guidance from their colleges in this domain (Redden, 2007). Bryant et al. (2003) suggested the importance of colleges providing supportive programs and curricula to provide students with "opportunities to reflect on life's big questions" (p. 740). They believe that sponsoring campus events that center on family visits, providing spaces for prayer and reflection and encouraging classroom discussions of religion and spirituality are all factors that can nurture students' faith development. The extensive Spirituality in Higher Education study of 14,527 students across 136 institutions found that self-reflection and meditation, service learning, and faculty encouragement of questions of meaning and purpose all supported spiritual questing (Astin & Astin, 2010). Dalton et al. (2006) offered additional useful suggestions gleaned from a survey of college and university chaplains.

Many studies of faith development (e.g., Cook et al., 2015; Barry & Nelson, 2005) suggest the importance of looking at EAs from specific religious traditions in specific secular and religious contexts and cultures. Lovik (2010) noted that required chapel attendance (characteristic of some very religious institutions) has the strongest effect on spiritual development. Required coursework in religion, theology or spirituality also positively impacts spiritual development. He is sensitive to the impact of college choice on college impact given that students interested in faith development are most likely to choose institutions that provide support for that interest. Yet even religious institutions that explicitly promote a faith perspective face challenges when EAs perceive their tenets as out of step with new social norms of tolerance. Cheah's (2016) excellent analysis of the challenges to traditional Catholic identities inherent in rising numbers of spiritual but not religious young people argues that because these EAs are open to multiple religious practices (PEW, 2015a), the Church needs to balance tradition with openness to less traditional practices that enhance spiritual growth. He believes that "too much tradition can lead to a formulation of Catholic identities that over-emphasize the form of tradition at the expense of the substance of spirituality. However, too little tradition can result in a loss in a sense of identity" (p. 315).

Applications and Implications for Helping Professionals

As with Piaget's and Kohlberg's theories, Fowler's conception of developmental progression in the capacity to grapple with the complexity of life's meaning is extremely helpful in taking the perspective of a client, student, or child whose questions about the meaning of life, values, and ideas may seem hard to understand. While Fowler's theory has been widely applied to religious education and pastoral care, Parker (2011) argued that secular counselors would also find Fowler's model useful, given its universal, inclusive definition of faith, and its orientation toward growth. With knowledge of Fowler's faith stages, counselors could guage clients' faith stages, supporting them in harnessing the strengths of those stages to confront a crisis, or challenging them to work through stage transitions. Parents may also be able to facilitate children's faith development. For example, late adolescents, in trying to assert their independence and develop their own system of values and beliefs, may be engaging in a developmentally healthy characteristic of Fowler's Stage 4, Individuative-Reflective Faith, by eschewing church attendance and questioning key tenets of their childhood faith. A family that responds with more authority and tighter control may stifle growth, while one who is open to and attempts to respond to doubt may enhance capacity for a self-reflective faith.

Fowler's theory is also of specific relevance to teachers, counselors, and university support staff who work with college students. While many students come to college seeking answers to spiritual answers, they often do not receive enough guidance from their institutions in this area of their lives (Redden, 2007). In the Higher Education Research Institute (HERI; 2010) large, national study almost half (48%) of first-year students believed it was "essential" or "very important" for their college to encourage their spirituality. However, Barry et al. (2010) noted that only "39% of college students reported their spiritual or religious beliefs to be strengthened from class discussions, and they generally were dissatisfied with their college experience because of a lack of opportunity for religious or spiritual reflection" (p. 315), suggesting that colleges could do more to engage students in purpose/meaning-based discussions. Challenging EAs to engage in purpose/meaning-based discussions within the context of support may encourage students to continue to grapple with spiritual questions central to some of the identity work of emerging adulthood (Arnett, 2000; Dalton et al., 2006). While students and faculty at secular institutions may find these discussions more challenging and less frequent than those at faith-based institutions (Fosnacht & Broderick, 2018), student-faculty interactions involving spirituality positively predict college students' meaning making and spiritual growth (Riggers-Piehl & Sax, 2018). However, providing adequate support for students through these meaning-based discussions is important as stepping out of the "lock-box" and engaging in such discussions may lead to spiritual struggle, which is associated with increased psychological distress, decreased physical health, lowered self-esteem, and less growth in religiosity and spirituality (Bryant & Astin, 2003).

Andrade (2014) explained how student affairs professionals could help meet college students' quest for meaning by using knowledge of Fowler's theory of faith development to help identify, as well as to support and challenge, students' individual stages, as well as to develop programming developmentally attuned to the changing needs of college students. For example, she provides the example of creating opportunities for those at lower stages to simply be introduced to new ideas and worldviews, while those at higher stages may be more equipped to grapple with, and actively respond to, issues of social justice and oppression. A common theme for suggestions for nurturing students' faith development is to encourage classroom discussions of spirituality and religion, as well as engagement in purpose/meaning-based discussions, to provide an informal space for EAs to continue to grapple with questions about spirituality and religion central to the identity work of this time period (Astin & Astin, 2010; Dalton et al., 2006).

Counselors, parents, teachers, and college staff may all find use in King and Furrow's (2004) investigation of *how* religion positively influences adolescents' and EAs' well-being, as they argue that religion does so by building social capital (especially through parents, peers, and non-familial adults), thus enhancing moral outcomes such as empathy and altruism. While the most direct applications of this study apply to congregations, faith-based organizations, and parents hoping to raise their children in their faith, the value of building trusting relationships and community could apply to secular communities, as well as natural interactions on college campuses (students with adult faculty, staff, and coaches), who "nurture intergenerational relationships that are characterized by social interaction, trust, and shared vision" (p. 711).

Conclusion

Regardless of whether one perceives development through the lens of stages or schemas, human development—both moral and faith—involves an increasingly complex and widening perspective on the world that allows individuals to grow in understanding of the self and become increasingly inclusive and tolerant of those unlike themselves (Hanford, 1991). As individuals live out their faith and ultimately seek to provide an answer to Tolstoy's universal moral question (cited by Gilligan, 1998) "how to live and what to do?"—faith development may interact with moral development and unique circumstances to determine whether an individual takes moral action. Just as Fowler highlighted that faith can provide the motivation for moral action at various stages, Kohlberg suggested that moral maturity requires the religious conviction necessary to live out values (Hanford, 1991). Consequently, as individuals progress through and find equilibrium within the faith stages, their present way of viewing the world interacts with various other developmental and situational factors, influencing both the schemata they pull upon to view the world and the actions they subsequently take. Just as many studies of faith development in the United States suggest the importance of examining EAs from specific religious traditions in specific secular and religious contexts and college cultures (e.g., Cook et al., 2015; Barry & Nelson, 2005; Padilla-Walker & Nelson, 2015), we imagine that future research with Jensen's (2015a) cultural-developmental theory of morality, with its inclusion of the Ethic of Divinity, will also enhance our knowledge of faith development across particular secular and religious contexts and cultures across the globe.

Discussion Questions

1. Wacker (2000, para. 8) found that discussing fundamentalism can be problematic. He notes that feelings can "run high" and that "many students, coming from the outside, will try to dismiss the movement as narrow-minded and even bigoted. Others, coming from the inside will try to defend it as the only valid form of Christianity (or any religion

for that matter)." Wacker suggests considering how fundamentalists are "similar to many other social and religious groups that looked backward to find resources for dealing with the troubling changes in the present." What do you think? Do you find Wacker's suggestion helpful? Have you observed this discomfort with discussing religion? Did the definition of fundamentalism at the beginning of this chapter help you?

2. The research suggests that college students frequently want to discuss spiritual matters, but often do not receive the guidance that they hoped for or anticipated from their colleges in this domain (Barry et al., 2010; Redden, 2007). Did your college experience influence your faith at all, either now or in the past? What about your college experience fostered or impeded your religious or spiritual growth? For example, think about your friends, classes, teachers, staff, religious groups on campus, residential life, etc.

Additional Resources

- For any of you interested in learning more about religious fundamentalism and radicalization, this European Union special report provides an excellent resource

  - Orva, A. (2015, March). Religious fundamentalism and radicalization. *European Parliamentary Research Service (EPRS)*. https://www.europarl.europa.eu/EPRS/EPRS-briefing-551342-Religious-fundamentalism-and-radicalisation-FINAL.pdf

- For any of you interested in conducting research, Jensen (2015a) gives away her research tools for assessing the Three Ethics in the appendixes of the following resource

  - Jensen, L. A. (Ed). (2015a). *Moral development in a global world: Research from a cultural-developmental perspective.* Cambridge University Press. https://doi.org/10.1017/CBO9781139583787

- Students and practitioners interested in additional research on faith development in globally diverse participants may be particularly fascinated by Jensen's (2015a)*Moral Development in a Global World: Research from a Cultural-Developmental Perspective.*
- If you are interested in global and national trends in key religious issues, you may want to bookmark the PEW Research Center: https://www.pewresearch.org/topic/religion/
- If you are interested in spirituality in higher education, you may find it useful to peruse the Higher Educational Research Institute (HERI) website for additional results of their longitudinal research, resources, key terms, and measures: https://spirituality.ucla.edu/

13 Conclusion: How to Live and What to Do?

You can't remake the world

Without remaking yourself

Each new era begins within.

(Ben Okri, "Mental Flight")

During her 1997 Kohlberg Memorial Lecture to the members of the Association for Moral Education, Carol Gilligan reflected on her scholarly and personal relationship with Larry Kohlberg (Gilligan, 1998) and talked about how their students in the 1960s, caught in the powerful currents of the antiwar movement and the emerging women's movement, struggled with Tolstoy's question of "How to live and what to do?" Don't we all in every era? In the wake of the financial crisis of 2008 and, more recently, the economic meltdowns during the pandemic, we watched our students grapple with tensions between choosing meaningful work and choosing a vocation that would pay the bills. As the global pandemic rages amidst the politicization of science, critical thinkers everywhere despair at their inability to overcome their fellow citizens' deep dive into misinformation and conspiracy theories. We see fellow professionals struggle to maintain a sustainable balance between the demands of work and home. And, at the macro level, the mounting global challenges of climate change, ethnic and religious hatreds, wars, poverty, disease, and hunger seem to have pushed many good people to psychic numbing if not to cynicism or despair. Despite all these challenges, we count ourselves as extraordinarily lucky to be working in a field where our colleagues have answered Tolstoy's question by promoting moral development and moral education. We know that morally mature and engaged young people and citizens not only are more likely to live ethical lives themselves but also to be motivated to help their fellow humans and tackle the big problems of their families, communities, and societies.

Back in Chapter 1, we shared with you our own moral motivation for writing this book:

DOI: 10.4324/9780429295461-15

This text's stress on application reflects our own sincere hope that whether you are a professional reading the book to enhance your practice or a student reading it in a course, you make the connections between theory and the pressing moral issues of our time. *Our ultimate goal has been to spark your interest to such an extent that you feel motivated to implement some of the field's ideas in your own professional life.* In a world fraught with challenges at every level—from the struggles of stressed families to the international scourges of terrorism, genocide, and war— we need a committed core of helping professionals dedicated to promoting both justice and care.

How exactly might you integrate the concepts of moral development theory and practice into your personal and work life? The knowledge that people at all ages and in all places are especially attuned to issues of justice and care has made both of us very curious about exactly how children and adults across the lifespan understand these concepts. For example, when Amie interviewed children from biblical families about the headmaster Dumbledore allowing young wizards to break rules, she was fascinated by their attempts to respect the caring and life-saving actions of beloved characters with their own respect for the justice-based norms and rules of their families and church. Turning from the world of research and hy- pothetical dilemmas to real-world observations of family life and lessons, when Elly visited her young grandchildren after the birth of the newest baby, it was evident that her 6-month-old granddaughter flourished in the caring environment of her extended Armenian-Italian family. Care was being held; smiled at, and cooed over by everyone; and being fed and changed and put down to sleep when she needed it. Justice for her then 3-year-old sister came to mean getting equal attention and time with that given to that adorable little interloper. Her 8-year-old brother, however, already exhibited the more complex conceptions of justice and care you would expect from an older child. He brought Elly a blanket when they watched his favorite cartoon and understood that the baby needed a lot of attention. (In fact, he was delighted to have someone who appreciated him making goofy faces!) In short, he could notice and respond to the needs of others in ways that his younger sisters couldn't yet understand but surely benefitted from seeing modeled.

It's extremely rewarding to be able to get a developmental fix on young children and come up with ways to respond appropriately. It's a lot harder to do so with what Marv Berkowitz calls "the tarnished pennies"—the kids who are angry or cruel or defiant—and who, of course, need us the most. Many of you reading this book will be going on into professional fields where you will be exposed to a wide range of people operating across a wide range of moral sensitivity, motivation, reasoning, and behavior. You may be teaching them, defending them in court, caring for them, or counseling them. We hope you are now sensitized to the idea that **every**

interaction you have with others is an opportunity for moral engagement. You may be that one person who listens to the wounded child or angry prisoner or lonely senior and makes a difference in their lives. When Elly taught adolescent development to undergraduate students, she encouraged them all to be aware that every teenager needs a "cool auntie or uncle"—people who accept them for who they are at the same time they encourage them to be the best person they possibly can be. As Norm Sprinthall would say: "**Challenge and support.**" That's the magic formula for promoting moral development, and we hope you now feel more able to use those powerful tools in your own professional lives.

In short, **moral development theories help us understand others.** Moral education and developmental counseling interventions and practices can help us to promote optimal growth, prevent future problems, and heal past ones. We hope you came away from reading about these applications with a broadened vision of what is possible in terms of human flourishing.

We'd like to end this chapter with one final reflection on why we believe it is so important to promote moral development at every possible turn. Albert Camus once wrote that in times of hatred (and surely we are living in such a time), intellectuals have the responsibility to "explain the meaning of words in such a way as to sober minds and calm fanaticisms" (Suleiman, 2013, p. 32). Let's return to Kohlberg's conception of moral reasoning as growth in complexity and see how we can connect it to that quote. The way we see it, for most of human history, people had little need for more than Stage 2 or Stage 3 thinking to guide their relationships. For the powerful, it made sense to control opportunities for education and growth. Promoting Stage 1 thinking where people believe that swift punishment will follow if they disobey, break rules, or challenge authority, is a brilliant strategy for keeping the masses servile. Stage 2 thinking could keep many others in line: an eye for an eye and a tooth for a tooth; you be good to me and I'll be good to you. It also served and serves as justification for wars and revenge.

When more of a population begins to regularly use Stage 3 thinking, we might expect more prosocial behavior. However, if Haidt (2012) is right, it is likely to be tribally focused. Kohlberg acknowledged this sort of limitation as well. But we no longer live in small tribes. We are a globally connected humanity. We can't all live upstream; smoke from raging forest fires in the US West and Canada kept our homes in Connecticut blanketed in smog during the summer of 2021. Problems such as climate change, war, overpopulation, and nuclear proliferation cannot be solved in any simple way.

So how to live and what to do? Throughout this text, we have argued that promoting the optimal moral development of all children has to be our first step. But that's not enough. We have to start caring about the communities in which that development is taking place. We know that stress drives down all aspects of development including moral development.

When you reach a point of mature moral sensitivity, it becomes clear that safe communities and societies are the bedrock of human rights. How can we think our job is done by teaching a child the virtue of the week and then tossing her out into a neighborhood where she is put at risk by drive-by shootings, omnipresent drug dealers, and sexual predators?

Theories of moral development suggest that higher (more complex) reasoning is better for solving the kind of complex problems facing the world today. As you saw in Chapter 9, social-emotional learning and moral education programs ideally also promote not only cognitive complexity but also an ever-expanding conception of "we." Yet privileging complex moral reasoning challenges Haidt's (2012) argument for tolerance of more traditional worldviews that incorporate hierarchy, loyalty/tribalism, and sanctity/purity as equal partners with justice and care. How can we respect differences in cultural perspectives, avoid the trap of ethnocentrism, and yet work for a more humane world? These are tough ethical questions with no easy answers. We've given you our perspectives, but you are going to have to grapple with these questions yourself.

You may recall from Chapter 7 how ethics professor Robert McNulty hypothesized that all societies (and major religions) have core concepts of justice and care but differ in whether they should be extended to all people or to some. The humanist vision, with which we agree, argues that there is only one answer: to all. From a humanist perspective, the moral person is obligated to respectfully but forcefully work towards a world in which *all* people's basic human needs are met, and their human rights respected.

What then should be the ultimate goal of moral development? We think it needs to be something much more than Kohlberg's concept of complexity in reasoning, or Hoffman's of mature empathy, or Haidt's of tolerance for multiple worldviews and moral foundations. We believe the goal should be one that is rarely mentioned in the literature and equally rarely reached without a great deal of life experience and the inevitable suffering that is part of all lives. Our hope for our children, grandchildren, students, and readers is that the goal they strive towards is **wisdom**—human goodness/care/empathy filtered through complex moral thinking. We began our exploration of moral development with Sagan's (1988) observation that "**Love is the great educator**." We think that's also a very good place to end.

References

Aharoni, E., Sinnott-Armstrong, W., & Kiehl, K. A. (2014). What's wrong? Moral understanding in psychopathic offenders. *Journal of Research in Personality*, *53*, 175–181. 10.1016/j.jrp.2014.10.002

Aknin, L. B., Broesch, T., Hamlin, J. K., & Van de Vondervoort, J. W. (2015). Prosocial behavior leads to happiness in a small-scale rural society. *Journal of Experimental Psychology: General*, *144*(4), 788–795. 10.1037/xge0000082

Aknin, L. B., Hamlin, J. K., & Dunn, E. W. (2012). Giving leads to happiness in young children. *PLOS ONE*, *7*(6), Article e39211. 10.1371/journal.pone.0039211

Aknin, L. B., Van de Vondervoort, J. W., & Hamlin, J. K. (2018). Positive feelings reward and promote prosocial behavior. *Current Opinion in Psychology*, *20*, 55–59. 10.1016/j.copsyc.2017.08.017

Althof, W. (2015). Just Community sources and transformations: A conceptual archeology of Kohlberg's approach to moral and democratic schooling. In B. Zizek, D. Garz, & E. Nowak (Eds.), *Kohlberg revisited* (pp. 51–91). Sense Publishing.

American Psychiatric Association (2013). *Diagnostic and statistical manual of mental disorders: DSM-5* (5th ed.). American Psychiatric Association.

Andrade, A. (2014). Using Fowler's faith development theory in student affairs practice. *College Student Affairs Leadership*, *1*(2), Article 2. https://scholarworks.gvsu.edu/csal/vol1/iss2/2/

Arnett, J. J. (1995). Adolescents' uses of media for self-socialization. *Journal of Youth and Adolescence*, *24*(5), 519–533. 10.1007/BF01537054

Arnett, J. J. (2000). Emerging adulthood: A theory of development from the late teens through the twenties. *American Psychologist*, *55*, 469–480.

Arnett, J. J. & Jensen, L. A. (2002). A congregation of one: Individualized religious beliefs among emerging adults. *Journal of Adolescent Research*, *17*(5), 451–467. 10.1177/0743558402175002

Astin, A. W. & Astin, H. S. (2010). Exploring and nurturing the spiritual life of college students. *Journal of College and Character*, *11*(3), 39–61. 10.2202/1940-1639.1724

Balthazar, N. (2007). *Ben X* [Film]. MMG Film & TV Production.

Bandura, A. (1999). Moral disengagement in the perpetration of inhumanities. *Personality and Social Psychology Review* [Special issue], *3*(3), 193–209. 10.1207/s15327957pspr0303_3

Bandura, A. (2002). Selective moral disengagement in the exercise of moral agency. *Journal of Moral Education*, *31*(2), 101–119. 10.1080/0305724022014322

Bandura, A. (2016). *Moral disengagement: How people do harm and live with themselves.* Worth.

Bandura, A., Ross, D., & Ross, S. A. (1961). Transmission of aggression through imitation of aggressive models. *The Journal of Abnormal and Social Psychology, 63*(3), 575–582. 10.1037/h0045925

Baron-Cohen, S. (1995). *Mindblindness: An essay on autism and theory of mind.* MIT/Bradford Books.

Baron-Cohen, S. (2011). *The science of evil: On empathy and the origins of cruelty.* Basic Books.

Barry, C. M., & Abo-Zena, M. M. (2014). *Emerging adults' religiousness and spirituality.* Oxford.

Barry, C. M., & Nelson, L. J. (2005). The role of religion in the transition to adulthood for young emerging adults. *Journal of Youth and Adolescence, 34*(3), 245–255. 10.1007/s10964-005-4308-1

Barry, C. M., Nelson, L., Davarya, S., & Urry, S. (2010). Religiosity and spirituality during the transition to adulthood. *International Journal of Behavioral Development, 34*(4), 311–324. 10.1177/0165025409350964

Baskin, T. W., & Enright, R. D. (2004). Intervention studies on forgiveness: A meta-analysis. *Journal of Counseling & Development, 82*(1), 79–90.

Baumsteiger, R., Mangan, S., Bronk, K. C., & Bono, G. (2019). An integrative intervention for cultivating gratitude among adolescents and young adults. *The Journal of Positive Psychology, 14*(6), 807–819. 10.1080/17439760.2019.1579356

Bebeau, M. J. (2014). An evidence-based guide for ethics instruction. *Journal of Microbiology & Biology Education, 15*(2), 124–129. 10.1128/jmbe.v15i2.872

Bergin, C. (2014). Educating students to be prosocial at school. In L. M. Padilla-Walker & G. Carlo (Eds.), *Prosocial development: A multidimensional approach* (pp. 279–301). Oxford University Press.

Berkowitz, M. W. (2002). The science of character education. In W. Damon (Ed.), *Bringing in a new era in character education* (pp. 43–64). Hoover Institution Press.

Berkowitz, M. W. (2011). What works in values education. *International Journal of Educational Research, 50*(3), 153–158.

Berkowitz, M. W. (2015, January 15). *The expanding universe of character education: One man's journey* [Invited Paper]. The Jubilee Centre for Character and Virtues, Insight Series, Oxford, England.

Berkowitz, M. W. (2021). *PRIMED for character education: Six design principles for school improvement.* Routledge.

Berkowitz, M. W., & Bier, M. C. (2006). *What works in character education: A research-driven guide for educators.* Character Education Partnership.

Berkowitz, M. W., & Bier, M. C. (2014). Research-based fundamentals of the effective promotion of character development in schools. In L. P. Nucci & D. Narvaez (Eds.), *Handbook of moral and character education* (2nd ed., pp. 248–260). Routledge.

Berkowitz, M. W., Bier, M. C., & McCauley, B. (2017). Toward a science of character education: Frameworks for identifying and implementing effective practices. *Journal of Character Education, 13*(1), 33–51.

Berkowitz, M. W., Lickona, T., Nast, T., Schaeffer, E., & Bohlin, K. (2020). The eleven principles of effective character education: A brief history. *Journal of Character Education, 16*(2), 1–10.

Berkowitz, M. W., Schaeffer, E. F., & Bier, M. C. (2001). Character education in the United States. *Education in the North, New Series, 9,* 52–59.

Bill, T. (Director). (1980). *My bodyguard* [Film]. Melvin Simon Productions.

Blasi, A. (1980). Bridging moral cognition and moral action: A critical review of the literature. *Psychological Bulletin, 88*(1), 1–45.

Blasi, A. (1983). Moral cognition and moral action: A theoretical perspective. *Developmental Review, 3*(2), 178–210.

Blasi, A. (2004). Moral functioning: Moral understanding and personality. In D. K. Lapsley & D. Narvaez (Eds.), *Moral development, self, and identity* (pp. 335–348). Lawrence Erlbaum Associates.

Blasi, A. (2009). The moral functioning of mature adults and the possibility of fair moral reasoning. In D. Narvaez & D. K. Lapsley (Eds.), *Personality, identity, and character: Explorations in moral psychology* (pp. 396–440). Cambridge University Press.

Bloom, P. (2013). *Just Babies: The origins of good and evil.* Crown.

Bloom, P. (2016). *Against empathy: The case for rational compassion.* HarperCollins.

Bock, T. (2001). *Ethical judgment: Activity booklet 2—Nurturing character in the middle school classroom.* Darcia Narvaez.

Bos, J., & Stokes, M. A. (2019). Cognitive empathy moderates the relationship between affective empathy and wellbeing in adolescents with autism spectrum disorder. *European Journal of Developmental Psychology, 16*(4), 433–446. 10.1080/17405629.201 8.1444987

Boustead, K. (2007). The French headscarf law before the European Court of Human Rights. *Journal of Transnational Law and Policy, 16*(2), 167–196.

Bronk, K. C., Baumsteiger, R., Mangan, S., Riches, B., Dubon, V., Benavides, C., & Bono, G. (2019). Fostering purpose among young adults: Effective online interventions. *Journal of Character Education, 15*(2), 21–38.

Bronk, K. C., & Mangan, S. (2016). Strategies for cultivating purpose among adolescents in clinical settings. In P. Russo-Netzer, S. E. Schulenberg, & A. Batthyany (Eds.), *Clinical perspectives on meaning* (pp. 407–421). Springer International Publishing.

Brosnan, S. F., & de Waal, F. B. M. (2014). Evolution of responses to (un)fairness. *Science, 346*(6207), 1–19. 10.1126/science.1251776

Broughton, J. M. (1983). Women's rationality and men's virtues: A critique of gender dualism in Gilligan's theory of moral development. *Social Research, 50*(3), 597–642.

Brown, J. D., Steele, J. R., & Walsh-Childers, K. (2002). *Sexual teens, sexual media: Investigating media's influence on adolescent sexuality.* Erlbaum.

Brown, P., Corrigan, M. W., & Higgins-D'Alessandro, A. (Eds.). (2012). *Handbook of prosocial education.* Rowman & Littlefield.

Brownell, C. (Ed.). (2013). Early development of prosocial behavior [Special edition]. *Infancy, 18*(1), 1–9.

Bryant, A. N., & Astin, A. W. (2008). The correlates of spiritual struggle during the college years. *The Journal of Higher Education, 79*(1), 1–27.

Bryant, A. N., Choi, J. Y., & Yasuno, M. (2003). Understanding the religious and spiritual dimensions of students' lives in the first year of college. *Journal of College Student Development, 44*(6), 723–745.

Bussey, K. (2020). Development of moral disengagement: Learning to make wrong right. In L. A. Jensen (Ed.), *The Oxford handbook of moral development: An interdisciplinary perspective* (pp. 306–326). Oxford University Press.

Cáceda, R., James, G. A., Ely, T. D., Snarey, J., & Kilts, C. D. (2011). Mode of effective connectivity within a putative neural network differentiates moral cognitions related to care and justice ethics. *PLOS ONE, 6*(2), Article e14730. 10.1371/journal.pone.0014730

Card, N. A., Stucky, B. D., Sawalani, G. M., & Little, T. D. (2008). Direct and indirect aggression during childhood and adolescence: A meta-analytic review of gender differences, intercorrelations, and relations to maladjustment. *Child Development, 79*(5), 1185–1229. 10.1111/j.1467-8624.2008.01184.x.

Carlo, G. (2013). The development and correlates of prosocial moral behaviors. In M. Killen & J. G. Smetana (Eds.), *Handbook of moral development* (2nd ed., pp. 208–226). Routledge.

Carlo, G., Knight, G. P., McGinley, M., Goodvin, R., & Roesch, S. C. (2010). The developmental relations between perspective taking and prosocial behaviors: A meta-analytic examination of the task-specificity hypothesis. In B. W. Sokol, U. Müller, J. I. M. Carpendale, A. R. Young, & G. Iarocci (Eds.), *Self and social regulation: Social interaction and the development of social understanding and executive functions* (p. 234–269). Oxford University Press. 10.1093/acprof:oso/9780195327694.003.0010

Carlo, G., Mestre, M. V., Samper, P., Tur, A., & Armenta, B. E. (2010). Feelings or cognitions? Moral cognitions and emotions as longitudinal predictors of prosocial and aggressive behaviors. *Personality and Individual Differences, 48*(8), 872–877. 10.1016/j.paid.2010.02.010

Carlo, G., Mestre, M. V., Samper, P., Tur, A., & Armenta, B. E. (2011). The longitudinal relations among dimensions of parenting styles, sympathy, prosocial moral reasoning, and prosocial behaviors. *International Journal of Behavioral Development, 35*(2), 116–124. 10.1177/0165025410375921

Centers for Disease Control and Prevention. (2020). Prevalence of autism spectrum disorder among children aged 8 years—autism and developmental disabilities monitoring network, 11 sites, United States, 2016. *Morbidity and Mortality Weekly Report, 69*(SS-04), 1–12. https://www.cdc.gov/mmwr/volumes/69/ss/ss6904a1.htm?s_cid=ss6904a1_w

Chapman, M. (1988). *Constructive evolution: Origin and development of Piaget's thought.* Cambridge University Press.

Cheah, J. (2016). Spiritual but not religious, multiple religious practice, and traditional Catholic identities. In J. Y. Tan & A. Q. Tran (Eds.), *World Christianity perspectives and insights: Essays in honor of Peter C. Phan* (pp. 300–317). Orbis Books.

Chodorow, N. J. (1978). *The reproduction of mothering: Psychoanalysis and the sociology of gender.* University of California Press.

Choi, Y-J., Han, H., Dawson, K. J., Thoma, S. J., & Glenn, A. L. (2019) Measuring moral reasoning using moral dilemmas: Evaluating reliability, validity, and differential item functioning of the behavioural defining issues test (bDIT). *European Journal of Developmental Psychology, 16*(5), 622–631. 10.1080/17405629.2019.1614907

Cohen, M. (2007, April 1). France uncovered [Review of the book *Why the French don't like headscarves: Islam, the state, and public space*]. *The New York Times.* https://www.nytimes.com/2007/04/01/books/review/Cohen.t.html

Colby, A., & Damon, W. (1992). *Some do care: Contemporary lives of moral commitment.* The Free Press.

Colby, A., & Kohlberg, L. (1987). *The measurement of moral judgment: Vol. 1. Theoretical foundations and research validation.* Cambridge University Press.

Conroy, J. C. (Ed.). (2021). Future directions for moral education, on the 50th anniversary of the *Journal of Moral Education* [Special issue]. *Journal of Moral Education, 50*(1).

Cook, K. V., Boyatzis, C. J., Kimball, C., & Leonard, K. C. (2015). Religiousness and spirituality among highly religious emerging adults. *Journal of Psychology and Christianity, 34*(3), 252–265.

Coyle, A. (2011). Critical responses to faith development theory: A useful agenda for change? *Archive for the Psychology of Religion, 33*(3), 281–298. 10.1163/157361211 X608162

Coyne, S. M., Padilla-Walker, L. M., & Howard, E. (2013). Emerging in a digital world: A decade review of media use, effects, and gratifications in emerging adulthood. *Emerging Adulthood, 1*(2), 155-137. 10.1177/2167696813479782

Cretton, D. D. (Director) (2019). *Just Mercy* [Film]. Warner Brothers.

Curry, O. S., Rowland, L. A., Van Lissa, C. J., Zlotowitz, S., McAlaney, J., & Whitehouse, H. (2018). Happy to help? A systematic review and meta-analysis of the effects of performing acts of kindness on the well-being of the actor. *Journal of Experimental Social Psychology, 76*, 320–329. 10.1016/j.jesp.2018.02.014

Dahl, A. (2018). New beginnings: An interactionist and constructivist approach to early moral development. *Human Development, 61*(4–5), 232–247. 10.1159/000492801

Dahl, A. (2019). The science of early moral development: On defining, constructing, and studying morality from birth. *Advanced Child Development Behavior, 56*, 1–35. 10.1 016/bs.acdb.2018.11.001.

Dahl, A., & Brownell, C. A. (2019). The social origins of human prosociality. *Current Directions in Psychological Science, 28*(3), 274–279. 10.1177/0963721419830386

Dahl, A., & Killen, M. (2018). A developmental perspective on the origins of morality in infancy and early childhood. *Frontiers in Psychology, 9*, Article 1736. 10.3389/fpsyg.2 018.01736

Dahl, A., & Paulus, M. (2019). From interest to obligation: The gradual development of human altruism. *Child Development Perspectives, 13*(1), 10–14. 10.1111/cdep.12298

Dahl, A., Satlof-Bedrick, E. S., Hammond, S. I., Drummond, J. K., Waugh, W. E., & Brownell, C. A. (2017). Explicit scaffolding increases simple helping in younger infants. *Developmental Psychology, 53*(3), 407–416. 10.1037/dev0000244

Dalton, J. C., Eberhardt, D., Bracken, J., & Echols, K. (2006). Inward journeys: Forms and patterns of college student spirituality. *Journal of College and Character, 7*(8), 1–19. 10.2202/1940-1639.1219

Damon, W. (1988). *The moral child: Nurturing children's natural moral growth.* The Free Press.

Damon, W., & Malin, H. (2020). The development of purpose: An international perspective. In L. A. Jensen (Ed.), *The Oxford handbook of moral development: An interdisciplinary perspective* (pp. 110–127). Oxford University Press. 10.1093/oxfordhb/ 9780190676049.001.0001

Davidov, M., Zahn-Waxler, C., Roth-Hanania, R., & Knafo, A. (2013). Concern for others in the first year of life: Theory, evidence, and avenues for research. *Child Development Perspectives, 7*(2), 126–131. 10.1111/cdep.12028

Davidson, M., Lickona, T., & Khmelkov, V. (2014). Smart & good schools: A new paradigm for high school character education. In L. P. Nucci & D. Narvaez (Eds.), *Handbook of moral and character education* (2nd edition, pp. 290–307). Routledge.

Davis, M. H. (1983). Measuring individual differences in empathy: Evidence for a multidimensional approach. *Journal of Personality and Social Psychology, 44*(1), 113–126.

Decety, J., & Cowell, J. M. (2014). Friends or foes: Is empathy necessary for moral behavior? *Perspectives on Psychological Science, 9*(5), 525–537. 10.1177/1745691 614545130

Denton, K., & Krebs, D. (2017). Rational and emotional sources of moral decision-making: An evolutionary-developmental account. *Evolutionary Psychological Science, 3,* 72–85. 10.1007/s40806-016-0067-3

de Saint-Exupéry, A. (1943/1971). *Le petit prince.* Harcourt, Brace & World.

DeVries, R. & Zan, B. (1994). *Moral classrooms, moral children: Creating a constructivist atmosphere in early education.* Teachers College Press.

de Waal, F. (1996). *Good natured: The origins of right and wrong in humans and other animals.* Harvard University Press.

de Waal, F. (2011). *Moral behavior in animals* [Video]. TED Conferences. www.ted.com/speakers/frans_de_waal.html

de Waal, F., & Sherblom, S. A. (2018). Bottom-up morality: The basis of human morality in our primate nature. *Journal of Moral Education, 47*(2), 248–258. 10.1080/03057240.2018.1440701

Dewey, J. (1916). *Democracy and education.* Macmillan.

Durkheim, E. (1961). *Moral education: A study in the theory and application of the sociology of education.* The Free Press.

Eagly, A. H. (2009). The his and hers of prosocial behavior: An examination of the social psychology of gender. *American Psychologist, 64*(8), 644–658.

Eisenberg, N., & Spinrad, T. L. (2014). Multidimensionality of prosocial behavior: Rethinking the conceptualization and development of prosocial behavior. In L. M. Padilla-Walker & G. Carlo (Eds.), *Prosocial development: A multidimensional approach* (pp. 17–39). Oxford University Press.

Eisenberg, N., Spinrad, T., & Knafo-Noam, A. (2015). Prosocial development. In R. M. Lerner (Ed.), *Handbook of child psychology and development science: Vol. 3. Socioemotional processes* (7th ed., pp. 610–656). John Wiley and Sons.

Eisenberg, N., Spinrad, T., & Morris, A. (2013). Empathy-related responding in children. In M. Killen, & J. G. Smetana (Eds.), *Handbook of moral development* (2nd ed., pp. 184–207). Routledge.

Elliott, M. L., Knodt, A. R., Ireland, D., Morris, M. L., Poulton, R., Ramrakha, S., Sison, M. L., Moffitt, T. E., Caspi, A. & Hariri, A. R. (2020). What is the test-retest reliability of common task-fMRI measures? New empirical evidence and a meta-analysis. *Psychological Science, 31*(7), 792–806. 10.1177/0956797620916786

Elkind, D., & Flavell, J. H. (Eds.). (1969). *Studies in cognitive development: Essays in honor of Jean Piaget.* Oxford University Press.

Emerson, M. O., & Hartman, D. (2006). The rise of religious fundamentalism. *Annual Review of Sociology, 32,* 1270144.

Endicott, L. (2001). *Ethical sensitivity: Activity booklet 1—Nurturing character in the middle school classroom.* Darcia Narvaez.

Enright, R. D., Freedman, S. R., & Rique, J. (1998). The psychology of interpersonal forgiveness. In R. D. Enright & J. North (Eds.), *Exploring forgiveness* (pp. 46–62). University of Wisconsin Press.

Enright, R. D., & North, J. (Eds.). (1998). *Exploring forgiveness.* University of Wisconsin Press.

Enright, R. D., & Song, J. Y. (2020). The development of forgiveness. In L. A. Jensen (Ed.), *Oxford handbook of moral development: An interdisciplinary perspective* (pp. 402–418). Oxford University Press.

Epstein, S. (1990). Cognitive-experiential self-theory. In L. A. Pervin (Ed.), *Handbook of personality theory and research: Theory and research* (pp. 165–192). Guilford Press.

Epstein, S. (1994). Integration of the cognitive and the psychodynamic unconscious. *American Psychologist, 49*(8), 709–724.

Epstein, S. (2003). Cognitive-experiential self-theory of personality. In T. Millon & M. J. Lerner, (Eds.), *Handbook of psychology: Vol. 5. Personality and social psychology* (pp. 159–184). Wiley & Sons.

Erikson, E. H. (1968). *Identity: Youth and crisis.* Norton.

Esterson, A. (2001). The mythologizing of psychoanalytic history: Deception and self-deception in Freud's accounts of the seduction theory episode. *History of Psychiatry, 7,* 329–352.

Farnsworth, J. K., Drescher, K. D., Nieuwsma, J. A., Walser, R. B., & Currier, J. M. (2014). The role of moral emotions in military trauma: Implications for the study and treatment of moral injury. *Review of General Psychology, 18*(4), 249–262. 10.1037/gpr0000018

Fengyan, W. (2004). Confucian thinking in traditional moral education: Key ideas and fundamental features. *Journal of Moral Education, 33*(4), 429–447. 10:1080/0305724 0420003279984

Flack, J. C., & de Waal, F. B. M. (2000). 'Any animal whatever.' Darwinian building blocks of morality in monkeys and apes. *Journal of Consciousness Studies, 7*(1–2), 1–29.

Flavell, J. H. (1963). *Developmental psychology of Jean Piaget.* D. Van Nostrand.

Flavell, J. H. (1982). On cognitive development. *Child Development, 53*(1), 1–10.

Flavell, J. H., Miller, P. H., & Miller, S. A. (2002). *Cognitive development* (4th ed.). Prentice-Hall.

Fordham University. (2021, January 26). *Faculty webpage: Ann Higgins-D'Alessandro.* https://www.fordham.edu/info/21660/psychology_faculty_and_staff/5425/ann_higgins-dalessandro

Forkus, S. R., & Weiss, N. H. (2021). Examining the relations among moral foundations, potentially morally injurious events, and posttraumatic stress disorder symptoms. *Psychological Trauma: Theory, Research, Practice and Policy, 13*(4), 403–411. 10.1037/tra0000968

Fosnacht, K., & Broderick, C. (2018). The role of religion and institution type in seniors' perceptions of the religious and spiritual campus climate. *Journal of College and Character, 19*(1), 18–31. 10.1080/2194587X.2017.1411274

Fowler, J. W. (1981). *Stages of faith: The psychology of human development and the quest for meaning.* HarperSanFrancisco.

Fowler, J. W. (1987). *Faith development and pastoral care.* Fortress Press.

Fowler, J. W. (2003). Faith development theory and the challenges of practical theology. In R. R. Osmer & F. L. Schweitzer (Eds.), *Developing a public faith: New directions in practical theology—Essays in honor of James W. Fowler* (pp. 229–250). Chalice.

Fowler, J. W., & Dell, M. L. (2006). Stages of faith from infancy through adolescence: Reflections on three decades of faith development theory. In E. C. Roehlkepartain, P. E. King, L. Wagener, & P. L. Benson (Eds.), *The handbook of spiritual development in childhood and adolescence* (pp. 34–45). Sage.

Fowler, J. W., Snarey, J., & DeNicola, K. (1988). *Remembrances of Lawrence Kohlberg: A compilation of the presentations given at the service of remembrance for Lawrence Kohlberg at Memorial Church, Harvard University, on May 20, 1987*. Atlanta, GA: Center for Research in Faith and Moral Development.

Frederickson, B. L. (2013, March 23). Your phone vs. your heart. *The New York Times*. https://www.nytimes.com/2013/03/24/opinion/sunday/your-phone-vs-your-heart.html

Freud, S. (1923). *The ego and the id*. (Standard ed., 19). Hogarth Press.

Freud, S. (1930). *Civilization and its discontents*. (Standard ed., 21). Hogarth Press.

Frimer, J. A., & Walker, L. J. (2008). Towards a new paradigm of moral personhood. *Journal of Moral Education, 37*(3), 333–356. 10.1080/03057240802227494

Frisancho, S., Moreno-Gutiérrez, M. C., & Taylor, M. (Eds.). (2009). Moral and citizenship education in Latin America: Towards reconciliation, community development and democracy [Special issue]. *Journal of Moral Education, 38*(4), 391–406.

Garmon, L.C., Glover, R.J., & Vozzola, E.C. (2018). Self-perceived use of popular culture media franchises: Does gratification impact multiple exposures? *Psychology of Popular Media Culture, 7*(4), 572–588. 10.1037/ppm0000153

George, T. (Director). (2005). *Hotel Rwanda*. Lion's Gate Entertainment and United Artists.

Georgiou, G., Demetriou, C. A., & Fanti, K. A. (2019). Distinct empathy profiles in callous unemotional and autistic traits: Investigating unique and interactive associations with affective and cognitive empathy. *Journal of Abnormal Child Psychology, 47*(11), 1863–1873. 10.1007/s10802-019-00562-1

Geraci, A., & Surian, L. (2011). The developmental roots of fairness: Infants' reactions to equal and unequal distributions of resources: Evaluation of fairness of distributive actions. *Developmental Science, 14*(5), 1012–1020. 10.1111/j.1467-7687.2011.01048.x

Getz, I. R. (1984). Moral judgment and religion: A review of the literature. *Counseling and Values, 28*(3), 94–116. 10.1002/j.2161-007X.1984.tb01153.x

Gibbs, J. C. (1995). The cognitive-developmental perspective. In W. M. Kurtines & J. L. Gewirtz (Eds.), *Moral development: An introduction* (pp. 27–48). Allyn & Bacon.

Gibbs, J. C. (2010). *Moral development and reality: Beyond the theories of Kohlberg and Hoffman* (2nd ed.). Allyn & Bacon.

Gibbs, J. C. (2019). *Moral development and reality: Beyond the theories of Kohlberg, Hoffman, and Haidt* (4th ed.). Oxford University Press.

Gibbs, J. C., Basinger, K. S., & Fuller, D. (1992). *Moral maturity: Measuring the development of sociomoral reflection*. Lawrence Erlbaum.

Gibbs, J. C., Moshman, D., Berkowitz, M. W., Basinger, K. S., & Grime, R. L. (2009). Taking development seriously: Critique of the 2008 *JME* special issue on moral functioning. *Journal of Moral Education, 38*(3), 271–282. 10.1080/030572409031 01432

Gibbs, J. C., Potter, G., & Goldstein, A. P. (1995). *The EQUIP program: Teaching youth to think and act responsibly though a peer-helping approach*. Research Press.

Gibbs, J. C., & Widaman, K. F. (1982). *Social intelligence: Measuring the development of sociomoral reflection*. Prentice Hall.

Gillberg, C. (1992). The Emanuel Miller lecture, 1991: Autism and autistic-like conditions: Subclasses among disorders of empathy. *Journal of Child Psychology and Psychiatry, 33*, 813–842.

Gilligan, C. (1982). *In a different voice: Psychological theory and women's development.* Harvard University Press.

Gilligan, C. (1998). Remembering Larry. *Journal of Moral Education, 27*(2), 125–140.

Gilligan, C., Ward, J. V., & Taylor, J. M. (Eds.). (1988). *Mapping the moral domain: A contribution of women's thinking to psychological theory and education.* Harvard University Graduate School of Education.

Gilligan, C., & Wiggins, G. (1987). The origins of morality in early childhood relationships. In J. Kagan & S. Lamb (Eds.), *The emergence of morality in young children* (pp. 277–305). Chicago University Press.

Gilligan, J. (1976). Beyond morality: Psychoanalytic reflections on shame, guilt, and love. In T. Lickona (Ed.), *Moral development and behavior: Theory, research, and social issues* (pp. 144–158). Holt, Rinehart and Winston.

Glover, R. J., Garmon, L. C., & Hull, D. H. (2011). Media's moral messages: Assessing moral content in media. *Journal of Moral Education, 40*(1), 89–104. 10.1080/0305724 0.2011.541773

Gorn, E. J. (Ed.). (1998). *The McGuffey readers: Selections from the 1879 edition.* Bedford/ St. Martins.

Graver, C., & Blumberg, F. C. (2020). Moral choices in digital games: Pixelated morality. In L. A. Jensen (Ed.), *The Oxford handbook of moral development: An interdisciplinary perspective* (pp. 708–724). Oxford University Press.

Grazzani, I., Ornaghi, V., Agliati A., & Brazzelli E. (2016). How to foster toddlers' mental-state talk, emotion understanding, and prosocial behavior: A conversation-based intervention at nursery school. *Infancy, 21*, 199–227. 10.1111/infa.12107

Haddon, M. (2003). *The curious incident of the dog in the night-time.* Doubleday.

Haidt, J. (2001). The emotional dog and its rational tail: A social intuitionist approach to moral judgment. *Psychological Review, 108*(4), 814–834.

Haidt, J. (2008). *The moral roots of liberals and conservatives* [Video]. TED Conferences. https://www.ted.com/talks/jonathan_haidt_the_moral_roots_of_liberals_and_conservatives?language=en

Haidt, J. (2012). *The righteous mind: Why good people are divided by politics and religion.* Pantheon Books.

Hall, T. W., Edwards, E., & Wang, D. C. (2016). The spiritual development of emerging adults over the college years: A 4-year longitudinal investigation. *Psychology of Religion and Spirituality, 8*(3), 206–217. 10.1037/rel0000051

Halstead, J. M. (Ed.). (2007a). Islamic values and moral education [Special issue]. *Journal of Moral Education, 36*(3), 283–296.

Halstead, J. M. (Ed.). (2007b). Islamic values: A distinctive framework for moral education? *Journal of Moral Education, 36*(3), 283–296.

Halstead, R. W. (2007). *Assessment of client core issues.* American Counseling Association.

Hamlin, J. K. (2013). Moral judgment and action in preverbal infants and toddlers: Evidence for an innate moral core. *Current Directions in Psychological Science, 22*(3), 186–193. 10.1177/0963721412470687

Hamlin, J. K., & Tan, E. (2020). The emergence of moral responses and sensitivity. In L. A. Jensen (Ed.), *The Oxford handbook of moral development: An interdisciplinary perspective* (pp. 267–287). Oxford.

Hamlin, J. K., Wynn, K., & Bloom, P. (2007). Social evaluation by preverbal infants. *Nature, 450*(7169), 557–559. 10.1038/nature06288

Han, H. (2017). Neural correlates of moral sensitivity and moral judgment associated with brain circuitries of selfhood: A meta-analysis. *Journal of Moral Education, 46*(2), 97–113. 10.1080/03057240.2016.1262834

Han, H., Dawson, K. J., Thoma, S. J., & Glenn, A. L. (2020). Developmental level of moral judgment influences behavioral patterns during moral decision-making. *The Journal of Experimental Education, 88*(4), 660–675. 10.1080/00220973.2019.1574701

Han, H., Kim, J., Jeong, C., & Cohen, G. L. (2017). Attainable and relevant moral exemplars are more effective than extraordinary exemplars in promoting voluntary service engagement. *Frontiers in Psychology, 8*, Article 283. 10.3389/fpsyg.2017.00283

Hanford, J. T. (1991). The relationship between faith development of James Fowler and moral development of Lawrence Kohlberg: A theoretical review. *Journal of Psychology and Christianity, 10*, 306–310.

Hardy, S. A., Zhang Z., Skalski, J. E., Melling, B. S., & Brinton, C. T. (2014). Daily religious involvement, spirituality, and moral emotion. *Psychology of Religion and Spirituality, 6*(4), 338–348. 10.1037/a0037293

Hare, R. D. (2003). *The Hare Psychopathy Checklist-Revised. 2.* Multi-Health Systems.

Harris, G. T., & Rice, M. E. (2006). Treatment of psychopathy: A review of empirical findings. In C. Patrick (Ed.), *Handbook of psychopathy* (pp. 555–572). Sage.

Hartley, H.V. (2004). How college affects students' religious faith and practice: A review of research. *College Student Affairs Journal, 23*(2), 111–129.

Haste, H. (2013). Deconstructing the elephant and the flag in the lavatory: Promises and problems of moral foundations research. *Journal of Moral Education, 42*(3), 316–329. 10.1080/03057240.2013.818529

Hay, D. F., Paine, A. L., Perra, O., Cook, K. V., Hashmi, S., Robinson, C., Kairis, V., & Slade, R. (2021). Prosocial and aggressive behavior: A longitudinal study. *Monographs of the Society for Research in Child Development, 86*(2), 7–103. 10.1111/mono.12427

Hayes, R. L. (1991). Counseling and clinical implications of Kohlberg's developmental psychology. In L. Kuhmerker (Ed.), *The Kohlberg legacy for the helping professions* (pp. 173–187). R.E.P. Books.

Hayes, R. L. (1994). The legacy of Lawrence Kohlberg: Implications for counseling and human development. *Journal of Counseling & Development, 72*(3), 261–267.

Hayes, R. L., & Paisley, P. O. (2002). Transforming school counseling preparation programs. *Theory into Practice, 41*(3), 169–176.

Henrich, J., Heine, S. J., & Norenzayan, A. (2010). The weirdest people in the world? *Behavioral and Brain Sciences, 33*, 61–83; discussion 83–135. 10.1017/S0140525 X0999152X

Hepach, R. (2017). Prosocial arousal in children. *Child Development Perspectives, 11*(1), 50–55. 10.1111/cdep.12209

Hertz, S. G., & Krettenauer, T. (2016). Does moral identity effectively predict moral behavior?: A meta-analysis. *Review of General Psychology, 20*(2), 129–140. 10.1037/gpr0000062

Higgins, A. (1995). Educating for justice and community: Lawrence Kohlberg's vision of moral education. In W. M. Kurtines & J. L. Gewirtz (Eds.), *Moral development: An introduction* (pp. 49–82). Allyn & Bacon.

Higgins-D'Alessandro, A. (2010). The transdisciplinary nature of citizenship and civic/ political engagement evaluation. In L. R. Sherrod, J. Torney-Purta, & C. A. Flanagan (Eds.), *Handbook of research on civic engagement in youth* (pp. 559–592). Wiley.

Higgins-D'Alessandro, A. (2015). Lawrence Kohlberg's legacy: Radicalizing the educational mainstream. In B. Zizek, D. Garz, & E. Nowak (Eds.), *Kohlberg revisited* (pp. 27–51). Sense Publishing.

Higher Education Research Institute. (2010). *The spiritual life of college students: A national study of students' search for meaning and purpose.* https://spirituality.ucla.edu/

Hill, J. P. (2009). Higher education as moral community: Institutional influences on religious participation during college. *Journal for the Scientific Study of Religion, 48*(3), 515–534. 10.1111/j.1468-5906.2009.01463.x

Hoffman, M. L. (1981). Is altruism part of human nature? *Journal of Personality and Social Psychology, 40*(1), 121–137.

Hoffman, M. L. (2000). *Empathy and moral development: Implications for caring and justice.* Cambridge University Press.

Hogan, R., & Emler, E. (1995). Personality and moral development. In W. M. Kurtines & J. L. Gewirtz (Eds.), *Moral development: An introduction* (pp. 209–228). Allyn & Bacon.

Horan, J. M., Higgins-D'Alessandro, A., Vozzola, E. C., & Rosen, J. (2010, May). *A qualitative analysis of student alumni reflective adult perceptions of the impact of a just community school (1972–2008)* [Poster presentation]. 22nd Annual Convention of the Association for Psychological Science (APS), Boston, MA.

Hui, B. P. H., Ng, J. C. K., Berzaghi, E., Cunningham-Amos, L. A., & Kogan, A. (2020). Rewards of kindness? A meta-analysis of the link between prosociality and well- being. *Psychological Bulletin, 146*(12), 1084–1116. 10.1037/bul0000298

Hymel, S., & Perren, S. (Eds.). (2015). Moral disengagement and aggression in children and youth [Special issue]. *Merrill-Palmer Quarterly, 61*(1), 1–9.

Imuta, K., Henry, J. D., Slaughter, V., Selcuk, B., & Ruffman, T. (2016). Theory of mind and prosocial behavior in childhood: A meta-analytic review. *Developmental Psychology, 52*(8), 1192–1205. 10.1037/dev0000140

Inhelder, B., & Piaget, J. (1964). *The early growth of logic in the child.* Harper & Row.

Iyer, R., Ditto, P., Graham, J., Haidt, J., Koleva, S., Motyl, M, Sherman, G., & Wojcik, S. (2019, October). *Moralfoundations.org.* https://moralfoundations.org/

Jacobs, T. (2012, March/April). My morals are better than yours. *Miller-McCune*, 68–70.

Jacobs, T. (2019, February). The complex ethical codes of anti-vaxxers. *Pacific Standard.* https://psmag.com/education/the-curious-morality-of-the-anti-vaxxer

Jaffe, S., & Hyde, J. S. (2000). Gender differences in moral orientation: A meta-analysis. *Psychological Bulletin, 126*, 703–726.

James, W. (1902/1985). *The varieties of religious experience.* Penguin Books.

Jankowski, P. J., Sandage, S. J., Bell, C. A., Davis, D. E., Porter, E., Jessen, M., Motzny, C. L., Ross, K. V., & Owen, J. (2020). Virtue, flourishing, and positive psychology in psychotherapy: An overview and research prospectus. *Psychotherapy, 57*(3), 291–309. 10.1037/pst0000285

Jensen, L. A. (Ed.). (2011). *Bridging cultural and developmental approaches to psychology: New syntheses in theory, research and policy.* Oxford University Press.

Jensen, L. A. (Ed). (2015a). *Moral development in a global world: Research from a cultural-developmental perspective.* Cambridge University Press. 10.1017/CBO9781139583787

Jensen, L. A. (2015b). Moral reasoning: Developmental emergence and life course pathways among cultures. In L.A. Jensen (Ed.), *The Oxford handbook of human development and culture: An interdisciplinary perspective* (pp. 230–254). Oxford University Press.

Jensen, L. A. (Ed.). (2015c). *The Oxford handbook of human development and culture: An interdisciplinary perspective*. Oxford University Press.

Jensen. L. A. (2015d). Theorizing and researching moral development in a global world. In L.A. Jensen (Ed.), *Moral development in a global world: Research from a cultural-developmental perspective* (pp. 1–17). Cambridge University Press. 10.1017/CBO9781139583787

Jensen, L. A. (Ed.). (2020a). *The Oxford handbook of moral development: An interdisciplinary perspective*. Oxford University Press. 10.1093/oxfordhb/9780190676049.001.0001

Jensen, L. A. (2020b). Moral development: From paradigms to plurality. In L. A. Jensen (Ed.), *The Oxford handbook of moral development: An interdisciplinary perspective* (pp. 3–8). Oxford University Press. 10.1093/oxfordhb/9780190676049.001.0001

Jensen, L. A., & McKenzie, J. (2016). The moral reasoning of U.S. evangelical and mainline Protestant children, adolescents, and adults: A cultural-developmental study. *Child Development, 87*(2), 446–464. 10.1111/cdev.12465

Johnson, L. V., Ziomek-Daigle, J., Haskins, N. H., & Paisley, P. O. (2016). An investigation of school counselor self-efficacy with English language learners. *Professional School Counseling, 20*(1), 44–53. 10.5330/1096-2409-20.1.44

Kagan, J. (1998). Morality and its development. In W. Sinnott-Armstrong (Ed.), *Moral psychology: Vol. 2. The cognitive science of morality: Intuition and diversity* (pp. 297–312). MIT Press.

Kahneman, D. (2003). A perspective on judgment and choice: Mapping bounded rationality. *American Psychologist, 58*(9), 697–720.

Kahneman, D. (2013). *Thinking fast and slow*. Farrar, Straus and Giroux.

Kahneman, D., & Tversky, A. (1973). On the psychology of prediction. *Psychological Review, 80*(4), 237–251. 10.1037/h0034747

Katz, L. D. (Ed.). (2000). *Evolutionary origins of morality: Cross-disciplinary perspectives*. Short Run Press.

Kegan, R. (1982). *The evolving self: Problem and process in human development*. Harvard University Press.

Kennett, J. (2002). Autism, empathy and moral agency. *The Philosophical Quarterly, 52*(208), 340–357.

Kiehl, K. A. (2008). Without morals: The cognitive neuroscience of psychopaths. In W. Sinnott-Armstrong (Ed.), *Moral psychology (Vol. 3): The neuroscience of morality: Emotion, brain disorders, and development* (pp. 119–149). MIT Press.

Killen, M., & Smetana, J. (Eds.). (2014). *Handbook of moral development* (2nd ed.). Psychology Press.

King, P. E., & Furrow, J. L. (2004). Religion as a resource for positive youth development: Religion, social capital, and moral outcomes. *Developmental Psychology, 40*(5), 703–713. 10.1037/0012-1649.40.5.703.

Klapwijk, E. T., Aghajani, M., Colins, O. F., Marijnissen, G. M., Popma, A., van Lang, N. D. J., van der Wee, N. J. A., & Vermeiren, R. R. J. M. (2016). Different brain responses during empathy in autism spectrum disorders versus conduct disorder and callous-unemotional traits. *Journal of Child Psychology and Psychiatry, 57*(6), 737–747. 10.1111/jcpp.12498

Klatt, J. S., & Enright, R. D. (2011). Initial validation of the unfolding forgiveness process in a natural environment. *Counseling and Values, 56*(1–2), 25–42.

Kohlberg, L. (1976). Moral stages and moralization: The cognitive-developmental approach. In T. Lickona (Ed.), *Moral development and behavior: Theory, research, and social issues* (pp. 31–53). Holt, Rinehart and Winston.

Kohlberg, L. (1981). *Essays on moral development: Vol. 1. The philosophy of moral development.* Harper and Row.

Kohlberg, L. (1984). *Essays on moral development: Vol. 2. The psychology of moral development.* Harper and Row.

Kohlberg, L. (1986). My personal search for universal morality. *Moral Education Forum, 11*(1), 4–10.

Kohlberg, L., & Power, C. (1981). Moral development, religious thinking, and the question of a seventh stage. In L. Kohlberg (Ed.), *Essays on moral development: Vol. 1. The philosophy of moral development: Moral stages and the idea of justice* (pp. 311–372). Harper & Row.

Kok, B. E., Coffey, K. A., Cohn, M. A., Catalino, L. I., Vacharkulksemsuk, T., Algoe, S. B., Brantley, M., & Fredrickson, B. L. (2013). How positive emotions build physical health: Perceived positive social connections account for the upward spiral between positive emotions and vagal tone. *Psychological Science, 24*(7), 1123–1132. 10.1177/0956797612470827

Kramer, P. D. (2006). *Freud: Inventor of the modern mind.* HarperCollins.

Krcmar, M., & Cingel, D. P. (2020). Media as a context for studying moral development. In L. A. Jensen (Ed.), *The Oxford handbook of moral development: An interdisciplinary perspective* (pp. 649–662). Oxford University Press.

Krebs, D. (2000). As moral as we need to be. In L. D. Katz (Ed.), *Evolutionary origins of morality: Cross-disciplinary perspectives* (pp. 139–143). Short Run Press.

Krebs, D. L. (2011). *The origins of morality: An evolutionary account.* University Press.

Krebs, D. L. (2020). The evolution and development of morality. In T. B. Henley, M. J. Rossano, & E. P. Kardas (Eds.). *Handbook of cognitive archaeology: Psychology in prehistory* (pp. 86–104). Routledge.

Krettenauer, T. (2021). Moral sciences and the role of education. *Journal of Moral Education, 50*(1), 77–91. 10.1080/03057240.2020.1784713

Kuhmerker, L. (1991). *The Kohlberg legacy for the helping professions.* R.E.P. Books.

Kuhn, T. S. (1970). *The structure of scientific revolutions* (2nd ed.). University of Chicago Press.

Kurtines, W. M., & Gewirtz, J. L. (Eds.). (1995). *Moral development: An introduction.* Allyn & Bacon.

Kwok, J. & Selman, R. (2017). From informed social reflection to civic engagement: How to interpret what youth say and do. In B. García-Cabrero, A. Sandoval-Hernández, E. Treviño-Villareal, S. Diazgranados Ferráns, M. Guadalupe, & P. Martínez (Eds.), *Civics and citizenship: Theoretical models and experiences in Latin America* (pp. 15–36). Sense Publishers.

Laible, D., & Karahuta, E. (2014). Prosocial behaviors in early childhood: Helping others, responding to the distress of others, and working with others. In L. M. Padilla-Walker & G. Carlo (Eds.), *Prosocial development: A multidimensional approach* (pp. 350–379). Oxford University Press.

Lancaster, S. L., & Miller, M. (2020). Moral decision making, religious strain, and the experience of moral injury. *Psychological Trauma: Theory, Research, Practice, and Policy, 12*(2), 156–164. 10.1037/tra0000518

Lapsley, D. K. (1996). *Moral psychology.* Westview Press.

Lapsley, D. K. (2006). Moral stage theory. In M. Killen & J. Smetana (Eds.), *Handbook of moral development* (pp. 37–66). Lawrence Erlbaum Associates.

Lapsley, D. K., & Narvaez, D. (Eds.). (2004). *Moral development, self, and identity.* Lawrence Erlbaum Associates.

Larsen, R. R., Jalava, J., & Griffiths, S. (2020). Are Psychopathy Checklist (PCL) psychopaths dangerous, untreatable, and without conscience? A systematic review of the empirical evidence. *Psychology, Public Policy, and Law, 26*(3), 297–311. 10.1037/law0000239

Larson, R. W., Walker, K. C., & McGovern, G. (2020). Youth programs as contexts for development of ethical judgment and action. In L. A. Jensen (Ed.), *The Oxford handbook of moral development: An interdisciplinary perspective* (pp. 552–569). Oxford University Press.

Leming, J. S. (2008). Research and practice in moral and character education: Loosely coupled phenomena. In L. P. Nucci & D. Narvaez (Eds.), *Handbook of moral and character education* (pp. 134–157). Routledge.

Levine, P., & Higgins-D'Alessandro, A. (2010). Youth civic engagement: Normative issues. *Handbook of research on civic engagement in youth* (pp. 115–137). Wiley.

Lickona, T. (Ed.). (1976). *Moral development and behavior: Theory, research, and social issues.* New Holt, Rinehart and Winston.

Lickona, T. (2004). *Character matters: How to help our children develop good judgment, integrity, and other essential virtues.* Touchstone Books.

Lickona, T., & Davidson, M. (2005). *Smart and good high schools: Integrating excellence and ethics for success in school, work, and beyond.* Character Education Partnership.

Lies, J., & Narvaez, D. (2001). *Ethical motivation: Activity booklet 3—Nurturing character in the middle school classroom.* Darcia Narvaez.

Lovik, E. G. (2010, November 20). *The impact of organizational features and student experiences on spiritual development during the first year of college* [Paper presentation]. Association for the Study of Higher Education 35th Annual Meeting, Indianapolis, IN, United States.

Lucca, K., Kiley, J., & Sommerville, J. (Eds.) (2019). Early moral cognition and behavior [Research Topic]. *Frontiers in Psychology* 10.3389/fpsyg.2019.02013

Lucca, K., Pospisil, J., & Sommerville, J. A. (2018). Fairness informs social decision making in infancy. *PLOS ONE, 13*(2), Article e0192848. 10.1371/journal.pone.0192848

Malatesti, L. (2010). Moral understanding in the psychopath. *Synthesis Philosophica, 24*(2), 337–348.

Malti, T., & Dys, S. P. (2018). From being nice to being kind: Development of prosocial behaviors. *Current Opinion in Psychology, 20,* 45–49. 10.1016/j.copsyc.2017.07.036

Malti, T., & Noam, G. G. (2016). Social-emotional development: From theory to practice. *European Journal of Developmental Psychology, 13*(6), 652–665. 10.1080/17405629.2016.1196178

Malti, T., Noam, G. G., Beelmann, A., & Sommer, S. (2016). Toward dynamic adaptation of psychological interventions for child and adolescent development and mental health. *Journal of Clinical Child & Adolescent Psychology, 45*(6), 827–836. 10.1080/15374416.2016.1239539

Maosen, L., Taylor, M. J., & Shaogang, Y. (Eds.). (2004). Moral education in changing Chinese societies [Special issue]. *Journal of Moral Education, 33*(4), 405–428.

Margoni, F., & Surian, L. (2018). Infants' evaluation of prosocial and antisocial agents: A meta-analysis. *Developmental Psychology, 54*(8), 1445–1455. 10.1037/dev0000538

Marshall, J., Watts, A. L., Frankel, E. L., & Lilienfeld, S. O. (2017). An examination of psychopathy's relationship with two indices of moral judgment. *Personality and Individual Differences, 113*, 240–245. 10.1016/j.paid.2017.03.034

Marshall, J., Watts, A. L., & Lilienfeld, S. O. (2018). Do psychopathic individuals possess a misaligned moral compass? A meta-analytic examination of psychopathy's relations with moral judgment. *Personality Disorders: Theory, Research, and Treatment, 9*(1), 40–50. 10.1037/per0000226

Maxwell, B., & Narvaez, D. (2013). Moral foundations theory and moral development and education. *Journal of Moral Education, 42*(3), 271–280. 10.1080/03057240.2013.825582

McAdams, D. P. (1993). *The stories we live by: Personal myths and the making of the self.* Guilford Press.

McAdams, D. P. (2009). The moral personality. In D. Narvaez & D. K. Lapsley (Eds.), *Personality, identity, and character: Explorations in moral psychology* (pp. 11–29). Cambridge University Press.

McGeer, V. (2008). Varieties of moral agency: Lessons from autism (and psychopathy). In W. Sinnott-Armstrong (Ed.), *Moral psychology (Vol. 3): The neuroscience of morality: emotion, brain disorders, and development* (pp. 227–257). MIT Press.

McKay, R., & Whitehouse, H. (2015). Religion and morality. *Psychological Bulletin, 141*(2), 447–473. 10.1037/a0038455

McKenzie, J. (2020). Globalization as a context for moral development. In L. A. Jensen (Ed.), *The Oxford handbook of moral development: An interdisciplinary perspective* (pp. 663–681). Oxford University Press. 10.1093/oxfordhb/9780190676049.001.0001

McNulty, J. K., & Fincham, F. D. (2012). Beyond positive psychology? Toward a contextual view of psychological processes and well-being. *American Psychologist, 67*(2), 101–110. 10.201037/a0024572

Mead, G. H. (1934). *Mind, self and society.* University of Chicago Press.

Menting, A. T., Orobio de Castro, B., & Matthys, W. (2013). Effectiveness of the incredible years parent training to modify disruptive and prosocial child behavior: A meta-analytic review. *Clinical Psychology Review, 33*(8), 901–913. 10.1016/j.cpr.2013.07.006.

Metz, T., & Gaie, J. B. R. (2010). The African ethic of Ubuntu/Botho: Implications for research on morality. *Journal of Moral Education, 39*(3), 273–290. 10.1080/03057240.2010.497609

Moreno-Gutiérrez, M. C., & Frisancho, S. (2009). Transitions to democracy: The role of moral and citizenship education in Latin America. *Journal of Moral Education, 38*(4), 391–406. 10.1080/03057240903321881

Næss, P. (Director). (2006). *Mozart and the whale* [Film]. Nu Image.

Narvaez, D. (2001). Moral text comprehension: Implications for education and research. *Journal of Moral Education, 30*(1), 43–54.

Narvaez, D. (2006). Integrative ethical education. In M. Killen & J. Smetana (Eds.), *Handbook of moral development* (pp. 703–732). Lawrence Erlbaum Associates.

Narvaez, D. (2008). Triune ethics: The neurobiological roots of our multiple moralities. *New Ideas in Psychology, 26*, 95–119.

Narvaez, D. (2010). Moral complexity: The fatal attraction of truthiness and the importance of mature moral functioning. *Perspectives on Psychological Science 5*(2), 163–181.

Narvaez, D. (2011). Neurobiology, moral education and moral self-authorship. In D. J. de Ruyter & S. Miedema (Eds.), *Moral education and development* (pp. 31–43). Sense.

Narvaez, D. (2014). *Neurobiology and the development of human morality: Evolution, culture, and wisdom.* W. W. Norton & Company.

Narvaez, D. (2016). *Embodied morality: Protectionism, engagement and imagination* (pp. 73–98). Palgrave MacMillan.

Narvaez, D. (Ed.) (2018). *Basic needs, wellbeing and morality: Fulfilling human potential.* Palgrave-MacMillan.

Narvaez, D., Endicott, L., Bock, T., & Lies, J. (2009). *Nurturing character in the classroom, EthEx series.* ACE Press.

Narvaez, D., & Lapsley, D. K. (Eds.). (2009). *Personality, identity, and character: Explorations in moral psychology.* Cambridge University Press.

Narvaez, D., Schiller, R., Gardner, J., & Staples, L. (2001). *Ethical action: Activity booklet 4—Nurturing character in the middle school classroom.* Darcia Narvaez.

Narvaez, D., & Snow, N. E. (Eds.). (2019a). Self, motivation, and virtue [Special Issue]. *Journal of Moral Education, 48*(1).

Narvaez, D., & Snow, N. E. (2019b). Introduction to self, motivation and virtue studies. *Journal of Moral Education, 48*(1), 1–6. 10/1080/03057240.20191556939

Narvaez, D., & Vaydich, J. L. (2008). Moral development and behaviour under the spotlight of the neurobiological sciences. *Journal of Moral Education, 37*(3), 289–312. 10.1080/03057240802227478

Narvaez, D., Wang, L., & Cheng, Y. (2016). The evolved developmental niche in childhood: Relation to adult psychopathology and morality. *Applied Developmental Science, 20*(4), 294–309. 10.1080/10888691.2015.1128835

Narvaez, D., Wang, L., Gleason, T., Cheng, Y., Lefever, J., & Deng, L. (2013). The evolved developmental niche and child sociomoral outcomes in Chinese 3-year-olds. *European Journal of Developmental Psychology, 10*(2), 106–127. 10.1080/17405629.2012. 761606

Narvaez, D., Woodbury, R., Cheng, Y., Wang, L., Kurth, A., Gleason, T., Deng, L., Gutzwiller-Helfenfinger, E., Christen, M., & Näpflin, C. (2019). Evolved developmental niche provision report: Moral socialization, social thriving, and social maladaptation in three countries. *International Journal of Behavioral Research, 9*(2), 1–16. 10.1177/2158244019840123

Needham-Penrose, J., & Friedman, H. L. (2012). Moral identity versus moral reasoning in religious conservatives. Do Christian evangelical leaders really lack moral maturity? *The Humanistic Psychologist, 40*, 343–363. 10.1080/08873267.2012.724256

Nelson, S. K., Layous, K., Cole, S. W., & Lyubomirsky, S. (2016). Do unto others or treat yourself? The effects of prosocial and self-focused behavior on psychological flourishing. *Emotion, 16*(6), 850–861. 10.1037/emo0000178

Noam, G. G. (1988a). A constructivist approach to developmental psychopathology. *New Directions for Child and Adolescent Development, 39*, 91–121. 10.1002/cd.2321 9883907

Noam, G. (1988b). The theory of biography and transformation: Foundation for a clinical-developmental therapy. In S. Shirk (Ed.), *Cognitive development and child psychotherapy* (pp. 273–317). Plenum.

Noam, G. G., & Malti, T. (2008). Responding to the crisis: RALLY's developmental and relational approach. *New Directions for Youth Development, 120*, 31–55. 10.1002/ yd.284

Noddings, N. (1984). *Caring, a feminine approach to ethics and moral education.* University of California Press.

Noddings, N. (1992). *The challenge to care in schools: An alternative approach to education.* Teachers College Press.

Noddings, N. (2002). *Educating moral people: A caring alternative to character education.* New Teachers College Press.

Noddings, N. (Ed.). (2005). *Educating citizens for global awareness.* Teachers College Press.

Noddings, N. (2008). Caring and moral education. In L. P. Nucci & D. Narvaez (Eds.), *Handbook of moral and character education* (pp. 161–174). Routledge.

North, J. (1998). The "ideal" of forgiveness: A philosopher's exploration. In R. D. Enright & J. North (Eds.), *Exploring forgiveness* (pp. 15–34). University of Wisconsin Press.

Nucci, L. P. (2001). *Education in the moral domain.* Cambridge University Press.

Nucci, L. P. (2009). *Nice is not enough: Facilitating moral development.* Pearson.

Nucci, L. P., & Narvaez, D. (Eds.). (2008). *Handbook of moral and character education.* Routledge.

Nucci, L., Narvaez, D, & Krettenauer. (2014). *The handbook of moral and character education* (2nd ed.). Routledge.

Nucci, L. P., & Powers, D. W. (2014). Social cognitive domain theory and moral education. In L. P. Nucci & D. Narvaez (Eds.), *Handbook of moral and character education* (2nd ed., pp. 121–139). Routledge.

Oliver, L. D., Neufeld, R. W. J., Dziobek, I., & Mitchell, D. G. V. (2016). Distinguishing the relationship between different aspects of empathic responding as a function of psychopathic, autistic, and anxious traits. *Personality and Individual Differences, 99,* 81–88. 10.1016/j.paid.2016.04.058

Ornaghi, V., Grazzani, I., Cherubin, E., Conte, E., & Piralli. F. (2015). "Let's talk about emotions!" The effect of conversational training on preschoolers' emotion comprehension and prosocial orientation. *Social Development, 24,* 166–183. 10.1111/scode.12091

Orva, A. (2015, March). Religious fundamentalism and radicalization. *European Parliamentary Research Service (EPRS).* https://www.europarl.europa.eu/EPRS/EPRS-briefing-551342-Religious-fundamentalism-and-radicalisation-FINAL.pdf

Oser, F. (1980). Stages of religious judgment. In C. Brusselmans (Ed.), *Toward moral and religious maturity* (pp. 277–315). Silver Burdett.

Oser, F., Fetz, R. L., Reich, H & Valentin, P. (2003). Religious judgement and religious world view: Theoretical relationship and empirical findings. *Archive for the Psychology of Religion, 25,* 165–179. https://www.jstor.org/stable/23912379

O'Toole, K. (1998, February 4). Noddings: To know what matters to you, observe your actions. *Stanford Online Report.* https://news.stanford.edu/news/1998/february4/noddings.html

Padilla-Walker, L. M., & Carlo, G. (2014). The study of prosocial behavior: Past, present, and future. In L. M. Padilla-Walker and G. Carlo (Eds.), *Prosocial development: A multidimensional approach* (pp. 1–16). Oxford University Press.

Padilla-Walker, L. M., & Nelson, L. J. (2015). Moral worldviews of American religious emerging adults: Three patterns of negotiation between development and culture. In L.A. Jensen (Ed), *Moral development in a global world: Research from a cultural-developmental perspective* (pp. 92–116). Cambridge University Press. 10.1017/CBO9781139583787

Padilla-Walker, L. M., & Memmott-Elison, M. (2020). Family and moral development. In L. A. Jensen (Ed.), *The Oxford handbook of moral development: An interdisciplinary perspective* (pp. 306–326). Oxford University Press.

Paisley, P. O., Bailey, D. F., Hayes, R. L., McMahon, H. G., & Grimmett, M. A. (2010). Using a cohort model for school counselor preparation to enhance commitment to social justice. *The Journal for Specialists in Group Work, 35*(3), 262–270. 10.1080/01933922.2010.492903

Paisley, P. O., & Hubbard, G. T. (Eds.). (1994). *Developmental school counseling: From theory to practice.* American Counseling Association.

Paisley, P. O., & Milsom, A. (2006). Group work as an essential contribution to transforming school counseling. *The Journal for Specialists in Group Work, 32*(1), 9–17. 10.1080/01933920600977465

Parker, S. (2010). Research in Fowler's faith development theory: A review article. *Review of Religious Research, 51*(3), 233–252. https://www.jstor.org/stable/20697343

Parker, S. (2011). Spirituality in counseling: A faith development perspective. *Journal of Counseling and Development, 89*, 112–119.

Parry, M. (2012, January 29). Jonathan Haidt decodes the tribal psychology of politics. *The Chronicle of Higher Education.* https://www.chronicle.com/article/Jonathan-Haidt-Decodes-the/130453

Patrick, R. B., Bodine, A. J., Gibbs, J. C., & Basinger, K. S. (2018). What accounts for prosocial behavior? Roles of moral identity, moral judgment, and self-efficacy beliefs. *The Journal of Genetic Psychology, 179*(5), 231–245. 10.1080/00221325.2018.1491472

Perry, W. G., Jr. (1970). *Forms of intellectual and ethical development in the college years: A scheme.* Holt, Rinehart, and Winston.

Pew Research Center. (2015a). *America's changing religious landscape: Christians decline sharply as share of population; Unaffiliated and other faiths continue to grow.* http://www.pewforum.org/2015/05/12/americas-changing-religious- landscape/

Pew Research Center. (2015b). *The future of world religions: Population growth projections, 2010-2050.* https://www.pewforum.org/2015/04/02/religious-projections-2010-2050/

Pew Research Center. (2019). *In U.S., decline of Christianity continues at rapid pace: An update on America's changing religious landscape.* https://www.pewforum.org/2019/10/17/in-u-s-decline-of-christianity-continues-at-rapid-pace/

Pew Research Center. (2020). *The global God divide.* https://www.pewresearch.org/global/2020/07/20/the-global-god-divide/

Piaget, J. (1928). *Judgment and reasoning in the child.* Routledge & Kegan Paul.

Piaget, J. (1932/1997). *The moral judgment of the child.* The Free Press.

Piaget, J. (1936). *The origins of intelligence in the child.* Routledge & Kegan Paul.

Piaget, J. (1960). The general problem of the psychobiological development of the child. In J. M. Tanner, & B. Inhelder (Eds.), *Discussions on child development* (Vol. 4, pp. 3–27). International Universities Press.

Piper, E. (2002). Faith development: A critique of Fowler's model and a proposed alternative. *Journal of Liberal Religion, 3*(1). https://www.meadville.edu/files/resources/v3n1-piper-faith-development-a-critique-of-fowlers.pdf

Plato. (380 BCE). *Meno.* http://classics.mit.edu/Plato/meno.html

Pollan, M. (2013, May 19). Some of my best friends are germs. *New York Times Magazine, 36–43*, 50, 58–59.

Potter, G. B., Gibbs, J. C., Robbins, M., & Langdon, P. E. (2015). *A comprehensive cognitive behavioral program for offenders: Responsible adult culture.* Springer.

Poushter, J., & Fetterolf, J. (2019). *A changing world: Global views on diversity, gender equality, family life, and the importance of religion.* PEW Research Center. https://www. pewresearch.org/global/2019/04/22/a-changing-world-global-views-on-diversity-gender-equality-family-life-and-the-importance-of-religion/

Power, F. C. (2015). Lawrence Kohlberg: The vocation of a moral educator. In B. Zizek, D. Garz, & E. Nowak (Eds.), *Kohlberg revisited* (pp. 187–198). Sense Publishing.

Power, F. C., & Higgins-D'Alessandro, A. (2008). The just community approach to moral education and the moral atmosphere of the school. In L. P. Nucci & D. Narvaez (Eds.), *Handbook of moral and character education* (pp. 230–247). Routledge.

Power, F. C., Higgins, A., & Kohlberg, L. (1989). *Lawrence Kohlberg's approach to moral education.* Columbia University Press.

Puka, B. (Ed.). (1994). *Moral development: A compendium.* Garland Press.

Rashid, R. (Executive Producer). (2017-2021). *Atypical* [TV Series]. Netflix.

Redden, E. (2007, February 1). *Spiritual accountability.* Inside Higher Ed. https://www. insidehighered.com/news/2007/02/01/spiritual-accountability

Redford, R. (Director). (1980). *Ordinary people.* [Film]. Paramount.

Reed, D. C. (1994, November). *Interpersonal community and impersonal justice: On the problem Lawrence Kohlberg's account of morality was meant to address.* Presentation to the Association for Moral Education (AME), Banff, Alberta, Canada.

Reed, D. C. (1997). *Following Kohlberg: Liberalism and the practice of democratic community.* Notre Dame Press.

Reed, D. C. (Ed.). (2008). Towards an integrated model of moral functioning [Special issue]. *Journal of Moral Education, 37*(3). doi:10.1080/03057240802227643

Reed, D. C. (2009). A multi-level model of moral functioning revisited. *Journal of Moral Education, 38*(3), 299–313. 10.1080/03057240903101523

Reed, D. C., & Stoermer, R. M. (2008). Towards an integrated model of moral functioning: An overview of the special issue. *Journal of Moral Education, 37*(3), 417–428.

Reiman, A. J., & Thies-Sprinthall, L. (1998). *Mentoring and supervision for teacher development.* Longman.

Renault, M. (2020, December 7). *Why are some scientists turning away from brain scans?* https:// apnews.com/article/why-some-scientists-turn-away-brain-scan-b778a88a0b7-c781e75e2f8c7c49e9421

Rest, J. R. (1983). Morality. In J. H. Flavell, & E. Markham (Eds.), *Handbook of child psychology: Vol. 3. Social, emotional, and personality development* (4th ed., pp. 556–629). Lawrence Erlbaum Associates.

Rest, J. (1984). Research on moral development: Implications for training counseling psychologists. *The Counseling Psychologist, 12*(3), 19–29 10.1177/0011000084123003

Rest, J. R. (1986). *Moral development: Advances in research and theory.* Praeger.

Rest, J. (1991). Kohlberg in perspective: A backward and a forward look. In L. Kuhmerker (Ed.), *The Kohlberg legacy for the helping professions* (pp. 201–204). R.E.P. Books.

Rest, J. R., & Narvaez, D. (Eds.). (1994). *Moral development in the professions: Psychology and applied ethics.* Lawrence Erlbaum.

Rest, J., Narvaez, D., Bebeau, M. J., & Thoma, S. J. (1999). *Postconventional moral thinking: A neo-Kohlbergian approach.* Lawrence Erlbaum.

Rideout, V. (2016). Measuring time spent with media: The Common Sense census of media use by US 8- to 18-year-olds. *Journal of Children and Media*, *10*(1), 138–144. 10.1080/17482798.2016.1129808

Rideout, V., & Robb, M. B. (2019). *The Common Sense census: Media use by tweens and teens.* Common Sense Media. https://www.commonsensemedia.org/research/the-common-sense-census-media-use-by-tweens-and-teens-2019

Ridley, M. (1996). *The origins of virtue: Human instincts and the evolution of cooperation.* Penguin Books.

Riggers-Piehl, T., & Sax, L. J. (2018). Encouraging the spirit: The role of student-faculty interactions in college students' meaning-making and spiritual quest. *Journal of College nd Character*, *19*(2), 101–119. 10.1080/2194587X.2018.1445642

Robb, M. B. (2020). *Teens and the news: The influencers, celebrities, and platforms they say matter most.* Common Sense Media. https://www.commonsensemedia.org/research/teens-and-the-news-the-influencers-celebrities-and-platforms-they-say-matter-most-2020

Rossen, I., Hurlstone, M. J., Dunlop, P. D., & Lawrence, C. (2019). Accepters, fence sitters, or rejecters: Moral profiles of vaccination attitudes. *Social Science & Medicine*, *224*, 23–27. 10.1016/j.socscimed.2019.01.038

Rowling, J. K. (1998). *Harry Potter and the chamber of secrets.* Bloomsbury.

Rubin, A. M. (1994). Media uses and effects: A uses-and-gratification perspective. In J. Bryant & D. Zillmann (Eds.), *Media effects: Advances in theory and research* (pp. 417–436). Lawrence Earlbaum Associates.

Rueda, P., Fernández-Berrocal, P., & Baron-Cohen, S. (2015). Dissociation between cognitive and affective empathy in youth with Asperger syndrome. *European Journal of Developmental Psychology*, *12*(1), 85–98. 10.1080/17405629.2014.950221

Sagan, E. (1988). *Freud, women, and morality: The psychology of good and evil.* Basic Books.

Santrock, J. W. (2018). *Adolescence* (17th ed.). McGraw-Hill.

Schonert-Reichl, K. A., Oberle, E., Lawlor, M. S., Abbott, D., Thomson, K., Oberlander, T. F., & Diamond, A. (2015). Enhancing cognitive and social–emotional development through a simple-to-administer mindfulness-based school program for elementary school children: A randomized controlled trial. *Developmental Psychology*, *51*(1), 52–66. 10.1037/a0038454

Schonert-Reichl, K. A., Smith, V., Zaidman-Zait, A., & Hertzman, C. (2012). Promoting children's prosocial behaviors in school: Impact of the "Roots of Empathy" program on the social and emotional competence of school-aged children. *School Mental Health*, *4*(1), 1–21. 10.1007/s12310-011-9064-7

Schrader, D. E. (2015). Evolutionary paradigm shifting in moral psychology in Kohlberg's penumbra. In B. Zizek, D. Garz, & E. Nowak (Eds.), *Kohlberg revisited* (pp. 7–27). Sense Publishing.

Schwadel, P. (2011). The effects of education on American's religious practices, beliefs and affiliations. *Review of Religious Research*, *53*(2), 161–182. 10.1007/s13644-011-0007-4

Selman, R. L. (1976). Social-cognitive understanding: A guide to educational and clinical practice. In T. Lickona (Ed.), *Moral development and behavior: Theory, research, and social issues* (pp. 299–316). Holt, Rinehart and Winston.

Selman, R. L. (2003). *The promotion of social awareness: Powerful connections from the partnership of developmental theory and classroom practice.* Russell Sage Foundation.

Selman, R. L., & Hickey Schultz, L. (1990). *Making a friend in youth: Developmental theory and pair therapy.* University of Chicago Press.

Selman, R. L., & Kwok, J. (2010). Informed social reflection: Its development and importance for adolescents' civic engagement. In L. R. Sherrod, J. Torney- Purta, & C. A. Flanagan (Eds.), *Handbook of research on civic engagement in youth* (pp. 651–683). Wiley & Sons.

Senland, A. K. (2017, November). *Moral reasoning and empathy across adolescence and emerging adulthood in autism spectrum disorder* [Invited talk]. Association for Moral Education, Saint Louis, MO.

Senland, A. K. (2019, November). Relationships among faith development, moral reasoning, and religious participation in the college years. In A. K. Senland (Chair), *The changing religious landscape of emerging adults' faith development in the college years* [Symposium]. Association for Moral Education, Seattle, WA.

Senland, A. K., & Higgins-D'Alessandro, A. (2016). Sociomoral reasoning, empathy, and meeting developmental tasks during the transition to adulthood in autism spectrum disorder. *Journal of Autism and Developmental Disorders, 46*(9), 3090–3105. 10.1007/s10803-016-2849-7

Senland, A. & Vozzola, E. (2007). Christian perspectives on Harry Potter: Tool of Satan or Christian parable? *Journal of Research in Character Education, 5*(2), 149–165.

Sherblom, S. (2008). The legacy of the 'care challenge:' Re-envisioning the outcome of the justice-care debate. *Journal of Moral Education, 37*(1), 81–98. 10.1080/0305724 0701803692

Sherrod, L., Torney-Purta, J., & Flanagan, C. A. (2010). *Handbook of research on civic engagement in youth*. Wiley.

Shortland, N., McGarry, P., & Merizalde, J. (2020). Moral medical decision-making: Colliding sacred values in response to COVID-19 pandemic. *Psychological Trauma: Theory, Research, Practice, and Policy, 12*(S1), S128–S130. 10.1037/tra0000612

Shweder, R. A. (1991). *Thinking through cultures: Expeditions in cultural psychology*. Harvard University Press.

Shweder, R. (2015). Acknowledgements. In L. A. Jensen (Ed.), Moral development in a global world: Research from a cultural-developmental perspective (pp. xii–xix). Cambridge University Press. 10.1017/CBO9781139583787

Shweder, R. (2018, December 6). *Richard Shweder Part 1: Morality, and Jonathan Haidt's Moral Foundations* [Video]. YouTube. https://www.youtube.com/watch?v=DiR8xRUWzSw

Shweder, R. A., Mahapatra, M., & Miller, J. G. (1987). Culture and moral development. In J. Kagan, & S. Lamb (Eds.), *The emergence of morality in young children* (pp. 1–82). University of Chicago Press.

Shweder, R. A., Minow, M., & Markus, H. R. (Eds.). (2002). *Engaging cultural differences: The multicultural challenge in liberal democracies*. Russell Sage Foundation.

Sinnott-Armstrong, W. (Ed.). (2008). *Moral psychology: Vol. 3. The neuroscience of morality: emotion, brain disorders, and development*. MIT Press.

Sizer, T. R., & Sizer, N. F. (1999). *The students are watching: Schools and the moral contract*. Beacon Press.

Skinner, B. F. (1948). *Walden two*. Hackett.

Sloane, S., Baillargeon, R., & Premack, D. (2012). Do infants have a sense of fairness? *Psychological Science, 23*(2), 196–204. 10.1177/0956797611422072

Smetana, J. G. (2006). Social-cognitive domain theory: Consistencies and variations in children's moral and social judgments. In M. Killen & J. Smetana (Eds.), *Handbook of moral development* (pp. 119–154). Lawrence Erlbaum Associates.

Smetana, J. G. (Ed.). (2018a). Early moral development [Special edition]. *Human Development, 61*(4–5).

Smetana, J. G. (2018b). Becoming moral: Introduction to the special issue on early moral development. *Human Development, 61*(4–5), 209–213. 10.1159/000492799

Smetana, J.G., Jambon, M., & Ball, C. (2014). The social domain approach to children's moral and social judgments. In M. Killen & J. G. Smetana (Eds.), *Handbook of moral development* (2nd Ed., pp. 23–45). Psychology Press.

Smith, C. (with Snell, P.) (2009). *Souls in transition: The religious and spiritual lives of emerging adulthood.* Oxford.

Smith, M. D. (2020). Nel Noddings, the ethics of care and education. *The encyclopedia of pedagogy and informal education.* https://infed.org/mobi/nel-noddings-the-ethics-of-care-and-education/

Snarey, J., & Samuelson, P. (2014). Moral education in the cognitive developmental tradition: Lawrence Kohlberg's revolutionary ideas. In L. P. Nucci & D. Narvaez (Eds.), *Handbook of moral and character education* (2nd ed., pp. 61–83). Routledge.

Song, Y., Nie, T., Shi, W., Zhao, X., & Yang, Y. (2019). Empathy impairment in individuals with autism spectrum conditions from a multidimensional perspective: A meta- analysis. *Frontiers in Psychology, 10*, Article 1902. 10.3389/fpsyg.2019.01902

Spinrad, T. L., & Eisenberg, N. (2017). Prosocial behavior and empathy-related responding: Relations to children's well-being. In M. E. Robinson (Ed.), *The happy mind: Cognitive contributions to well-being* (pp. 331–347). Springer International Publishing.

Spinrad, T. L., & Gal, D. E. (2018). Fostering prosocial behavior and empathy in young children. *Current Opinion in Psychology, 20*, 40–44. 10.1016/j.copsyc.2017.08.004

Sprinthall, N. A. (1994). Counseling and social role taking: Promoting moral and ego development. In J. R. Rest & D. Narvaez (Eds.), *Moral development in the professions: Psychology and applied ethics* (pp. 85–99). Lawrence Erlbaum Associates.

Sprinthall, N. A., Peace, S. D., & Kennington, P. A. D. (2001). Cognitive-developmental stage theories for counseling. In D. C. Locke, J. E. Myers, & E. L. Herr (Eds.), *The handbook of counseling* (pp. 109–129). Sage.

Stigler, J. W., Shweder, R. A., & Herdt, G. (Eds.). (1990). *Cultural psychology: Essays on comparative human development.* Cambridge University Press.

Stoppa, T. M., & Lefkowitz, E. S. (2010). Longitudinal changes in religiosity among emerging adult college students. *Journal of Research on Adolescence, 20*(1), 23–38. 10.1111/j.1532-7795.2009.00630.x

Straughan, R. (1985/1994). Why act on Kohlberg's moral judgments? (Or how to reach stage 6 and remain a bastard). In B. Puka (Ed.), *Moral development: A compendium* (Vol. 4, pp. 169–177). Garland Press.

Streib, H. (2001). Faith development theory revisited: The religious styles perspective. *The International Journal for the Psychology of Religion, 11*(3), 143–158.

Streib, H. (2007). Faith development and a way beyond fundamentalism. In C. Timmerman's *Faith based radicalism: Christianity, Islam and Judaism between constructive activism and destructive fanaticism* (pp. 151–167). Peter Lang.

Streib, H., Chen, Z. J., & Hood, R. W. (2020). Categorizing people by their preference for religious styles: Four types derived from evaluation of faith development interviews. *The International Journal for Religious Education, 30*(2), 112–127. 10.1080/105 08619.2019.1664213

Suleiman, S. R. (2013, May 12). The postcolonial: Albert Camus's writing on Algeria reveals both hope and dread [Review of the book *Algerian chronicles*]. *The New York Times Book Review*, p. 32.

Svetlova, M., Nichols, S. R., & Brownell, C. A. (2010). Toddlers' prosocial behavior: From instrumental to empathic to altruistic helping. *Child Development*, *81*(6), 1814–1827. 10.1111/j.1467-8624.2010.01512.x

Swartz, S. (Ed.). (2010a). Moral education in sub-Saharan Africa—culture, economics, conflict and AIDS [Special issue]. *Journal of Moral Education*, *39*(3).

Swartz, S. (Ed.). (2010b). The pain and the promise of moral education in sub-Saharan Africa. *Journal of Moral Education*, *39*(3), 267–272.

Takeda, T., Kasai, K., & Kato, N. (2007). Moral judgment in high-functioning pervasive developmental disorders. *Psychiatry and Clinical Neurosciences*, *61*(4), 407–414. 10.1111/j.1440-1819.2007.01678.x

The Best Schools. (2019, June 14). The 50 most influential living psychologists in the world. https://thebestschools.org/features/most-influential-psychologists-world/

Thoma, S. J. (1986). Estimating gender differences in the comprehension and preference of moral issues. *Developmental Review*, *6*(2), 165–180.

Thoma, S. J. (1994). Moral judgments and moral action. In J. Rest & D. Narvaez (Eds.), *Moral development in the professions: Psychology and applied ethics* (pp. 199–212). Lawrence Erlbaum Associates.

Thoma, S. J. (2002). An overview of the history of the Minnesota approach to morality research in moral development. *Journal of Moral Education*, *31*(3), 225–246. 10.1080/0305724022000008098

Thoma, S. J. (2006). Research on the Defining Issues Test. In M. Killen & J. Smetana (Eds.), *Handbook of moral development* (pp. 67–92). Lawrence Erlbaum Associates.

Tomasello, M. (2019). *Becoming human: A theory of ontogeny*. Belknap Press: An Imprint of Harvard University Press.

Trommsdorff, G. (2015). Cultural roots of values, morals, and religious orientations in adolescent development. In L. A. Jensen (Ed.), *The Oxford handbook of moral development: An interdisciplinary perspective* (pp. 377–395). Oxford University Press. 10.1093/oxfordhb/9780190676049.001.0001

Tully, E. C., & Donohue, M. R. (2017). Empathic responses to mother's emotions predict internalizing problems in children of depressed mothers. *Child Psychiatry & Human Development*, *48*(1), 94–106. 10.1007/s10578-016-0656-1

Turiel, E. (1983). *The development of social knowledge: Morality and convention*. Cambridge University Press.

Turiel, E. (2002). *The culture of morality: Social development, context, and conflict*. Cambridge University Press.

Turiel, E. (2008). Foreword. *Journal of Moral Education*, *37*(3), 279–288. 10.1080/0305724080222 7452

Turiel, E. (2018). Moral development in the early years: When and how. *Human Development*, *61*(4–5), 297–308. 10.1159/000492805

Uecker, J. E., Regnerus, M. D., & Vaaler, M. L. (2007). Losing my religion: The social sources of religious decline in early adulthood. *Social Forces*, *85*(4), 1667–1692. 10.1353/sof.2007.0083

U.S. Department of Education, Office of Safe and Drug Free Schools, Office of Character Education and Civic Engagement. (2007). *Mobilizing for evidence-based character education*. U.S. Dept. of Education, Office of Safe and Drug-Free Schools.

Van Sant, G. (Director). (1997). *Good Will Hunting* [Film]. Miramax Home Entertainment.

Viglas, M., & Perlman, M. (2018). Effects of a mindfulness-based program on young children's self-regulation, prosocial behavior and hyperactivity. *Journal of Child and Family Studies, 27*(4), 1150–1161. 10.1007/s10826-017-0971-6

Vozzola, E. C. (1991). Gender influences on moral reasoning: An analysis of the Kohlberg/Gilligan controversy in a Kuhnian framework. *Conference, 2*(2), 22–28.

Vozzola, E. C. (1996). The Kohlberg paradigm and beyond. *New Ideas in Psychology 14*(2), 197–206.

Vozzola, E. C. (Spring, 2017). The case for the Four Component Model vs. Moral Foundations Theory: A perspective from moral psychology. *Mercer Law Review, 68*(3), 633–647.

Vozzola, E. C. (2019, November). Faith in a lockbox: Conceptions of a higher power and religious affiliation. In A. K. Senland (Chair), *The changing religious landscape of emerging adults' faith development in the college years* [Symposium]. Association for Moral Education, Seattle, WA.

Vozzola, E., Rosen, J., & Higgins-D'Alessandro, A. (2009, July). *Looking back: Student, teacher, and researcher reflections on the Scarsdale Alternative just community school (1972–2009)*. Symposium presentation to the 35th Conference of the Association for Moral Education, Utrecht, Netherlands.

Wacker, G. (2000, November). *The rise of fundamentalism*. National Humanities Center. http://nationalhumanitiescenter.org/tserve/twenty/tkeyinfo/fundam.htm

Walker, L. J. (1984). Sex differences in the development of moral reasoning: A critical review. *Child Development, 55*(3), 677–691.

Walker, L. J. (1989). A longitudinal study of moral reasoning. *Child Development, 60*, 157–166.

Walker, L. J. (2004). Gus in the gap: Bridging the judgment–action gap in moral functioning. In D. K. Lapsley & D. Narvaez (Eds.), *Moral development, self and identity* (pp. 1–20). Lawrence Erlbaum Associates.

Walker, L. J. (2006). Gender and morality. In M. Killen & J. Smetana (Eds.), *Handbook of moral development* (pp. 93–115). Lawrence Erlbaum Associates.

Walker, L. J. (2020). The character of character: The 2019 Kohlberg Memorial Lecture. *Journal of Moral Education, 49*(4), 381–395. 10.1080/03057240.2019.1698415

Walker, L. J., & Frimer, J. A. (2009). 'The song remains the same:' Rebuttal to Sherblom's re-envisioning of the legacy of the care challenge. *Journal of Moral Education, 38*(1), 53–68. 10.1080/03057240802601599

Walker, L. J., & Reimer, K. S. (2006). The relationship between moral and spiritual development. In E. C. Roehlkepartain, P. E. King, L. Wagener, & P. L. Benson (Eds.), *The handbook of spiritual development in childhood and adolescence* (pp. 224–238). Sage.

Warneken, F. & Hepach, R. (Eds.). (2018). Early prosocial development [Special edition]. *Current Opinion in Psychology, 20*.

Warneken, F., & Tomasello, M. (2009). The roots of human altruism. *British Journal of Psychology, 100*, 455–471. 10.1348/000712608X379061

Watters, E. (2013, March/April). We aren't the world. *Pacific Standard, 6*(2), 46–53.

Weiten, W. (2016). *Psychology: Themes and variations* (10th ed.). Cengage.

Wentzel, K. (2015, May). *Prosocial behavior and schooling*. In A. Knafo-Noam (Ed.), The *Encyclopedia of early childhood development: Prosocial behaviour* (pp. 57–61). https://www.child-encyclopedia.com/prosocial-behaviour/according-experts/prosocial-behaviour-and-schooling

Whitney, M., Vozzola, E., & Hofmann, J. (2005). Children's moral reading of Harry Potter: Are children and adults reading the same books? *Journal of Research in Character Education, 3*(1), 1–24.

Wrangham, R. (2019). *The Goodness Paradox: The strange relationship between virtue and violence in human evolution.* Pantheon Books.

Wright, R. (1994). *The moral animal: Why we are the way we are: The new science of evolutionary psychology.* Vintage Books.

Wynn, K., & Bloom, P. (2013). The moral baby. In M. Killen & J. G. Smetana (Eds.), *Handbook of moral development* (2nd ed., pp. 435–451). Routledge.

Wynne, E. A., & Ryan, K. (1993). *Reclaiming our schools: A handbook on teaching character, academics, and discipline.* Merrill.

Yonker, J. E., Schnabelrauch, C. A., & DeHaan, L. G. (2014). The relationship between spirituality and religiosity on psychological outcomes in adolescents and emerging adults: A meta-analytic review. *Journal of Adolescence, 35*, 299–314. 10.101 6/j.adolescence.2011.08.010

You, D., Maeda, Y, & Bebeau, M. J. (2011). Gender differences in moral sensitivity: A meta-analysis. *Ethics & Behavior, 21*(4), 263–282. 10.1080/10508422.2011.585591

Young, J. E., Klosko, J. S., & Weishaar, M. (2003). *Schema therapy: A practitioner's guide.* Guilford Press.

Zahn-Waxler, C., & Schoen, A. (2016). Empathy, prosocial behaviour and adjustment: Clinical aspects of surfeits and deficits in concern for others. In A. Knafo-Noam (Ed.), The *Encyclopedia of early childhood development: Prosocial behaviour* (pp. 42–51). https:// www.child-encyclopedia.com/prosocial-behaviour/according-experts/empathy-prosocial-behaviour-and-adjustment-clinical-aspects

Zahn-Waxler, C., & Van Hulle, C. (2011). Empathy, guilt, and depression: When caring for others becomes costly to children. In B. Oakley, A. Knafo, G. Madhavan, & D. S. Wilson (Eds.), *Pathological Altruism* (pp. 322–344). 10.1093/acprof:oso/97801 99738571.003.0224

Zaki, J. (2017). Moving beyond stereotypes of empathy. *Trends in Cognitive Sciences, 21*(2), 59–60. 10.1016/j.tics.2016.12.004

Ziv, T., & Sommerville, J. A. (2017). Developmental differences in infants' fairness expectations from 6 to 15 months of age. *Child Development, 88*(6), 1930–1951. 10.1111/cdev.12674

Zizek, B., Garz, D., & Nowak, E. (Eds.). (2015). *Kohlberg revisited.* Sense Publishing.

Index

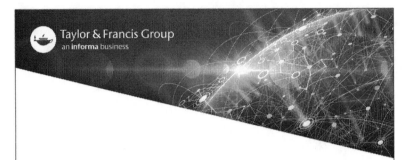